PATHFINDERS

People with Developmental Disabilities and Their Allies Building Communities That Work for Everybody

John O'Brien & Beth Mount

With Contributions by

Muriel Grace, Vici Clarke & Rob Clarke, Deb Hall, Gail Jacob, Helen Jones,

Diana McCourt & Judith McGill

INCLUSION

Library and Archives Canada Cataloguing in Publication

O'Brien, John, 1946-, author
    Pathfinders : people with developmental disabilities and their allies building communities that work for everybody / John O'Brien & Beth Mount ; with contributions by Muriel Grace, Vici Clarke & Rob Clarke, Deb Hall, Gail Jacob, Helen Jones, Diana McCourt & Judith McGill.

Issued in print and electronic formats.
ISBN 978-1-987935-02-8 (paperback). --ISBN 978-1-987935-03-5 (pdf)

    1. Developmentally disabled--Services for. 2. Social integration.
3. Community life. I. Mount, Beth, author II. Title.

HV1570.O2785 2015   362.4'048   C2015-904771-4
                                              C2015-904772-2

ISBN: 978-1-987935-02-8

Images incorporating Theory U on page 132, page 133, page 2, page 148, page 149, page 152, page 153, page 154, page 155, and page 157 are modified from materials licensed under Creative Commons by Otto Scharmer and The Presencing Institute, www.presencinginstitute.com/permissions.

Images from *Christmas in Purgatory* on page 138 and page 140 by permission of the Center on Human Policy, Law & Disability Studies, Syracuse University.

Words on page 39 and images on page 231 by permission of Simon Duffy

Cover images and images on page 21 © 2011 Beth Mount All rights reserved

PO Box 8335
Madison, WI 53708
www.ddnetworkinc.org

The mission of the Developmental Disabilities Network is to inspire, inform, and point the way to best practice of daily support for people with developmental disabilities and to promote greater opportunities for people with developmental disabilities to:

- Contribute to community life
- Control their own lives
- Secure good health and a stable home
- Work and earn an income
- Learn and grow

INCLUSION PRESS

47 Indian Trail, Toronto
Ontario Canada M6R 1Z8
p. 416.658.5363 f. 416.658.5067
inclusionpress@inclusion.com

inclusion.com BOOKS ·WORKSHOPS · MEDIA · RESOURCES

Contents

Introduction

*I do not think of political power as an end. Neither do I think of economic power as an end. They are ingredients in the objective that we seek in life. And I think that objective is the **creation of the beloved community.***

–Martin Luther King

We have written this book because we have been privileged to learn from courageous and creative people who have remade the world for people with developmental disabilities. In so doing these pathfinders have built up communities that come a little closer to the beloved community because they work a bit better for everybody. These creators are people with developmental disabilities, family members, providers of personal assistance or professional help, and leaders of significant changes in the way publicly funded assistance is organized. They come from North America, Europe, Australia and New Zealand. Some of our learning partners and teachers have left this life and many others are now young people. All of them recognize that people with developmental disabilities have a moral claim on the responsibilities and benefits of citizenship that far too often goes unredeemed. They know that things are not as they should be for people with developmental disabilities and that this is wrong and unjustly limiting, not only for people with disabilities and their families, but for our communities and our society as a whole. Keeping people on the sidelines of community life impoverishes everybody. Most important, our teachers have set out to discover what will move us along a path that makes things right. Their action has led to positive change that justifies our belief that current reality can move closer to the vision of the beloved community.

Our joy is to be among the riders on the waves of creativity involved in forming lasting good relationships between citizens with and without developmental disabilities, bringing infants

I want a cultural change, I want to contribute to a work of art in the domain of human existence, I want to contribute to evoke a manner of coexistence in which love, mutual respect, honesty and social responsibility arise spontaneously from living instant after instant.

–Humberto Maturana

and children out of residential programs and into permanent families, designing and managing local service systems that make institutions unnecessary for anybody, offering families flexible supports to their flourishing, discovering how to make preschools and schools and universities fully inclusive for all children and young people, organizing people with developmental disabilities to find their public voice, creating the means for people with developmental disabilities to live with support in their own home, opening the ways to good jobs in ordinary workplaces, building bridges to membership in community associations, recognizing and enhancing the value brought by direct support workers, and creating ways that people can be in control of the assistance they require.

Mostly we work as independent partners in learning. In company with friends, especially Connie Lyle O'Brien, we design, facilitate and document ways that people and families, organizations and systems can clarify the contributions that life calls them to make, describe where they are now, and figure out a way forward. We have walked with some people and families and assisted some organizations for thirty years and more. These partnerships give us the opportunity to listen to people who are committed to building a more just and inclusive community and support them to make sense of their situation, plan and take action.

We are interested in what our friend Judith Snow calls great questions. She says,

> A great question refuses to be answered. So it keeps leading us into deeper connections with each other and into deeper thinking.

The presence of people with developmental disabilities in the world produces great questions. Thinking about what we have learned with people whose everyday lives creatively engage these questions produced the ideas we offer in this book.

Our ambition is to present a useful story of the work of supporting people with developmental disabilities and their families. We don't claim that ours is THE STORY, we present a set of frames for action that we have found helpful. We develop connections among six ideas, pictured on the facing page.

- Our common purpose as citizens is to contribute, each in our own way, to building **communities that work better for everybody**. Communities will work better as citizens struggle to develop a sustainable relationship between the earth's human population and our planet and find ways to

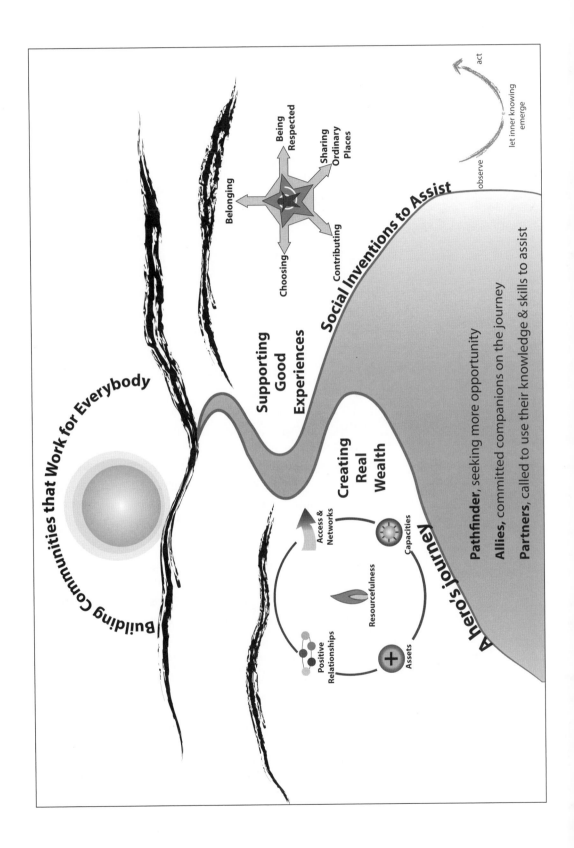

overcome social exclusion and the common tendency to disregard some people's dignity on the basis of difference.

- A community that works better for everyone is a place where citizens offer one another opportunities to create **real wealth**. Real wealth includes money and what money buys but only in the context of other values: good relationships, access to networks that channel flows of knowledge and support, development of capacities, and nurturing resourcefulness.

- People with developmental disabilities are vulnerable to social exclusion because they have differences that often lead others to disregard their dignity and exclude them from opportunities for contributing citizenship. Today, social inclusion is the result of a **hero's journey**. It involves courageous and creative pathfinding, even when the destination is such an ordinary matter of social justice as the key to one's own home, a job, opportunities to learn and the chance to pursue one's interests through participation in civic life.

- The journey to the dignity of contributing community roles is most likely to be successful when pathfinders recruit committed allies and skillful **partners**. Allies are people who act from personal commitment to the person with a developmental disability. Partners are people who use their knowledge, skills and authority to put specialist and public resources at the disposal of pathfinders and their allies. The task of publicly funded services is to develop and support creative partnerships with people and their families and allies.

- A key difference that exposes people with developmental disabilities to social exclusion and devaluation is their need for accommodation and continuing assistance. Our system expends far too many public dollars on services that demand separation from community life and intrusive supervision as the price of assistance. Good partners on the journey to social justice learn how to assist people to have **valued experiences**, including being respected, sharing ordinary places with their fellow citizens, developing their capacities and contributing, exercising choice and directing their lives, and belonging.

- Developing and sustaining contributing community roles calls for **social invention**. Personalized discovery and design are at the core of good support. Theory U, which we will summarize in Chapter 5, guides a process of invention that

A Note on Words

Unless we can use a person's name, it's hard to decide on the way to identify the people we have learned with. We don't accept the assumption that labels like intellectual disability and autism are diagnoses of a medical condition that calls for treatment. We see these terms as having migrated from the diagnostic clinic in order to define a legal status, bureaucratically assigned under color of medical authority as a condition of receiving benefits, services and protection for specific rights.

Practice and preference vary with geography. "Intellectual disability" is probably the term currently in widest use world wide, "learning disability" or "learning difficulty" commonly refers to the same status in the UK. These terms narrow the group of people we know best to people with cognitive impairments, so we have settled on "developmental disability" when we need a general term and, when it seems clear that we are referring to those who receive support, just people. When we talk about people when they are subjected to staff or management control we refer to them as "clients."

We are aware that some disabled and autistic people object to the usage that puts "people first". They argue that autistic or disabled describes an identity they are proud to have, not an accidental characteristic. This criticism, like every effort to contest the terms of identity imposed on people by others, is instructive. In general, we refer to "people with developmental disabilities" and change our usage when writing about disabled or autistic people who refer to themselves that way. When we are writing about history, we use the terms in common use in the period we write about.

The term we choose as least worst, "**developmental disability**", is a coinage of 1970's US federal law. To influence public policy and expenditures the status clumps together people whose impairments are evident by age 18 and require life-long, coordinated assistance because of limitations those impairments impose on performing life activities.

We follow a social model of disability in understanding **impairments** to be persistent differences of body and mind that limit a person's opportunities and activities unless the person has effective accommodation or assistance. Impairments may be evident at birth, they may result from an accident, they may come as a consequence of chronic disease. From this perspective, elders don't require publicly funded assistance because they are old but because they acquire impairments in old age. Some impairments require adjustments to a physical or social setting or individually tailored equipment if the person is to function comfortably and competently there. Some impairments require that the person have effective personal assistance some or all of the time in order to function comfortably and competently in settings that matter to them, whether home, work, leisure, or civic life. Restrictive definitions of **assistance** are unhelpful. It is best understood as whatever it takes –that a capable, ethical and well supported assistant can sustainably do– to enable each person with impairments to live a life that they, and the people who love them, have good reasons to value.

Disability is the disadvantage that people with impairments experience when they encounter barriers to opportunities and experiences that would be available to them if they were not impaired. Creative action to name and remove barriers to full participation in ordinary life and mainstream services is an urgent and continuing necessity.

System means the whole network of relationships, structures, policies and practices concerned with assistance to people with developmental disabilities and purposeful support to their action as full citizens. This network is reproduced and changed by the interaction of people with disabilities and their families and allies, advocacy groups, service providers, administrators charged with managing services, and legislators and courts as they take an interest in policy and resources for people with disabilities. We call it **our system** because we are among its members, shaped by and shaping its culture. This usage differs from identification of the service bureaucracy as "the system". We see **publicly funded assistance** as one possible source of support for good lives, but we don't use the terms interchangeably because people can rely on many other sources of support in addition to publicly funded assistance and because the delivery of publicly funded assistance can deprive people of the conditions necessary to good lives (think of the millions squandered on survival level assistance in nursing homes).

Within our system, a**dministrators** are people who accept responsibility for the healthy development and operation of the whole publicly funded enterprise of offering assistance in a region or state. **Managers** accept responsibility for the healthy development and operation of an organization that offers publicly funded assistance.

Person-centered work co-creates the means for a person to live a life that they and the people who love them have good reasons to value. Person-centered work takes three forms. **I. Person-centered planning** facilitates a person and their allies discernment of the person's purposes, gifts, and capacities so as to identify and coordinate access to the opportunities and supports necessary to show up in community life as a valued friend and a contributing citizen. **II. Person-centered direct support** develops and sustains respectful and productive relationships with personal assistants who align their capacities with the person's chosen path to contributing citizenship. **III. Person-centered design** orchestrates available resources and constraints at the personal, organizational, and system levels to reliably offer the assistance and support a person requires to show up in community life as a contributing citizen.

References we point to a variety of books and websites that we have found helpful. Books from Inclusion Press simply refer to inclusion.com as their source. Long web addresses have been shortened with Google URL Shortener; links worked as of 1 June 2015.

creates new capacities and opportunities. The design question that engages us is,

How might we make it much easier for people and their families to choose self-directed journeys to contributing roles and social inclusion?

We hope these six ideas create a story of inventing and supporting new opportunities, a story that helps people celebrate and build on what is meaningful in their own journeys. We hope that the lessons we have learned from many efforts to support real change will be of use to pathfinders and their partners.

Some books promise a guide that guarantees success to those who follow the steps outlined between their covers. This isn't one of them. We notice that many investments in change, whether personal, organizational or systemic, produce variations on more of the same rather than the deep change necessary to build a more inclusive community. Two generations of service reform show that conditions for excluded and supervised people can improve remarkably without much real increase in self-direction or access to contributing community roles and relationships. We speak from experience of tough and shifting terrain: partial successes,

This kind of organizing takes a lot of patience because changing people and people changing themselves requires time. Because it usually involves only small groups of people, it lacks the drama and visibility of angry masses making demands on the power structure. So it doesn't seem practical to those who think of changes only in terms of quick fixes, huge masses, and charismatic leaders.

–Grace Lee Boggs

frustration, disappointment, unexpected turns and reversals, remarkable changes for individuals and slow change for a dis- appointingly small set of organizations. And all this calling for celebration as committed leaders formulate more interesting and more powerful questions and move organizations to better assist people with developmental disabilities to take their rightful place in community life.

We respect the work of researchers committed to investigating the paths to social inclusion and self-direction, but this book reports neither the results of statistical analysis nor coding pages of field notes. We constructed these pages by making sense of our partnership with people, families and organizations who struggle to make social inclusion and self-direction real in their lives. We don't claim objectivity; we care about the people whose stories inform us and we speak from inside the effort to change things. Shared commitment to action for inclusion biases the experience we reflect on; there is no more convenient sample than this one. We question the ways people understand social inclusion and self-direction and the actions that follow from that understand- ing, but from a position of commitment to these values.

We like the system's thinking metaphor of the iceberg as a guide to reflection. We look for signs of growth in people's engagement in community and their ability to direct their lives. We notice where action for social inclusion and self-direction is absent or stuck. We ask people in the situation, and then we ask our friends and ourselves, what lets action flow freely toward a rich life in community and what inhibits move- ment. The idea that the multiple influences on what we observe can be arranged to show different levels of power and visibility keeps us thinking together. In stuck situations people often start by blaming other people –clueless staff, controlling parents, heartless community members. We've discovered that more options show up when we consider the mental models (stories) that structures and practices express. In our understanding, stories that people take as the way things are can be invisible to those who live inside them. Sometimes they hide behind words that float free of what is hap- pening. Words like person-centered can mask untested assump- tions about the inevitability of social exclusion and control by

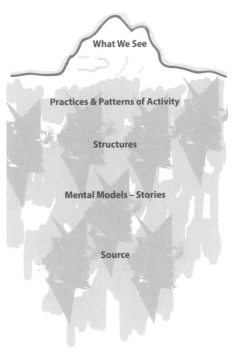

others –*he could never…; the community won't….* We have found
leverage for positive change when people intentionally revise
mental models to test assumptions that compete with expressed
values. To bring mental models into the light we ask, *What story
could we be in that makes what's happening seem like the best or
only possibility?* Theory U, which gives us a grammar for social
invention, draws attention even deeper under the waterline to
consider the source of action in the social field of attention. The
quality of attention that we bring to our shared world powerfully
affects what shows up. Inattention to capacities and gifts traps us
in a story of fear and isolation. Intentional opening to the highest
potential of a community that works better for everyone energizes
co-creation.

We have learned much from disabled people who have led the
independent living movement and articulated the social model of
disability. Our experience, and our focus in this book, however,
is more narrowly on people and families who rely on assistance
from publicly funded services for those assigned the status of
intellectual or developmental disability. This includes some people
diagnosed with autistic spectrum disorder. Their lives raise questions about the design and delivery of assistance that the social
model doesn't fully consider.

As you read, remember that we write about what we are learning
from people and families and service workers who choose to go
for something more than is currently easy to find in their community. We are not prescribing for those fulfilled by their current
relationships and roles. It would be awful to try to drag people
satisfied with their lives down the paths our teachers have broken.
We do hope, though, that the stories and lessons here encourage
more pathfinders to set out on their own self-directed journeys.

Something darker in our environment also motivates our writing. At just the time when we have enshrined in law and policy
the highest aspirations in history for people with disabilities, at
just the time when we know more than ever about how to offer
good assistance, we are collectively hellbent on shrinking the
space for personal journeys of discovery. In announced pursuit of
health, safety, self-direction, person-centered support, inclusion
and partnership, we are choking the life out of those who want to
do the work necessary to realize these very values.

We see this irony as an invitation to look deeper into our understanding of these commonly espoused values, and we'll do so in
these pages. Along our way we have developed a perspective that
can seem quirky. Because so many words have lost the savor they

once brought to people's thinking. We have tried to tell the truth we know. Our slant on familiar terms and practices like person-centered planning, system change or self-direction may seem odd and our observations puzzling, at least at first.

One reason for this is the considerable tension we experience between what we have found that it takes to make significant change and the working assumptions about change most common among administrators. Common practice would have us believe that professional strangers can reliably conduct life and system changing person-centered plans in no more than a couple of hours for each of 75 people on their caseload or that a strategic plan or change of rule or performance contract will galvanize service managers to transform their organizations. Our experience of these and other current managerial certainties is otherwise.

Our perspective may seem weird for another reason. We encounter mystery in a field that prefers to solve problems and count the outcomes of tool use. We take inclusion as mutual welcoming and mutual accommodation. Inclusion cannot be done to or for people with developmental disabilities by application of a technique. It is relational work in which people with developmental disabilities must do their share. All who participate do most of this work spontaneously and beneath verbal communication. We have repeatedly participated in and frequently observed people who do the work of inclusion stepping out of their typical roles and into an everyday mystery, a relationship that dissolves the distance created by fear of difference and allows diverse gifts to flow among them. We speak of everyday occurrences. Nina relaxes to Cori's music. Evan exchanges greetings with his co-workers at the grocery store. Steve and Mark play Metallica in a guitar lesson. Angie reads to the preschool children she assists. If angels sing as these things happen those involved are too absorbed in the ordinary to hear them. What is mysterious is invisible without a sense of the sheer improbability of these things happening, given the history of deprivation driven by the social devaluation of people with developmental disabilities.

Reflection can point towards, but not explain, the mystery of gifts flowing in all directions. Anna has assisted Rebecca for many years (for more of their story see page 45). She says,

> *I had never been around someone like Rebecca who wasn't able to respond to me in words. Someone who physically couldn't move in a way that would show me her interests or passions for things. So it was a real learning process for me. I didn't know what to expect.*

I think at the time I very much felt like I was doing Rebecca a favor, that I was helping her. I've come to see that it's Rebecca who has pushed me on to do all the things that we have done together. She encourages me to be a better person in everything that I do. So even when we're not together her presence is with me and I bring that to each encounter that I have.

Whether our perspective seems resonant or weird, we ask busy readers to stop, at least long enough to reflect and test our experience with their own. Try on our perspective as if it is a pair of differently tinted glasses and see if something that adds usefully to your work shows up.

We remain confident that people with developmental disabilities and their families will continue to recruit allies and push toward better lives. We are less confident about publicly funded services supplying creatively flexible partners, at least in the short term. If our worry that systems will get even more mired in "no" turns out to be justified, this will limit the numbers of people able to make the journey to a better life without extensive support from their biological or chosen families. Others will be confined by services that will grow increasingly mechanistic unless service workers and managers succeed in heroic efforts to reverse the trend to impose ever more meticulous external control on their work. Our concern is especially strong for the US. Our estimate of the odds on a favorable climate for large scale social invention have shifted toward nations where there is somewhat more "yes space" in the bureaucracy and a somewhat less individualistic bias in social policy.

Whether conditions favor social invention or not, our hope rests in the spirit that animates people with developmental disabilities and their families to resist exclusion, imagine better and to go for it. We know that these pathfinders will continue to find ways to grow beautifully, if vulnerably, through the cracks in society and its organized systems.

Thanks

We have been on this learning journey for more than a generation. Evidence of our debts fill the pages of this book. We stopped listing names of the people we have learned with when we got to 100 names and were nowhere near finished. Our learning has happened in a network of networks that we can name in a reasonable space. In rough chronological order our webs of connection include networks formed around these people and projects.

- Wolf Wolfensberger created an international network to try, test and teach his ideas about comprehensive community services, normalization and citizen advocacy. People worked together across state and national borders to promote these ideas and related practices. Many of our friendships and collaborations began in these networks. Intensive work grew over many years in Georgia, Massachusetts, Connecticut, Ohio, Washington State, Wisconsin, Kentucky, Michigan, Rhode Island, Vermont, New Hampshire, Ontario, Manitoba and Alberta, England, Scotland, Wales, New Zealand and Australia. Work in these places has ebbed and flowed over decades, but refection on many experiences, conversations and conflicts in this network, sustained over decades, are the source of many of the ideas on these pages.

- The Canadian National Institute on Mental Retardation (as it was known in the mid 1970's), led by Alan Roeher, harnessed Wolfensberger's ideas to a national dissemination effort. NIMR connected to systems design and development built on the work of Eric Trist and his colleagues. ComSERV, a nationwide change effort focused on developing comprehensive systems of community services, brought many more lessons on the politics and adaptive demands of change. NIMR also supported for a time the work of our friends Marsha Forest, Judith Snow and Peter Dill on inclusive education, organizing families and circles of support.

- CMH brought PASS, Wolfensberger's method for teaching normalization and evaluating programs, to the UK under the leadership of Alan Tyne and Paul Williams. This network grew into connections with the King's Fund Ordinary Life Initiative and David Towell and with the Northwest Training and Development Team.

- Organized self-advocates in Washington State, Ontario, New York, Pennsylvania, California, the UK and Australia have shown us the power of the desire for better lives.

- Pat Beeman and George Duscharme founded Communitas to hold their efforts to walk with people with disabilities and families in Connecticut. Collaboration with them has produced a deeper understanding of what works to change communities one person at a time.

- Under Steve Taylor's leadership, the Center on Human Policy at Syracuse University became a host for dialogs and provided colleagues and financial support for John and Connie Lyle O'Brien's learning and writing.

- Marsha Forest and Jack Pearpoint, among a great many other good things, founded Inclusion Press and an annual Summer Institute on Inclusion. Jack and Lynda Kahn continue this work and are the publishers of this book.

- Marcie Brost and Howard Mandeville have organized and financed multiple learning opportunities and writing projects in Wisconsin, first under the sponsorship of the Wisconsin Council on Developmental Disabilities and then through DD Network, the co-publisher of this book. In addition to providing consultation, project management and training, DD Network supports in depth inquiries into individualized supports, self-direction, support to families, organizational and system change, and community development. Dane County, Wisconsin exemplifies a system committed to inclusion and self direction. So it is the site of many social inventions, including Options in Community Living, an early innovator in supported living and a rich source of learning for us.

- Washington State remains a leader in employment for people with developmental disabilities. Linda Rolfe made administrative space for supported employment to grow. A sustained commitment to developing capacity, implemented by Mary Romer and Candace O'Neill, produced many lessons on changing systems. Cross boundary investment in exploring community building supported Carolyn Carlson to work on inclusion from inside the Seattle Department of Neighborhoods.

- Simon Duffy has harnessed his creativity to fundamental reform of the relationship between citizens who require assistance to enact their citizenship and the state. He founded in Control and has moved on to found The Centre for Welfare reform..

- Fredda Rosen, Carole Gothelf, Bernard Carabello, Jen Teich, Diana McCourt, Clara Berg and Kathy Broderick have sourced a variety of initiatives in New York City that create new options for young people in transition from high school. A twenty year thread connects these transition initiatives beginning with the Pathfinder projects formed in the 1990s, the FAR Fund Initiatives, and the more recent Urban Innovations initiative in Harlem, New York. Kate Buncher and Cathy James spark the energy and initiative of self advocates, their families, and direct support allies, through their Mentoring for Excellence, activism and artistic collaborations.

- Under Ann Hardiman's leadership, The New York State Association of Community and Residential Agencies (NYSACRA) created a series of Learning Institutes (from 2008 to present) to support innovation in individualized supports using Theory U practice. A core group of ARC Executive Directors including Ric Swierat, Laurie Kelley, Hanns Meissner, Michael Goldfarb and Chris Fortune co-hosted the 2009 Garrison Institute Theory U Workshop to deepen organizational understanding of social invention.

- Cathy Stevenson, as Developmental Disabilities Division Director in New Mexico, has invested in multiple initiatives to inspire inclusion throughout the state. The seeds of community building have been nurtured by Angela Pacheco, Anysia Fernandez, Rebecca Shuman, Kay Lilley, and Marc Kolman and others.

- Julie Stansfield leads in Control in England as it becomes a citizen movement oriented to social inclusion and self-direction. Lynne Elwell and Julia Erskine have built a powerful network of champions through intensive leadership development centered on families and people with disabilities.

- More recent collaboration with David Towell has provided opportunities to explore the contributions that people with developmental disabilities can make to efforts to discover sustainable local and national economies. goo.gl/IU90P7

- Hanns Meissner is our partner in developing and delivering a number of multi-organizational change efforts. He has told the thirty year story of developing individualized supports in the organization he now directs, Renssalaer ARC, in *Creating Blue Space* from inclusion.com

- Through Inclusion Alberta, Bruce Uditsky and Anne Hughson and their colleagues assist families who choose an inclusive life pathway. Their contributions provide opportunities to better understand families as social inventors.

- The work of Otto Scharmer, Katrin Kaufer, Arawana Hayashi and the Presencing Institute provides a coherent approach to deep change and connections to practitioners in many other fields.

- Real Communities, a project of the Georgia Council on Developmental Disabilities organized by Caitlin Childs and Eric Jacobsen, tests community building as a path to social inclusion and leadership development for people with developmental disabilities.

- New Paths to Inclusion has opened a window into the work of change makers exploring person-centered work, community engagement and organizational change in 17 European countries www.personcentredplanning.eu.

Close to the book you are holding we are grateful to Connie Lyle O'Brien and Hanns Meissner for careful reading and many good suggestions for improvement. Carol Blessing, Gail Jacob and Sheli Reynolds provided encouraging and helpful readings.

The Cover Images

The images on the front cover and those on the next page are taken from the quilt, *Garden of Soul*, pictured on the back cover. Beth created this quilt to explore the resonance between this insight from Carl Jung's *The Undiscovered Self* and the experience of making real change in partnership with people with developmental disabilities, work that brings everyone involved into awareness of their own imperfections, weakness and need for relationship:

> *A human relationship is not based on differentiation and perfection, for these only emphasize the differences or call forth the exact opposite; it is based, rather, on imperfection, on what is weak, helpless, and in need of support –the very ground and motive for dependence. The perfect have no need of others, but weakness has for it seeks support and does not confront its partner with anything that might force him [sic] into an inferior position...It is from need and distress that new forms of existence arise.*

Beth's commentary on her quilt:

> *The great healer, Carl Jung, helped us see that each of us possesses a higher level of self, at least in embryonic form, and that under favorable circumstances the higher self emerges. Therefore, in a generative community, the most important problems of life are never really solved, but only outgrown in the context of widening circles of mutuality.*

> *The star represents the defining image that calls us to our destiny. The cross in the circle is a universal symbol of the sacred soul space in which we live or hope to live. Our capacity to live out our call is directly related to the fertility of our environment, our relationships, our sense of belonging, purpose, and access to opportunities and resources that enrich our development. In contrast, discrimination, injustice, intolerance, poverty, and economic exploitation distort development and weaken the entire social fabric. This image challenges us to create a fertile garden of soul for all people, not just a chosen few.*

The quality of the journey to a better life is determined by the quality of our attention and commitment to the person, allies and community. Everyone has a higher purpose and gifts that relate to their highest purpose.

We build communities that nurture the highest potential of all members. We reach for the highest potential in all of us.

Our role is to discover, reveal, and clarify a pattern language for assistance that allows our communities to benefit from each citizen's gifts. We discover ways to connect with roles, relationships, places, and organizations that call forth personal initiative and contribution.

Highest purpose is expressed by the ways we co-create and multiply valued roles. Devaluation, social exclusion, isolation and segregation are the biggest threats to quality of life.

Our job is to resist the devaluation, cynicism, despair and fear that disconnects people from one another and from the highest potentials in human life.

We amplify gifts, strengthen relationships, and create places to belong.

We align with others who share common passions and concerns. Possibilities are endless as more people care, share action, and create deeper relationships. Nothing happens when nobody cares.

We know that communities are made of assets and opportunities for contribution. Pathfinder's journeys always include creating relationships that deepen people's belonging and strengthen local community.

We get outside of ourselves, our organizations and our isolation and discover the interests and concerns of others. We join with others to create real wealth.

We take the next step to deepen relationships with family and friends, create jobs and volunteer roles, make neighborhood connections, and connect to associations.

We continually question what more is possible and cultivate ways that one thing leads to another good thing.

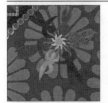

We invest in design teams to generate social inventions.

We practice opening our minds, hearts, and wills to harvest new energy to sense, discover and embody new possibilities for our communities to work better for everybody.

We know that deep change is tough. We live with the discomfort of letting go of our certainties and not knowing. We develop the resourcefulness to stick with the creative process. We wrestle with voices and forces of judgment, cynicism, and fear. We fiercely confront conditions that hurt people and create conditions that nurture.

1

Communities that Work Better for Everybody

The beloved community is not a utopia, but a place where the barriers between people gradually come down and where the citizens make a constant effort to address even the most difficult problems of ordinary people. It is above all else an idealistic community.

–Jim Lawson

In a community that works for everybody, citizens intentionally generate opportunities for one another to create real wealth.*

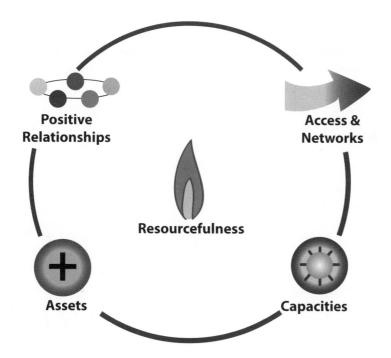

* We are grateful to our Centre on Welfare Reform colleagues, Pippa Murray and Simon Duffy, for introducing us to the idea of real wealth. We have revised and expanded their definitions of the components of real wealth while remaining indebted to their insights. For the original account, see goo.gl/AK26bl

Real wealth

The idea of real wealth describes the means to create well being. It offers people the freedom to pursue lives that they, and those who love them, have good reasons to value. Assets with money value are one kind of wealth, but real wealth includes other resources that people can develop, enjoy and exchange to serve their own highest purposes.

- **Assets** are goods that a person can direct toward their purposes. Disposable income, savings and investments, real estate, tools and equipment, stored and organized information all count as assets. Money spent by government agencies to purchase services that clients cannot effectively control doesn't count as real wealth for the person who is the object of that expenditure.

- **Capacities** are qualities of being, gifts, powers, talents, knowledge, wisdom, skills and abilities that a person can enjoy, develop and contribute. Time, attention and energy are capacities. Capacities are the inheritance of culture and genetic endowment and the fruit of individual development. Capacities embody interests and enable understanding, enjoyment, problem-solving, creation and practical action. As capacities develop they shape a person's identity and chosen roles. Capacities enrich the time a person spends alone or with intimates and friends and form a person's contributions to workplace, social and civic life. People employ capacities to create products or performances of value to the people and communities that matter to them

- **Access & networks** identify the physical and social pathways open to a person and the means a person can employ to navigate them. Access includes good connections to contacts who support the person to gather information and knowledge of interest and use in finding opportunities for membership, enjoyment, exchange, contribution and development. Knowledge and availability of the aids, accommodations and technology that make engagement with people, experiences and information easier and more rewarding are critical elements of real wealth.

- **Positive relationships** are connections with others who share time and activity enjoyably and meaningfully and count on each other to exchange support and practical help. Relationships are a source of sense-making, encouragement, challenge and consolation. Relationships shape and support a person's sense of identity, purpose and plan.

- **Resourcefulness** is the confidence that one can take action that achieves meaningful results, even in difficult circumstances, and the belief that effort improves competency and the odds of success. It arises from a sense of purpose and mobilizes assets, capacities and connections in response to challenging circumstances. It encourages appreciation of opportunities and moves a person to set ambitious goals and persevere in the face of failure. Resourcefulness supports resilience in response to loss, trauma or tragedy. It is the spirit that makes a way from no way.[*]

The idea of real wealth invites citizens to imagine and do more than is allowed by the more common understanding of wealth as money and the consumption that money allows. When many citizens face a shortage of money despite spending more and more time and energy to earn it and many families are insecure about continuing to have enough money to live decently, investment in real wealth may seem like an idle daydream. We think otherwise. We believe that putting assets that can be measured in money in the context of developing capacities, networks of trust, positive relationships and resourcefulness opens more possibilities for cooperative action with people nearby us on issues that matter to all of us. Recognition that making commodities of every need closes off many possibilities for gift exchange encourages more mindful use of material assets. Realizing that our sense of wellbeing and our experience of community depends on tending to and counting on our interdependencies guides our search for meaningful activity.

As real wealth grows, more people can act as citizens. They have the freedom to say, *We belong to this place and act from responsibility for it*. Acting from responsibility for a community means joining others in making a constant effort to make progress on the difficult issues that affect ordinary people. These issues are difficult because making progress demands learning and change, involves loss, and challenges the way power is distributed. Climate change. A sustainable economy that offers enough good work and a just share of material assets for everyone. Reclamation and preservation of the natural world and public space. Security and good health. Equality of access to the conditions for a decent life. Progress on each of these connected issues depends on enough citizens acting together from their care for each other and their world to mobilize next steps forward.

The Canadian writer Margaret Laurence urged us "to feel, in your heart's core, the reality of others."…One of the great values of belonging to any group with a purpose is that we act with other people, for the benefit of other people, knowing that we could not accomplish anything without other people. Thoughts and actions have to be coordinated with those of others in order to reach a goal. And it is in these smaller groups, all looking in the same direction and defining friendship in the context of a mutual goal, that the true nature of belonging lies.

–Adrienne Clarkson

---

[*] For helpful psychological perspectives on resourcefulness, see Albert Bandura (1997). *Self-efficacy: The exercise of control.* New York: W.H. Freedman and Carol Dweck (2006). *Mindset: The new psychology of success.* New York: Random House.

75 Actions That Build Community

1. Attend a political meeting
2. Support local merchants
3. Volunteer your special skills to a community organization
4. Donate blood (with a friend)
5. Work in a community garden
6. Mentor a person of a different ethnic group
7. Surprise a new or favorite neighbor by taking them food
8. Avoid destructive gossip
9. Help another person outside your home fix something
10. Attend local school or children's athletics, plays, & recitals
11. Get involved with youth
12. Sing in a choir
13. Attend a party in someone else's home
14. Get to know the clerks and salespeople at your local stores
15. Audition for community theatre or support a production backstage or volunteer to usher
16. Attend a lecture or concert
17. Give to your local food or clothing bank
18. Play cards or games with friends or neighbors
19. Walk or bike to support a cause and meet others
20. Participate in a political campaign
21. Attend a local festival or parade
22. Find a way to show personal appreciation to someone who builds your local community
23. Coach or help out with local (youth) sport
24. Offer to help a neighbor with garden work or shopping or a ride
25. Start or participate in a discussion group or book or film club
26. Start or join a carpool
27. Plan a "Walking Tour" of a local historic area
28. Tutor or read to children or have children read to you
29. Run for public office
30. Invite neighbors over for a meal
31. Host a party
32. Offer to serve on a committee outside of work
33. Form a walking group (or a swimming group) with at least one other person & encourage each other
34. Play a sport
35. Go to church
36. Ask an elder to teach you something
37. Host a potluck supper
38. Take dance lessons with a friend
39. Become a trustee
40. Join a campaign & take action that brings you into contact with others (not just a donation)
41. Gather a group to clean up a local park or cemetery
42. Bake something for neighbors or work colleagues
43. Plant trees
44. Volunteer at the library or primary school
45. Call an old friend
46. Sign up for a class & meet your classmates
47. Accept or extend an invitation
48. Log off and go to the park
49. Say hello to strangers
50. Find out more by talking with a neighbor you don't know very well yet
51. Host a movie night
52. Help out with or create a newsletter
53. Collect oral histories to discover the interesting things people have done
54. Cut back on TV
55. Join in to help carry something heavy
56. Make gifts of time
57. Greet people
58. If you think someone needs help, ask to find out & do what you can
59. Fix it even if you didn't break it
60. Pick up litter even if you didn't drop it
61. Attend gallery openings & art exhibits
62. Organize a neighborhood yard sale
63. Read or listen to the local news faithfully
64. Attend a public meeting or hearing & speak up
65. When inspired write a personal note or send a card to friends
66. Offer to watch a neighbor's home while they are away.
67. Help out with recycling
68. Ask to see a friend's photos
69. Invite a local politician or official to speak to a group you belong to
70. Start talking to people you see regularly
71. Listen to the children you know and find out what matters to them
72. Plan a reunion of family, friends, or people with whom you had a special connection
73. Hire local young people for odd jobs
74. Write a letter to the editor
75. Join a group that is likely to lead to making new friends of different ethnicity, or religion, or income, or life experience*

---

* Adapted from www.bettertogether. org which identifies 150 community building actions.

Social relationships produce real wealth. Societies with richer and more varied networks of ties and connections and higher levels of citizen activity in a greater variety of civic associations generate trust and security and more opportunities for people to initiate new enterprises, exchange their gifts, develop capacities and produce assets than societies in which individuals are more disconnected and less organized do. People with secure attachments to significant others, memberships that support their interests and demand their contributions, and more extensive and diverse networks of personal connections can be more resourceful, better develop their capacities, enjoy broader access and command more assets than isolated and disconnected people can.[*]

> The well connected are more likely to be hired, housed, healthy and happy.
> –Robert Putnam

The issues that communities must face are complex and troubled. Deeply conflicting interests are at stake. But any citizen can strengthen the foundation for making progress by engaging in simple actions like those identified on the facing page. These actions may look irrelevant to the serious business of increasing wealth or saving the planet, but as these small shared experiences accumulate in a place, their effects multiply a community's stock of trust and opportunity for civic action and entrepreneurial activity.[†]

A community that works cares for the planet

Some issues are so big that people feel powerless to do anything about them. The options seem to boil down to denial or indirect action such as signing an online petition or writing a check to a big organization that lobbies on the issue. Direct, local efforts to address sustainability are not enough to overcome the economic and political structures that perpetuate inequality and environmental destruction, but they increase the real wealth of the people involved and create social relationships that strengthen the foundations for meaningful action.

Those who want to build a community that works for everybody recognize the value in turning to one another to address difficult questions such as these:

- How might we significantly reduce our local carbon footprint?
- How might we cultivate a more sustainable local economy?
- How might we preserve and renew the natural environment in the interest of future generations?

---

[*] See Robert Putnam (2002). *Democracies in flux: The evolution of social capital in contemporary society.* New York: Oxford University Press and Joseph Rowntree Foundation (2009). *Contemporary social evils.* London: Policy Press.

[†] Robert Putnam (2001) *Bowling alone.* New York: Simon & Schuster.

- How might we become more resilient to the consequences of climate change and shifting populations?

- How might we strengthen local democracy and mobilize diverse interests to respond more effectively to these challenges?

- How might we contribute to and benefit from regional, national and global efforts to care for the planet?*

A bigger we

Citizens create opportunities for each other to build real wealth. A community that works for everybody multiplies local platforms for contribution and engages people with more and more diverse identities, interests and gifts to join in common projects.

Local people can create many different platforms for contribution. Starting, investing in, operating or expanding a business and providing good jobs at decent wages gives people chances to build real wealth. Supporting workers to organize and develop their capacities and networks multiplies real wealth. Patronizing local businesses builds real wealth. Operating a local timebank, community garden, farmer's market, child care co-op, ride sharing or tool sharing initiative channels mutually beneficial exchange of capacities and assets. Participation brings these structures alive. Organizing around local issues from safe streets to food justice, clean water and downtown renewal strengthens connectedness while improving the physical and social environment in ways that promote greater engagement. Putting on an art show, a concert, a play, a festival or a parade builds connectedness through celebration, develops capacities and creates a marketplace for the fruits of artistic gifts. Sharing skills and experience by teaching, mentoring and peer support increases assets and capacity for people of every age. Civic associations build the soil for real wealth to grow as people organize to pursue shared interests from quilting to wooden boat building.

Summarizing their study of successful efforts, Robert Putnam and Lewis Feldstein identify the way citizens create platforms for contribution:

> *What people who [create real wealth] do is understand and emphasize the importance of relationships and personal connections to achieving their objectives.*[†]

> The hope of a poverty-free society is the hope of a society in which faithful and constructive relationships are normal and there is a robust common life – cultural and productive– to share in.
>
> –Rowan Williams

---

* For an inspiring description of local practices that address the transition to a lower carbon, more environmentally aware future see Rob Hopkins (2012). *The transition companion: Making your community more resilient in uncertain times.* White River Junction, VT: Chelsea Green Publishing. For more on the intersection of sustainability and social justice for disabled people, see the on line discussion led by our friend David Towell at www.centreforwelfarereform.org

† (2004) *Better Together: Restoring the American Community.* New York: Simon & Schuster. The original sentence uses the term "social capital" rather than real wealth.

A community that includes everybody in opportunities to create real wealth makes steady progress on two issues that encourage a more generous sense of who we are as a community. Citizens create solidarity by finding ways to act together around shared interests that bridge differences in race, ethnicity, religion, economic class, culture, gender identity and disability. And citizens find ways to tackle the social and economic structures that reduce some people's chances to build real wealth by producing social exclusion and inequality,.

Bridging obvious difference

As visible diversity grows, strengthening community means finding more encompassing identities and new ways to build social solidarity, a **bigger we**. Evidence from the US suggests that growing diversity can lead ethnic groups to become more exclusive and draw closer together in a *smaller we* surrounded by an alien, even threatening, *them*. This has negative effects on real wealth both within and across the diverse groups: trust declines, altruism and cooperation is rarer, and friendships fewer.[*]

When platforms for contribution engage only those members of a community who already share a sense of common identity, they strengthen **bonding** social relationships. They reinforce a more closely gathered sense of who **we** are –a smaller we. The bonds of culture, language, race, ethnicity, religion or social class are important sources of identity and resourcefulness. So are groups that define themselves by embracing a difference as an defining boundary of identity, as some advocates of disability culture do.

When platforms for contribution purposely include those with different identities, without demanding the denial of differences, they strengthen **bridging** social relationships. Both bridging and bonding relationships are vital resources, but without purposeful effort to create bridges, communities of more tightly bonded groups will miss many opportunities to create real wealth.

Our vision of a new social settlement aims to achieve: social justice and well-being for all, a fairer and more equitable distribution of power, and environmental sustainability. We need solidarity to reach these goals.

By solidarity, we mean feelings of sympathy and responsibility between people that promote mutual support. It involves collective action towards a shared objective, to tackle a common challenge or adversary. For a new social settlement, it must be inclusive, expansive and active, both between groups who are 'strangers' to each other, and across generations. The 'adversary' is not other people, but the systems and structures that shore up inequalities, foster short-term greed, plunder the natural environment and blight the prospects of future generations.

Solidarity is essential to a new social settlement because none of the goals can be achieved by individuals or groups simply fending for themselves and pursuing their own interests. They depend on collective policy and practice: sharing resources and acting together to deal with risks and problems that people cannot cope with alone. So it is vital to create conditions for different groups and individuals to feel sympathy and responsibility for each other.

Social justice and well-being for all can only be achieved by pooling the means to meet common needs, by subscribing to shared values and obligations, and by encouraging mutually supportive relations between people.

–New Economics Foundation

---

[*] Robert Putnam (2007). *E pluribus unum*: Diversity and community in the twenty-first century. *Scandinavian Political Studies 30*, 2: 137-174.

Overcoming social exclusion

The healing social life is
found

When in the mirror of each
human soul

The entire community
finds its reflection,

And when in the community

The virtue of each one is
living.

–Rudolf Steiner

Social exclusion and structural inequality of money and property significantly depress real wealth.* Communities that marginalize people by negative discrimination –expressed in insecure housing and unsafe neighborhoods, inadequate health care and restricted access to good food, poorly resourced early education and schools, ineffective transport and lack of good jobs– pay a high cost in lost real wealth and increased ill health.

Social exclusion increases the social distance people have to travel to form productive relationships with people they see as unlike them. Greater social distance makes difference more a threat and less a potential source of richness and resourcefulness. Communities that contain people with apparent differences fragment into *US vs THEM* subgroups. Energy goes into reinforcing walls that keep *THEM* away from *US* rather than bridging social distance to create beneficial alliances. Those who are materially privileged are vulnerable to political narratives that blame the consequences of social exclusion entirely on those who are excluded and frame them as dangerous. These practices and the mental models that generate them lock a community into social exclusion.

In order to make progress, those with privilege recognize their responsibility to a bigger we, reconsider stories that separate them from people who are socially excluded, and find ways to invest in increasing real wealth for the whole community. They risk reshaping privileges that benefit them. Those who experience exclusion risk extending trust to others who have different interests and greater assets, reconsider stories that separate them from participation in common platforms for contribution, and find ways to invest their capacities and assets in creating real wealth with the whole, diverse population around them.

Conflict and failure are very likely experiences along this path, but the rewards of even a small decrease in social exclusion makes the journey worthwhile.

From ME to WE

Progress toward a community that works for everybody can only happen with a deep change in mental models. The one dimensional idea that wealth equals money and social effectiveness is adequately measured by a single bottom line in profit statements cuts off too many possibilities. This way of thinking hides in-

---

* See Kate Pickett & Richard Wilkinson (2010). *The spirit level: Why equality makes societies stronger.* New York: Bloomsbury Press and Joseph Stiglitz (2012). *The price of inequality: How today's divided society threatens our future.* New York: W. W. Norton.

terdependencies among people and with our environment. It reinforces the twin beliefs that each individual or family is on its own and that responsibility for the whole can be satisfied by each individual's vigorous and single-minded pursuit of their own idea of just what is good for me and mine. Worth equals cash value. The best answer to the challenges of our time is more of the same: more consumption, sharper competition and more financial instruments that accelerate money chasing money around the globe. When citizens act as if this were the only true story of the way things are, and that this story does not have dangerous consequences, progress on the big challenges of social inclusion and sustainability slows.

A more adaptive mental model recognizes each dimension of real wealth. This mindset celebrates the possibilities and struggles that come along with looking for productive co-creations in a community that contains and offers resources for exchange to a network of diverse me's. Each citizen's capacity to pursue a life that he or she has good reasons to value results from individual effort and development in relationship with diverse others, within the environmental spheres from neighborhood to planet. Money assets are one result of co-creative effort, especially when material inequality is steadily reduced, but development of capacities, networks, relationships and resourcefulness matter even more.

A community that wants to work better for everybody will intentionally encourage a shift of mental model from ME to WE. ME is seeing and acting as isolated individuals rationally striving to accumulate material assets in order to consume more in an economy unsustainably geared to exhaust our planet. WE is seeing and acting as purposeful co-creating actors embedded interdependently with one another and the earth. This shift is not simply a matter of using new words. New experiences result from a shift in the quality of our awareness that expands our sense of connectedness through empathic listening to diverse perspectives, makes room to appreciate the highest potential in our shared situation, and energizes learning to actualize that potential. We shift the quality of our awareness by becoming more and more conscious of the patterns of thinking and emotion that limit our ability to sense and act on the highest possible future available to us. Doing the personal work of deepening our awareness leads us into a new social field in which the work of moving into a sustainable future can flourish.[*]

Emerging systems conditions require new leadership capacities that enable us to feel and act from interdependence. The three capacities we need to develop are: a knowledge of suffering, altruism and courage. All can be cultivated.

–Karma Ura
Centre for Bhutan Studies

From

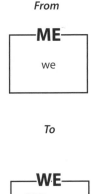

---
[*] See Otto Scharmer & Katrin Kaufer (2013). *Leading from the emerging future.* San Francisco: Barrett-Koehler.

People who are shifting into a mental model that recognizes WE…

> … notice and question the assumptions of the ME focused stories that narrow their perceptions and limit their options for shared and inclusive action.

> … decide to co-create new ways rather than consume existing options off the shelf or complain about others' inability to satisfy their desires by providing what they wish to consume.

> … reach outside their comfort zone and cross existing borders with an attitude of openness and curiosity in order to connect with co-creators who are different from them in important ways.

The role of people with developmental disabilities

Disabled people are fighting for a society which celebrates difference, a society which does not react to physical, sensory or intellectual impairments, or emotional distress,with fear and prejudice. We want a society that recognizes the difficulties we face, but which also values us for what we are.

Our hopes for the future are based on the justice of our wish for control over our lives, the strength of our demands for equal participation, the passion of our belief in the value of our contribution to the communities in which we live.

–BBC: Disabled Lives

As a group, people with developmental disabilities mark a limit to the common sense of citizenship. Through the lens of wealth as money they are vulnerable to being seen and treated as social junk, a drain on the economy and the productivity of the families burdened with their care and the workers diverted from productive efforts by the supervision their dependency demands.[*] At best they are objects of charity to be occupied and amused when economic surplus permits and neglected or warehoused at lowest cost when economic times are tight, at worst they are sub-humans whose lives are not worth the cost of their keep.[†]

Under this devaluing view, people with developmental disabilities are at great risk of social invisibility and imposed lack of voice. They carry social projections of otherness and incapacity that obscure their gifts. Their fellow citizens move inside a story that portrays them as incompetent to meet the responsibilities and rights of contributing citizenship. This story justifies a form of professional control that isolates them from ordinary places and activities and places them under supervision in groups of others seen as "their own kind".

As these "others" overcome social exclusion and discover pathways to the interdependencies that create real wealth they under-

---

[*] For reasons related to the dominant economic story and deep rooted fear of dependency, in the US the work of providing assistance to disabled people is very poorly compensated and seen as having little economic value.

[†] If this seems excessive, remember that the Nazi drive to exterminate threats to racial purity began in institutions for people with developmental disabilities where methods of mass killing were tested and perfected. Today, prenatal screening in money rich countries results in the termination of a high percentage of pregnancies when Down Syndrome is detected. See Simon Duffy (2013). *The unmaking of man: Disability and the holocaust.* goo.gl/zrvNdR

mine narratives that lock communities in too narrow a sense of citizenship and too small a sense of who **we** really can be together. Their gifts and capacities, once engaged, celebrate the power of interdependency and a form of social inclusion that does not extinguish differences but benefits from diversity. .

Members of Urban Innovations, an example of this kind of co-creation, generate opportunities for meaningful participation by joining and linking the hopeful efforts of grass roots organizations committed to building real wealth in neighborhoods of New York City's Harlem. Their co-creations, one of which is described on the following pages, includes actions to improve literacy, offer access to healthy food, celebrate cultural diversity, and revitalize public space. The many connections they have made open paths to individually meaningful employment and their engagement in a rich variety of community initiatives has increased their relationships, capacities and resourcefulness.

Real Communities

The Georgia Council on Developmental Disabilities (GCDD) is co-inventing a new pathway to social inclusion called Real Communities.* The Council invests some of its resources in local groups organized to make progress on issues of concern to a whole community and willing to actively recruit and include interested citizens with developmental disabilities in contributing roles.

Real Communities supports social invention by strengthening local connections to three sets of practices: community development to guide the process of community building; person-centered supports to guide the discovery of people's gifts and offer the conditions necessary for their contribution; and purposeful learning.†

GCDD's interest is based on the conviction that an important privilege of citizenship is the choice to join with others to build a stronger community. The purpose of Real Communities is to learn how to make this

---

* There are links to descriptive materials and videos at goo.gl/vqWtRW Real Communities was initially organized around practices from Mike Green. *ABCD in Action: When People Care Enough to Act* inclusion.com.As it has developed, ideas and practices from Popular Education and Visionary Organizing have also been helpful.

† Real Communities draws on Theory U, described in Chapter 5, for purposeful learning practices.

choice real for more people with developmental disabilities so that they can exercise the responsibility to act as contributing citizens through membership in a local group that is at work on making their community better for everyone.

In return for a modest stipend to support a part time community builder, opportunities to learn, and active support from GCDD staff, local groups make these four commitments.

Commitment	...this means learning
People with developmental disabilities are active members who influence the group's direction and participate in doing its work. Action is with people with developmental disabilities, not for them.	...to keep asking "Whose gifts are missing?" and discovering how to reach out, invite and actively involve people who need personalized support in order to contribute to their community.
Action focuses on making the community better for everyone. The initiative is not about specialized responses to disability but about engaging people who care about working together on local issues of common interest.	...to listen carefully to fellow citizens outside the circle of those primarily concerned with disability to discover what local issues people care about enough to take action together.
Over time, the initiative builds up local capacity for collective action by creating and strengthening continuing relationships with a variety of associations and groups. The initiative is not about single victories but about building communities where people have a growing capacity to act together.	...to build and strengthen local alliances and networks.
Participants take responsibility for sharing what they are learning. The initiative creates new ways for people with developmental disabilities to do the work of active citizenship and makes what they have found available to other communities.	...to reflect together on the work and identify and communicate its lessons.

The story of The Little Green Wagon on the next page describes the creation of a pathway to contribution. Learning Asset Based Community Development prompted farmer's market leaders to ask *Whose gifts are missing?* when they were planning to expand. Personal networks identified a few people with developmental disabilities willing to get involved. Some people, disabled and not, found meaning in their involvement and have stayed active, others have drifted away. Engagement results from mindfulness about invitation, asking *will you help with...*, not setting individual goals, project milestones or applying service world tools to organize people's lives. Person-centered support matters for everyone, regardless of their defined disability status.

I take care of the Little Green Wagon and water it. I like to talk with school kids about the plants. Parents learn what we do with gardening too. That makes me feel happy.

–Johnny Smith

The Little Green Wagon - A Way of Organizing

The Little Green Wagon invites children and young people who visit the **Forsyth Farmers' Market** to plant a seed, watch it grow from one Saturday to the next, and take their plant home when it is ready to transplant. Plants that don't find a home with the children who planted them are given away.

This project, designed and implemented by members of **Mixed Greens** a group of Forsyth Farmer's Market supporters, serves the market's mission by promoting young people's understanding and participation in the local food system.

The Little Green Wagon embodies a way of organizing that mirrors the market's commitment to *give priority to organic production over conventional, whole foods over prepared foods, craft or artisan production of staples over more processed food.*

- It has grown organically from the creative efforts of people who care about the market and want to craft new routes to active participation.

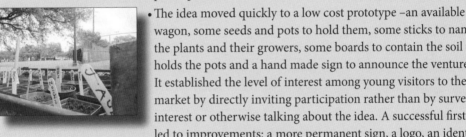

- The idea moved quickly to a low cost prototype –an available wagon, some seeds and pots to hold them, some sticks to name the plants and their growers, some boards to contain the soil that holds the pots and a hand made sign to announce the venture. It established the level of interest among young visitors to the market by directly inviting participation rather than by surveying interest or otherwise talking about the idea. A successful first day led to improvements: a more permanent sign, a logo, an identity for the project on *facebook*.

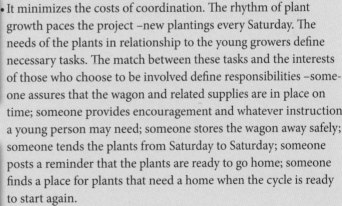
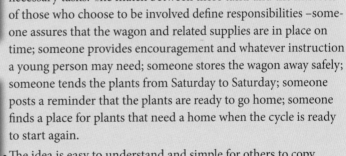

- It minimizes the costs of coordination. The rhythm of plant growth paces the project –new plantings every Saturday. The needs of the plants in relationship to the young growers define necessary tasks. The match between these tasks and the interests of those who choose to be involved define responsibilities –someone assures that the wagon and related supplies are in place on time; someone provides encouragement and whatever instruction a young person may need; someone stores the wagon away safely; someone tends the plants from Saturday to Saturday; someone posts a reminder that the plants are ready to go home; someone finds a place for plants that need a home when the cycle is ready to start again.

- The idea is easy to understand and simple for others to copy.

John O'Brien & Teri Schell wrote this in 2012. The photos are Teri's. The Mixed Greens group includes several members with developmental disabilities, one of whom continues to play a key role in providing the Little Green Wagon to children.

• Success can be estimated easily, at a glance: how many pots does the wagon hold at the end of a day of planting? how many growers stop by to check on their plants? how many pots find a home with their planters? A deeper sense can be gained by listening for the stories that flow around the Little Green Wagon.

• The idea can find its limits naturally. Will the bigger area allowed by an offered truck bed encourage more participation or will it become unwieldy? Trying will tell and retreat to a smaller scale is easy.

• Like any sort of human scale farming, The Little Green Wagon is completely vulnerable to the will of those who tend it. It can continue only as long as young people want to plant and see their plants grow. It is sustained and improved only if people choose to cultivate it. When care fades, the project will die. But even if the project ends, if people choose, the knowledge gained and relationships strengthened will fertilize a new effort.

Organizing for an inclusive and sustainable community can puzzle people who think at an industrial scale. Somewhat like farmers concerned to build living soil, the strategy exemplified by The Little Green Wagon aims to build increasingly diverse relationships through shared experience of acting on care for a place and all of its people. Much more depends on what emerges from the ways engaged people care to invest their energy than on achieving measured milestones in a grand strategy. This can be frustrating to people who want a sense of control or the satisfaction of quick returns on well defined projects, but ignoring the reality that community depends on recognizing and enabling one another's gifts deprives people of the conditions necessary to create the organic, the whole, and the artisanal.

In addition to the Farmer's Market GCDD has partnered with a church, a city government, an organization that advocates for women whose lives are impacted by prison, an organization that advocates against the death penalty, a citizen group advocating for rural public transportation and groups of Korean immigrant families with developmental disabled members, family advocates seeking to increase local opportunities for inclusion, and refugee families who created a community garden.

GCDD has learned from these investments.

- People with developmental disabilities can build real wealth and find meaning and enjoyment in contributing to civic action intended to benefit their whole community.

- It is difficult to escape a world circumscribed by developmental disability specific concerns. Organizing efforts aimed to include and benefit a larger community have had difficulty achieving escape velocity from the world of services because so many issues caused by their requirements for assistance interrupt and take priority. Social justice organizations unrelated to disability experience a gravitational pull toward the world of services created by the common belief that people with developmental disabilities have special needs that can only be met by experts. Three groups have moved on from Real Communities to become successful disability advocacy groups.

- The presence of a part-time paid, well supported person who is responsible for organizing community building efforts multiplies the contributions a group makes. A story from the work of one community builder follows.

- Purposeful learning activities make a difference in groups' ability to penetrate the fog of specialness that seems to envelop people with developmental disabilities, see fellow contributors and respond in commonsense ways to their requirements for accommodation and assistance. This learning process matters as much for people with developmental disabilities, who have frequently come to expect separation and passivity, as it is for those who are not identified as disabled. Learning journeys to places of potential and regular opportunities for retreat and reflection have been helpful in revealing possibilities and useful practices.

Preparing the soil in which social inclusion can flourish can be a long and difficult process. As we will see in the next four chapters, increasing real wealth depends on people with developmental disabilities and families who choose to be pathfinders and find willing allies and partners to co-create the conditions for a good life. Otherwise people with developmental disabilities will remain on the sidelines, excluded, supervised and impoverished no matter how much public money goes into containing and maintaining them.

Growing Leadership

In 2012, Basmat Ahmed began work as a Community Builder in Clarkston, GA, a richly diverse small city where people speak 60 languages and half the residents were born outside the US and resettled as refugees, including Basmat whose family moved from Sudan in 2006. Hired through a partnership between the GCDD Real Communities Initiative and the Global Growers Network, Basmat's first round of learning conversations brought together 12 families from 10 different countries, some of whom have family members with disabilities, who were interested enough in growing vegetables to reclaim a vacant lot in a neglected county park and turn it into a thriving community garden.

As the garden has grown to involve 50 families, those involved in the garden have assumed responsibility for it. Basmat has moved on to organize a group interested in creating a local grassroots leadership network and developing new community builders. Her work has multiplied her cross cultural relationships and her understanding of person-centered support for inclusion has grown –learning that has benefited her own brother, who has a developmental disability. Others in the community see her as a resource, which brought her to Maha.

Maha, a refugee from Iraq, was recently resettled with her four children in Clarkston. Her 3 year old son, Mohamed, has cerebral palsy and the whole family struggled with isolation. Basmat developed a relationship that allows her to encourage Maha to identify and act on matters she cares about: an early educational setting that includes Mohamed and other children in learning both English and Arabic and a safe, accessible playground in her apartment complex. Recognition that she can make a difference for her own family and others broke Maha out of isolation and into a growing variety of new connections. She attended meetings of the Clarkston Early Learning Network, enrolled in an English as a Second Language Course, and attended Mommy and Me with her baby, Adam.

With coaching from Basmat and help from Roberta Malavenda, an Early Education specialist for CDF: A Collective Action Initiative, Maha negotiated with the owner of her apartment complex to create a safe and accessible play space. The landlord also offers free space in the complex for a Ready School, where 12 children age three and four with and without disabilities learn in English and Arabic. Maha and other parents were active in planning the Ready School and Roberta was able to win a small grant for the school. The grant employs a part time teacher and three mothers, including Maha, as parent aides.

While young people with developmental disabilities and their families benefit, Basmat's focus is on progress on issues that build community leadership and include people with disabilities, not providing a disability service. Maha moved from isolation and passivity to connection, part-time employment, contribution and leadership. Her children moved from isolation to participation and learning. Basmat shared her experiences and connections, encouraged and coached Maha to take action with other parents to offer their children safe play space and culture appropriate learning, mobilized and multiplied local resources, and added another grassroots leader to the community.

Simon Duffy on Full Citizenship*

Citizenship for people with intellectual disabilities is exactly the same as citizenship for anyone else. That's one of the good things about the idea of citizenship –citizenship is important for all of us.

At the heart of citizenship is a simple idea of how we combine two important moral principles…

> *…we are all different, and being different is good and*

> *…we are all equal, with equal rights and equal value.*

A society that is committed to citizenship is one that knows how to support all of its members to flourish as unique individuals.

Citizens all have equal rights, but there are also some very practical things that help us be citizens:

> *Purpose –have our own unique sense of who we are and how we should live*

> *Control –the ability to shape and direct our own life*

> *Money –enough money so we can act freely and be independent*

> *Home –a place of our own, where we belong*

> *Help –getting help and support from other people*

> *Giving –making a contribution to the community*

> *Love –being connected, valued and enjoying the many sides of love*

Of course some people do need a bit more help than others to take advantage of these things. Some people need help to communicate, to manage money or to join in their community. But everybody can do it.

The first big threat [to citizenship] is that society still sees support to people with intellectual disabilities as a financial cost –and then when money seems tight– people start trying to reduce this cost in ways which are damaging. We must see each human being for who they really are –a gift.

The second big threat is eugenics. Some people seem to prefer the idea that there be no people with intellectual disabilities in our world. Silently, by testing, abortion, neo-natal death, poor healthcare and institutionalization those people who are different are being removed. And the more this happens the more likely it is that those who remain will also come under threat.

---

* From an interview in the *Yearbook of the Finnish Service Foundation for People with an Intellectual Disability.* (2012) goo.gl/cu2X8H

Urban Innovators Bring Little Free Libraries to Harlem

Urban Innovations is the collective effort of a group of graduates of New York City's special school district and their partners from two agencies, Job Path and AHRC. Their purpose is to create alliances that let them discover and contribute to what wants to be born to make their Harlem neighborhoods communities that work better for everybody.

Urban Innovators meet as a whole group for a few hours each month to explore what they are discovering about opportunities for positive engagement in their neighborhoods and their own capacities to make a difference. A very active closed Facebook page shares news and coordinates action between meetings. Members have strengthened their own voices and capacities for observation by participating in hip hop, spoken word and drama workshops, making art and sharing poetry.

Small teams work with their allies around areas of shared interest. In their first year members participated in a rich and welcoming fabric of community action and focused their diverse interests on contribution. Their next challenge is overcoming the service system's many barriers to paid employment that matches their individual capacities.

The practice of approaching grass roots groups from a position of openness to understanding their purposes and supporting their activities has created a network that reveals four complementary fields for local action: availability of healthy food; cultivation of good safe spaces for people to share; celebration of the rich and diverse local mix of cultures and identities; and promotion of literacy. Four themes for action weave through these efforts: a commitment to mobilize local capacities; the aim of developing leadership, particularly leadership among young people; investment in strengthening the local economy: and the creation of art, music and poetry.

As the Urban Innovators act with their allies, new possibilities emerge. Their approach follows a pattern. One thing leads to another when you engage with others who care for the same place with different purposes, stay open to the call in their agenda, imagine the possibilities of adding your capacities to theirs, and find ways to do things together. By working systematically to connect across boundaries, Urban innovations has been a bridging agent, bringing their allies into shared activities that would not have happened without their presence and participation.

This emergent approach contests sharply with typical human service planning. Typical individual plans state goals and outline steps to reach them. Urban Innovators discover, pursue and renew personally and civilly meaningful goals as they walk and roll through their neighborhoods, sensing new possibilities for constructive action with open minds, open hearts and willingness to join those they meet who are acting with hope for a community that works for everybody.

There are challenges. System wide fear and risk aversion limit the ability of agency partners to move with people as they explore new possibilities. Neighborhoods are shaped by the interaction of creative efforts to build real wealth and violently destructive forces. Most families struggle with compounding effects of severe income inequality and racism. Many Urban Innovators themselves have had limited opportunities to discover, develop and offer their capacities because they are products of a special education system designed to produce clients for services that congregate and control the socially excluded and professionally designated incompetent.

Shared desire for a rich life is strong enough to energize Urban Innovators and make a productive way through these challenges. The story on the facing page sketches just one of the paths they have found. Little Free Libraries are a small scale platform for generating real wealth through reciprocal exchange, *Take a book, bring a book*. Their creation mobilizes many talents –carpentry, decoration, negotiation with authorities– and maintaining them creates the role of Steward, responsible for stocking the libraries and keeping them in good shape.

- Collaborates with Urban Innovations & inspires interest in literacy, especially in reading with & for children.
- Later, connects **Urban Innovations** to **Marcus Garvey Park Alliance** after establishing the Success Garden Library

Emergence: observing & acting so that one good thing leads on to another

- Gets the idea for Little Free Libraries from a Facebook friend & forms a crew to make one happen.
- Builds on previous relationship with **Harlem Grown** to create a space for the first library.
- Organizes members & allies to acquire, decorate, plant & steward the first library.

- Connects with **Marcus Garvey Park Alliance** to plant & steward two more libraries & to provide mentors for children's reading activities.

- Provides space for the first Little Free Library in **The Harlem Success Garden** despite concerns that it will be vandalized & plundered.

- Sees the connection of Little Free Libraries to its vision of a renewed park filled with local people of all ages & offers hospitality to Urban Innovators.

- Negotiates with NYC Parks Department for necessary permissions & permits & quiets concerns about Little Free Libraries becoming a nuisance.

- Joins in installing & dedicating the new libraries.
- Invites Urban Innovators into additional activities including children's reading & renewing the Park's Watchtower

What people who create real wealth do is understand and emphasize the importance of relationships and personal connections to achieving their objectives.

2

Pathfinders and Allies

*Failing to meet the fundamental human
needs of autonomy, empowerment, and
freedom is a potent cause of ill health...
changing social conditions to ensure that
people have the freedom to lead lives they
have reason to value would lead to marked
reductions in health inequalities.*

–Michael Marmot*

Pathfinders are people with developmental disabilities who
want more in their lives than their communities and available
forms of assistance currently offer and choose to risk a quest
in search of a better life. Their desire recruits allies who join as
companions on their journey. Often, a successful quest involves
people and their allies entering into partnership with an organization that invests public money in developing and providing the
individualized accommodations and assistance people need in
order to participate successfully in community life. Their quest
develops capacities in themselves and in their allies and partners.
It opens new possibilities that inspire others to imagine better
and want more for themselves. As others receive the gift of pathfinders' action, communities increase real wealth and offer better
life chances to people with developmental disabilities.

Allies are people who respond to the pathfinder's call with
personal commitment to share their real wealth in service of the
pathfinder's purpose. They accept responsibility for contributing
what they can to enable the pathfinder to find the way to a life
they have even more reasons to value. They stick with the pathfinder even when the way is uncertain or when the journey gets
stuck in defeat or discouragement.

Allies draw on their capacities and assets to recognize the pathfinder's gifts and offer practical help in finding and traveling the

_____

* Chair of the World Health
Organization's Commission
on Social Determinants of
Health. More at instituteof-
healthequity.org

path. They open their social networks to recruit trustworthy connections and discover missing knowledge. Entrained by a feeling
of connection to the pathfinder's purpose, their resourcefulness
motivates invention and persistence. They form a personal bond.

Recruitment can seem mysterious. It does not depend on verbal proficiency. Some allies report joining a journey of social invention in response to a call for deep change expressed through
challenging behavior. Others, often family members, sense a
person's purpose and desire for more in their lives despite very
limited understanding of a person's communication.

Now is the time for pathfinders
to make a difference

Pathfinders have a vital part to play at this moment in history.
December 2006 marked the culmination of more than 50 years
of international advocacy for the rights of people with disabilities when The UN General Assembly adopted *The Convention
on the Rights of Persons with Disabilities.* * *The Convention* recognizes that respect for the dignity and worth of every person with
a disability demands purposeful and sustained effort to overcome discrimination and equalize opportunity so that people
have the necessary support to participate fully and effectively in
society. *The Convention* specifies 27 areas for action to establish
the rights and responsibilities of people with disabilities. Taken
together they express the highest aspirations of the worldwide
movement for disability rights.

Pathfinders contribute in important ways to making the practical meaning of three Articles of *The Convention* clear and real
by pursuing their desires for real homes, real learning, real jobs
and full participation in community life. *Article 19* defines the
right to choose where and with whom one lives, with the personal
assistance necessary to support inclusion and prevent isolation or
segregation from the community. *Article 24* calls for an inclusive
system of education that ensures adults access to post-secondary
education and opportunities for lifelong learning. *Article 27* estab-
lishes the right to opportunities to make a living by work freely
chosen in a labor market that is open, inclusive and accessible.

The language of these articles seems clear enough, but when it
comes to putting them to work for people with developmental
disabilities they open-up three big uncertainties.

---

* Read this historic document at goo.gl/zOfSsW Quotes on this page are
excerpted from the full text.

Rebecca Beayni Shapes the UN Convention

In August 2005, supported by her family and circle of friends, Rebecca Beayni journeyed from Toronto to UN headquarters in New York to share her experience with the committee charged with drafting *The Convention on the Rights of Persons with Disabilities*. Rebecca's pathfinding life as a contributing citizen who depends on and trusts others to understand her dreams, pursue meaningful opportunities and assist her with daily life makes her a powerful messenger for peace, interdependence, inclusion and choice. This is her statement, composed by members of her circle and read by her friend and dance partner Anna Mongillo.

Rebecca has been blessed, ironically, with cerebral palsy and an intellectual disability which makes her dependent on others for almost everything. Despite this, Rebecca had led and continues to lead a favored life where she is an integral, functional, and impactful member of her society. She represents persons with disabilities who demand to invoke their rights as citizens to be seen, heard, and allowed to make meaningful contributions to the community. Usually, when people see Rebecca, they do not initially see her as able to share and contribute. It is not her physical limitations but rather an attitude of unwillingness to see beyond them that can bar her from becoming a full citizen.

A part of being a whole society or a democratic society is making certain ALL voices are heard, however, some of our society's most vulnerable citizens are ignored. Rebecca forces people to slow down to communicate with her and this is a gift to the world, slowing people down to the point where they have to listen to those otherwise-ignored voices. This guides us in the direction of a good society; which is measured by how people treat, listen deeply to, empathize and interact with its most vulnerable members.

Rebecca was fully included and integrated into the regular classroom since elementary school and she has had wonderful teachers who planned creatively and effectively to cater to her learning needs. Part of this was having Rebecca's classmates play critical roles in assisting her and helping her teachers to create accommodations that would be to her benefit. Not only did these youngsters learn the importance of responsibility for others, task commitment and community building, they also gained from an educational perspective as well; since teaching strategies used to assist Rebecca helped all levels of learners. Teachers, administrators, fellow students, and co-workers say that Rebecca's mere presence changes the very fabric of their relationships, making them more collaborative, more compassionate, and more intuitive to strategies that advantage all persons.

Rebecca continues to disseminate citizenship education in her pursuits as an adult. She listens to Grade 1 students read at her old elementary school, [and as she cannot speak the children] are able to read freely with no expectation of criticism. Rebecca is also a facilitator at the Royal Ontario Museum in the Bio-Diversity Hands-On exhibit, helping people discover things that they might not otherwise notice. She also brings hope and inspires the vulnerable and dispossessed through her own vulnerability when she volunteers at the Mustard Seed Drop-In Centre with its community kitchen, library, and sewing room. Salt and Light TV is another place that Rebecca contributes her gifts. Her presence reminds this Catholic community of the values that form the foundation of their faith.

Most inspiring to many is the fact that Rebecca is a dancer. She dances with the Spirit Movers liturgical dance group and testifies to her strong faith using this medium. Her success in overcoming obstacles is mainly due to the deep and committed relationships she has developed with family, friends, her support circle as well as collaboration with community groups such as the church, schools and other venues. Her support circle, who has met regularly for the past 13 years, help interpret her goals and dreams. Rebecca does not speak, so those around her ensure that she has many other ways to express her feelings and desires. It is  *imperative that she have long term relationships, both paid and unpaid, who can help build the capacity of the community to welcome her gifts. In return Rebecca helps them create a better world for all. This is citizenship, and Rebecca is an esteemed educator in this regard.*

Susan, Rebecca's mother, describes what it takes to support Rebecca in her roles as a messenger for social justice through creative interdependence in the spirit of *ubuntu* –the realization that I can't be free to be fully me unless you are free to be fully you.

In order for Rebecca to live the life she does, she needs one-on-one support for everything, including communication. The fact that Rebecca lives a rich and textured life while making a meaningful contribution to her community is significant. This is due to the fact that she has a committed support circle around her and has financial support which is individualized so that she can choose and train her own staff.

Rebecca's story is powerfully told in two videos: *Revel in the Light* and *Dance in the Shadow*. To learn more about Rebecca's interests, contributions and further adventures, and to order the videos, visit her website, www.rebeccabeayni.com

First, there is considerable variation in desire for change among people with developmental disabilities and their families. A real say in decision making is fundamental to *The Convention*, which formalizes the demand of disabled activists, *Nothing about us without us!* It would contravene the convention, and worse, disrespect people, to simply demand that people abandon their day center cohort and fall in line for placement in a community job.

Second, the limits of accommodating and assisting people with complex impairments are not clear, and knowledge of what does work is unevenly distributed from place to place, so what is possible keeps changing and what people in any given place think is possible varies considerably.

Third, people read the words inclusion and choice in different ways. We understand these words as a call for deep change in the relationship between people with developmental disabilities and other citizens that demands the invention of new ways to organize assistance. Others see current organizations as fully able to deliver without much disruption to their current mental models, structures and investments.

Pathfinders don't usually set out to implement *The Convention*, They simply seek a better life. But their journeys have the good effect of informing the uncertainties that come along with the rights *The Convention* enshrines. When pathfinders and their allies and partners pursue their desire for good lives as contributing citizens they create grounded knowledge that pushes the limits of what inclusion and choice can mean and what it takes to equalize opportunities for full and effective participation in an inclusive society. They add to the stock of approaches that other people can adapt and increase capacity for solving problems and designing good support. Pathfinders become models and sources of inspiration and knowledge for other people and the organizations that serve people with developmental disabilities. Organizations and administrations that want to realize *The Convention's* promise will encourage pathfinders in their quests and gather and share the gifts of practical knowledge that they create.

Marian Jackson, then President of Georgia People First, expressed the change she wants to be in the world with this image. Her purpose is to build a bridge that she & other people with developmental disabilities can cross to exchange their gifts with other community members. She sees herself as crossing over and going back to encourage the next person to risk crossing to more happiness. Her chosen model is Harriet Tubman, who escaped slavery and then repeatedly traveled back South to guide others to freedom while she worked for the abolition of slavery.

Heroes with a thousand faces

We love quest stories. Dorothy finds the way home to Kansas. Harry, Hermione and Ron play their part in restoring the freedom to flourish in ordinary wizarding lives. Frodo and Sam take the ring to the place of its making and return home to reestablish order in the Shire. The crews of one Starship Enterprise after another boldly go where no one has gone before. Buffy comes to terms with her calling as a vampire slayer and awakens the world's young women to their power. Luke Skywalker becomes a Jedi and the Death Star dies. Unique characters and circumstances follow a deeper common pattern and remind us that leaving the familiar and risking the uncertainties of a quest attracts unanticipated difficulties and unexpected help, clarifies purpose and develops capacities and brings gifts won along the way back to the questor's community.[*]

What people want is simple: someone to love, somewhere to live, somewhere to work and something to hope for.

–Norman Kirk

Pathfinders mostly search for commonplace good things in ordinary community places. Friends and someone to love who loves you back. A secure place that deserves to be called home with the freedom to fully inhabit it. The chance to learn what is personally meaningful and liberating. The opportunity to earn a living through dignified work. The means to participate in associations and events that express personal interests and contribute to community well being. A placard attached to a demonstrator's wheelchair at a protest against confining people with disabilities in nursing homes set Star Trek's explorations in a new key, *Our mission: to boldly go where everyone else has already been.*

Pathfinders are more likely to be found weeding their patch in a community garden, setting up chairs for a public meeting, serving coffee in a church fellowship hall, entering data or shredding confidential documents in an office, pursuing an apprenticeship in auto mechanics, or taking a university drama class than they are to be seen climbing Mount Doom or confronting Darth Vader. And yet, in most places, these ordinary experiences are the exceptional result of intentional effort to open new pathways by building new relationships.

Seeking your own home or a community job that suits you or the opportunity to play a contributing community role gets the feel of a hero's journey because of the surplus difficulty that people with developmental disabilities typically encounter in establishing

---

[*] Joseph Campbell (1972) describes the classic version of the hero's journey in *Hero with a thousand faces, 2nd edition*. Princeton, NJ: Princeton University Press. Our version is drawn from listening to the stories of pathfinders with his idea in mind but it identifies the journey's path in somewhat different terms.

themselves in ordinary community roles. The UN debated the need to add a disability specific convention on top of the Universal Declaration of Human Rights and decided to do so because they judged that without particular focus on creating better life chances people with disabilities will remain disadvantaged.

Surplus difficulty has many sources. Almost every person with a developmental disability who wants to play valued roles in ordinary community life must deal with these constraints, which work together to reproduce social exclusion and limit the creation of real wealth.

- Disability imposes financial costs that other citizens don't face. Some of these costs are met by a benefits system that discourages work, limits people's disposable income and, unless income is carefully managed, threatens loss of necessary assistance. These systems have complex requirements that create anxiety for many people and their allies. People are easily locked into material poverty that inhibits participation in community life.

- People with developmental disabilities rely significantly on public services for transportation, leisure, housing and medical care. When these services work well for all citizens this is less a problem than it is in much of the US, where public transit is likely to be inconvenient if it exists at all, housing policy leaves many people insecurely housed, and access to medical care depends on physicians' and dentists' willingness to take Medicaid. Where there is a political bias against public goods, good quality options are limited and there is an untested assumption that dependence on benevolence and charity is sufficient.

- Eligibility for disability services depends on regular proof of incompetence, but proof of eligibility does not necessarily entitle people and their families to adequate assistance or funds. Access to assistance remains a professional gift within funding limits and access conditions set by interaction among levels of government.

- Public funds usually buy places in group settings whose operators must comply with complex rules, some of which limit people's freedom to participate in community life. Even when administrators offer the option of self-directed individual budgets, there are very likely to be bureaucratically imposed constraints on how people can use the funds, which can limit social mobility.

CURRENT REALITY FOR PEOPLE IN THE US DEVELOPMENTAL DISABILITIES SERVICE SYSTEM*

Choose where and with whom they live?

72% live in a "family caregivers" home. An estimated 268,000 people are "waiting for a residential service."

Of the remaining people

14% live in a facility with more than 16 residents

9% live in a facility with 7-15 residents

65% live with a group of 6 or fewer people

12% live with support in their own home

Work freely chosen in an environment that is open, inclusive & accessible?

20% are employed in community integrated jobs.

Integrated employment ranges across states from 2% to 88% of adults funded for developmental disability services.

---

* See D. Braddock (2013) *The state of the states in developmental disabilities.* Washington: AAIDD & *StateInfo.data* www.statedata.info

- Low expectations result in underinvestment in developmentally powerful assistance and accommodation. This creates a self-fulfilling prophecy that inhibits the growth of people's capacities.

- Despite a growing appreciation of diversity, a shadow of otherness falls on many contacts between people with developmental disabilities and their fellow citizens. Hate crimes and an increased incidence of bullying blight some people's lives and discourage leaving home. Discrimination, shaming and rejection play out in many ways. Accommodations may be resented as unreasonable impositions. Public cluelessness yields disregard for people's dignity. Even workplaces, schools and community associations that welcome people with developmental disabilities can have difficulty fully including them. If the still common sense of us vs them is not overcome, people with developmental disabilities will not be able to make the contributions and gain the rewards that they want. This limits the size and range of the social networks that people can call on and respond to.

- People with developmental disabilities, and their families, can come to see themselves as devalued others with no choice but to make the best life they can in professionally protected spaces at the margins of community life.

When faced with a difficult question, we often answer an easier one instead, usually without noticing the substitution.

– Daniel Kahneman

Prevailing public investment in real estate and group-based assistance influences the way professionals and policy makers understand the rights established by *The Convention* and the practical action necessary to satisfy it. Differences in interpretation can be substantial, as the following table shows. Our perspective is on the left. Others, represented on the right, see far less need to radically shift current investments toward individualized assistance. This is because they understand people in special buildings and groupings as full members of ordinary communities and we do not.

The right to employment in a labor market that is open, inclusive & accessible is satisfied by…	
… customized development of the accommodations, systematic instruction & assistance that people require to individually get & succeed in paid community jobs	… places in sheltered workshops, work crews of disabled people or day and community experience programs for people who are professionally assessed as unqualified for employment in integrated jobs

The right to choose where & with whom you live is satisfied by…	
… working one person at a time to determine how to use all available resources to find a good place of one's own to live & the assistance necessary to live there securely & well	… a choice among group residences that have vacant beds available

The hero's journey

When there is no clear path to realize your purpose in your everyday world, you have a choice. Set aside your desire or set out into new territory and make a way toward more. While finding the path to greater real wealth involves lots of practical tasks that can be broken into logical steps, we think it makes better sense to also think of people with developmental disabilities who want more and better as hearing a call to gather companions and set out on a hero's journey.

For many people with developmental disabilities, a real home, a decent and secure address of one's own, is the real goal of the quest and not just a metaphor. This journey may begin from sharing a home with parents or from a facility where the pathfinder has been placed. The destination is a home of the person's choice with individualized assistance that the person and their allies direct. Getting there involves negotiating budgets for housing and support, deciding whether to share your home and with whom, finding a good place and making modifications, figuring out the adjustments and assistance you need, and recruiting trustworthy assistants and developing their commitment and competence.

In many places the tasks necessary to establish a real home, a job or a meaningful role in community life are alien to providers, so this is a journey of discovery through which pathfinders generate the social inventions necessary to make the rights established by *The Convention* real for them. In many places, public funds and personal assistance are tied to *beds* or *slots* designed for a group of *service users* drawn from an anonymous pool of clients. Local housing resources and local employers, and even physicians and dentists, have assumed that disability organizations will take care of people with developmental disabilities by providing programs that will allow them to spend their lives with *their own kind*. Administrator's methods of managing costs and risk and assuring compliance with regulations typically constrain choice and self-direction and lock people into a narrow range of assistance.

Beyond task performance and invention, pathfinding is an emotional adventure. A person has to ask more of themselves, recruit allies and find a position from which to negotiate more individualized assistance and ask more of their community. There are dragons to face and new capacities to mobilize along the path. Barb moved from a group home where agency staff directed her daily routine into a home of her own, with personal assistants she and her allies select, develop and supervise with help from a new

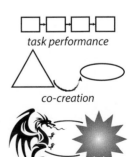

task performance

co-creation

imaginative adventure

kind of organization that she and her mother helped to found. She looks back on her journey:

> *I wanted my own place, but for a long time my fears were bigger than my want to. So I said 'no' to myself and kept it secret from other people, even my mom. Then I came to a conference and met some other people who made the move. Then my want to was just a little bit bigger than my fears and I told people I wanted my own home. I was the first in my area, so it took a long while to figure it out and there were times I almost gave up. I still have fears and troubles, but I got what I wanted and I won't ever go back. I like to tell my story to other people so they know that a real home can happen for them too.*

Barb is not the only participant in her quest for an ordinary home. Others whose cooperation is necessary have to consent to the risks of the journey as well. Her mother had to reconsider attaching Barb's security to full time staff supervision in a group home run by a well established organization and rethink Barb's capacity to find security in her own home with the support of her allies, the personal assistants she and Barb recruit and supervise together, and the technology that she counts on. Allies among current staff have to face the facts that they have underestimated her capacities and failed to listen well enough to discover a clear desire Barb has had for a long time. This hurts their pride in the person-centered planning they have done and their belief that their agency functions at the leading edge. One current staff member has to decide whether or not to give up the security and seniority in her current job and say yes to the invitation to lead Barb's new support team as her family's employee.

No two quests are the same, but when finding a path in unknown territory it can help to have a sense of what may come up along the way. Other pathfinders have made gifts of the practical solutions invented on their journey's to their own homes, jobs and community memberships. At the task level, much can be adapted from what others have learned.[*] We have found Theory U, which we introduce in Chapter 5 (page 131), a helpful guide to navigate the social invention level of the journey. The pattern of the hero's journey captures the emotional experience of the

---

[*] Neighbours, Inc. has compiled a helpful set of guides to the practical tasks involved in being in control of your own home. Patti Scott & David Hasbury: *You and your home, You and your budget,* and *You and your personal assistants.* Available at inclusion.com or neighbours-inc.com,

The hero's journey

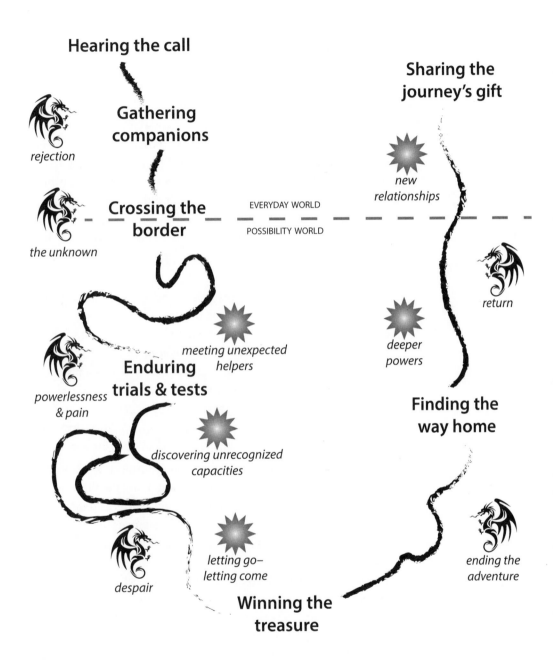

Hearing the call

rejection

Gathering companions

Sharing the journey's gift

new relationships

Crossing the border

EVERYDAY WORLD

POSSIBILITY WORLD

the unknown

return

meeting unexpected helpers

Enduring trials & tests

powerlessness & pain

deeper powers

discovering unrecognized capacities

Finding the way home

despair

letting go– letting come

ending the adventure

Winning the treasure

quest and provides a sense of the challenges and surprises that will show up in their own way and in their own time.

Hearing the call

THE UNKNOWN

The journey begins when the pathfinder says yes to a call that can only be answered by recruiting companions and leaving the familiar behind. The calls that concern us in this book move people beyond the familiar world constructed around developmental disability and into a search for new roles in a bigger, more diverse community. Some calls come with great clarity. Waiting for sleep in his bed on a crowded institution ward Larry could imagine every room in the little white shotgun house that called to him. Many calls come in an idea or image that only hints. Barb knew that she was mighty tired of being told what to do by staff and a bossy roommate and the words *my own home* expressed her deep desire. Details emerged as others listened to her respectfully and asked to hear more.

Pathfinder's calls are far bigger than wanting to consume a commodity. A call is a message from a person's highest purpose. Each person's desire to be more fully and distinctly themself activates their search for a place to call home and contributing social roles. Larry imagines helping out his neighbors. Barb wants a place she can invite friends to share the muffins she will bake in her own oven and join her in knitting for her church's silent auction. Rebecca's quest to dance new and more just social relationships offers beautiful images of a community that works better for everyone.

It's easy to deny a call that rearranges a community's relationships. A generation of progress means that many people have secure and pleasant lives within the orbit of family and developmental disabilities services. Even in circumstances that fit people's identity and aspirations poorly, compromise their dignity and stunt their growth, people find ways to feel safe enough and good enough. Calls are disruptive. They question what's assumed to be possible and pull people into uncharted territory. Drowning out a call with fantasies of winning the lottery or becoming a star athlete or famous singer fends off risk and hard work. Dismissing calls to the realm of daydreams and staying put can be the safest course, especially for people lacking allies who respect their possibilities.

Gathering companions and making partnerships

Companions are necessary to the journey. Without company it will be nearly impossible for most people to cross the border from their everyday world into the uncertain world of possibility. Companions add knowledge, skill and judgment to meet the tests and spot the resources the journey brings. Finding companions can be hard for people whose networks are limited to other clients and staff who have little more freedom of movement and control of resources than they do. And asking is hard. Even people with strong allies have reason to fear rejection and disappointment.

REJECTION

Those with the courage to risk rejection often discover that a real quest has power to recruit people. Those who have been invited to be on a journey, as companions, or guides to resources, or supporters along the way often say they are grateful to have been part of the person's journey. Many citizens can find a meaningful connection to their own higher purpose in joining a person's efforts toward a better life.

Sometimes assistance has isolated a person to the extent that staff and other people with developmental disabilities are the only available allies. Larry is a survivor of early efforts to relocate people from institutions and a very early seeker of a home of his own. From the point of diagnosing him as mentally deficient and separating him from his family in early childhood, the state arranged his life around the expectation that he would someday be buried under a number in an institution's graveyard.

Grave marker for an inmate of the institution that Larry left. The name of the person identified as 220 has been lost.

Even when legal action compelled a move to the community, it was an administrator controlled placement, far from his known family, with seven strangers in a big house organized to provide active treatment according to professional specifications. Fear that speaking out about his desire for his own home would get him sent back to the institution made him passive. It was years before he risked trusting a staff person with the dream of his own home.

The quest moved from his imagination into an alliance with committed staff. Finding a secure place of his own to live, a reasonably straightforward matter for most citizens, became a trip though a bureaucratic maze. Their steps were dogged by unanticipated disappointments and the need to try one way after another to reach their goal. Persistence, the unexpected help of bureaucrats who found reason to bend, excellent local connections in the rental market, and administrative willingness to assume the risk that providing Larry's assistance might no longer return full reimbursement finally put the key in Larry's hand. The house of his dreams became the site for many new challenges and difficulties along with some of the satisfactions he hoped for. Larry's move inspired other residents of the group home and soon the agency faced the problem of organizing, funding and offering in-

POWERLESSNESS & PAIN

WINNING THE
TREASURE

dividualized supports for them. They also had to find another use for a big house that the state had financed on the assumption that a group of people with developmental disabilities would live there for at least the 40 years necessary to repay the bonds that financed its purchase.

In their time, a generation ago, Larry and his companions had many novel technical challenges to figure out. There were no informative manuals to guide them. In addition to problem solving, the staff who joined Larry's journey had to do the emotional work of losing their role as benevolent rescuers who supervised Larry and taught him, step by tiny step, to acquire skills from their independent living checklist. They had to find new ways to relate to Larry as a man, an equal who needs thoughtful and respectful assistance in order to be in charge of his own life. They did, however, have a real advantage over most pathfinders today. They had the space to be companions on a journey of their own choosing.

Today it is harder to gather allies, make partnerships and cross the border into the world of possibilities. People's rights to their own homes and opportunities for meaningful work have never been more clearly stated in policy or more widely embraced in mission statements. Many pathfinders have returned from their journeys with valuable knowledge of how to make these good things real. But it is as if the whole system intended to serve people with developmental disabilities has dedicated itself to shutting out the world of possibility.

The dragons from the old stories appear in new forms, as earnest bureaucrats straining under a huge burden of financial calculations and regulations while rolling out the latest public management ideas and marketing a vision of person-centered assistance that supports community inclusion. More and more of the space for relationship and action is taken over by complex rules intended to protect confidentiality, avoid risk, control costs and, ironically, assure rights. Citizens who are not under administrative control are treated with suspicion, as if every neighbor were a likely abuser whose fingerprints must be taken and checked. A mirage of equitable provision governs: everyone everywhere will access the same assistance of identical quality if we treat assistance like the output of a machine. Those responsible for public funds act as if establishing one's own home, doing a real job and finding meaningful ways to engage in community life could be produced as the neat and homogenized outcomes of bureaucratically prescribed and controlled procedures. Fear pervades the system and drives hyper-vigilance and near paranoid anxiety about the punishing consequences of failure or error. Many organizations are frozen solid, unwilling to actually step outside their current box, no matter how frequently their managers admonish their staff to think outside it.

Even so, people and their allies persist in their search. Bureaucratic enclosure of the space for alliance and innovation makes it harder to encourage pathfinders to undertake journeys toward communities that work for everybody. The difficulty makes the journey more important. Only people persistently on the move toward a better life have a chance of waking others to the possibilities that come with deep and difficult change.

Building on the gifts of the quest

Success in the quest for a real home or job or opportunity for learning or civic engagement is one thing. Sustaining the gifts of the quest in the everyday world is continual work. What has been won is often vulnerable to changing priorities in the administration people rely on to finance the assistance they need to act as full citizens. Recruiting and developing capable personal assistants is a recurring and challenging task, especially when the work is undervalued and underpaid. So is navigating the changing policies and requirements that come with employing people with public funds. So is staying aware of new knowledge that will improve assistance or increase necessary resources. So is negotiating changes in funding as needs shift. As more organizations develop commitment and capacity to partner with people to sustain what they have won, more people can choose to be pathfinders.

A lifelong journey out of the institution

Tom Allen engaged in a life long quest to liberate himself and other people with developmental disabilities from the grip of institutionalization. Institutionalized for 69 years, mostly through the period of overcrowding and neglect depicted in institutional exposés, Tom found ways keep his sense of agency alive and act to serve his highest purpose as he understood it: to be a man of peace and free people with disabilities and staff from routine institutional abuse and its dehumanizing consequences.

Although professionals interpreted substantial physical impairments as signals of severe intellectual disability and inability to develop language, over the years Tom was able to recruit and trust a few institution staff who were willing to learn how he communicated. They became allies in one of his projects, writing his autobiography. He wrote because he wanted to teach staff how not to hurt people and to advise other people with disabilities on how to resist the effects of institutionalization. Progress was slow and the remarkable document that resulted is brief as autobiographies go, about 13,000 words. In the institution the project had to be done in secret. One draft was found and destroyed by staff who felt Tom's account of his life on the ward reflected badly on staff. Sometimes years went by with no allies to take dictation from him. Sometimes despair claimed his voice. At the best of times understanding Tom's communication was very difficult. The project was finished, in the open and with eager assistants, only a short time before his death.*

Conditions improved in Tom's final years in the institution. Staff listened to and supported his desire to join a church and a self-advocacy group. He recruited allies who helped him petition a court for community placement. The judge had to intervene because the state's plan for deinstitutionalization assumed that people who had grown old in an institution would want to stay in a facility until they died. This age discrimination was unacceptable to Tom and his allies.

Living in a group setting with a local address, Tom learned that the institution is not just a physical place but a mental model that generates restriction, control and isolation, mostly outside the awareness of the mostly well intentioned staff who serve the smaller and physically nicer institution. Tom's deep disappointment at the reproduction of many institutional conditions in what was supposed to be a life in community finally awakened staff and mobilized his allies. They joined him to create an individualized retirement program to replace a day activity program that never inquired about or engaged his interests. His retirement program was, for its time and place, a significant social invention. Tom chose a staff person he trusted to listen to him and act with him on what he wanted. With her practical and emotional support he improvised a schedule from day to day as opportunities came up to pursue what he cared about: reconnecting with his extended family, exploring his city and meeting people, fighting back against institutions through public presentations and legislative testimony, and finishing his autobiography. More and more days became, in themselves, brief quests for new connections and new ways to actualize the struggle against institutionalization.

---

* Read Tom's autobiography and more of his story in Kelley Johnson and Rannveig Traustadottir, Editors.(2005). *Deinstitutionalization and People with Intellectual Disabilities: In and Out of Institutions*. London: Jessica Kingsley Publishers.

When kidney failure produced a medical recommendation for nursing home placement and dialysis, Tom affirmatively chose to die at home. His public activism for institution closure in the last years of his life and the charisma that touched the people he met earned him an extensive obituary in the local newspaper.

THOMAS ALLEN was confined to a wheelchair at an apartment run by ENABLE for the disabled. Allen, who spent most of his life in institutions, found a home at the apartment.

Thomas Allen, 78, fought back from institutions

By Ellen Flood
Editorial Assistant

treatments. "God, no," Allen had said. "It's not a good place to be. I want to be home." And he was, until the end.

Like most pathfinders in the time of large scale deinstitutionalization, Tom expended most of his creative energy within the boundaries of disability services. His purpose was to break the physical and mental bonds of institutionalization for himself and for other people with developmental disabilities. His networks and relationships were mostly among staff allies and advocates for deinstitutionalization. This work is important and far from finished. Many tens of thousands of people remain in institutional settings and smaller places that reproduce too much of the institutional pattern. But the social innovations that Tom and his generation of allies and partners created have also opened the way for others to build and cross bridges to contributing roles in a more diverse community.

A reflective reading of Tom's autobiography produced this outline of the ways the institutional mental model clings and reproduces the destructive effects of closed and controlling settings. More important, it identifies Tom's strategies for resisting the corrosion of people's sense of agency caused by institutional practices. Tom makes it clear that these are not easy strategies to employ. In his life the implacable grind of devaluing routines and restrictions sometimes got him down, even to points of despair when he believed that God had forgotten him. But, difficult as it may be to heed, this advice is a gift to those on today's heroes' journeys from a man who came through a lifelong quest for freedom. It would be a sad error to read this as though the institution Tom speaks of were a thing of the past rather than a continuing force that shapes the life of every citizen who does not consciously and courageously resist it.

The institution wants to isolate you.

Reach out and make friends.

The institution wants to cut you off from your family.

Remember the people who have loved you. Remember their love even if they have also let you down or hurt you.

The institution wants to control the smallest details of your daily life.

You can find spaces to be free if you figure out exactly how the institution controls you.

The institution wants to silence you.
Find safe ways to use your voice. Don't give up when others don't listen.

The institution makes decisions for you "for your own good".
Be a decision maker whenever you can be.

The institution makes you dependent.
Learn to do whatever you can for yourself, even if it is hard and it takes a long time.

The institution has low expectations of you.
Make a positive difference to other people.

The institution wants to get inside your head and the heads of the people who care about you.
Don't think like the institution. The institution wins when you give up and believe you are no more than the institution thinks you are.

The institution wants to own you and your past.
Tell and retell your own life story in your own way to anybody you can trust to listen.

The institution wants to own your future.
Keep your dream alive and guard it from people who want to kill it.

Tom's disappointing discovery that the institutional mental model found ways to survive the move to a small group home and day activity program holds an important message. It is common to measure progress toward community life by reporting the number of people resident in smaller residential settings. A steadily growing percentage of people living with five or fewer others can be taken to mean progress toward replacing the institution. It's also easy for managers who recognize a need for change to assume that changing a mental model (or shifting a paradigm, as some describe it) is a simple matter of changing language and procedure, not struggling to re-form a deeply rooted culture of segregation and control. It took far more than a change of address and new mission statements for Tom and his allies to finally move outside the grip of the institutional regime, even for a few daytime hours a week.

Tom portrays the institution as an active force that he must fight against in order to live a life he has good reasons to value. Because for most of his life Tom had remarkably little real wealth besides his own resourcefulness, his relationships with other powerless inmates, and occasional, limited access to networks through exceptional staff, this was a profoundly unequal fight until the final few

Ontario's Government Takes Responsibility for the Injustice of Institutionalization

From 1876 to 2009 many thousands of children and adults with developmental disabilities and other conditions resided in the wards, called "cottages", of this institution. In 2013, the Government of Ontario issued an apology to the former residents for the conditions over time.

Survivors of the largest and oldest institutions in Ontario sued the Provincial Government for abuses they experienced. After exploring its case in detail, the Government chose not to contest the case. The settlement includes $70 million in cash compensation, the formal apology from the Government quoted below, historical markers like the one on the left, and allocation of funds to support the continuing advocacy of People First, increase Person-Directed Planning, document the stories of survivors, and implement ways to teach the history and lessons of institutionalization.

The Premier of Ontario, Kathleen Wynne, made this statement to the Legislative Assembly on 9 December 2014.

One of a government's foremost responsibilities is to care for its people, to make sure they are protected and safe. And therein lies a basic trust between the state and the people.

It is on that foundation of trust that everything else is built: our sense of self, our sense of community, our sense of purpose. And when that trust is broken with any one of us, we all lose something –we are all diminished.

I stand to address a matter of trust before this house and my assembled colleagues, but I am truly speaking to a group of people who have joined us this afternoon and to the many others who could not make it here today.

I am humbled to welcome to the legislature today former residents of the Huronia Regional Centre and Rideau Regional Centre in Smiths Falls and to also address former residents of the Southwestern Regional Centre near Chatham, along with all their families and supporters.

I want to honour them for their determination and their courage and to thank them for being here to bear witness to this occasion.

Today, Mr. Speaker, we take responsibility for the suffering of these people and their families.

I offer an apology to the men, women and children of Ontario who were failed by a model of institutional care for people with developmental disabilities.

We must look in the eyes of those who have been affected, and those they leave behind, and say: "We are sorry."

As Premier, and on behalf of all the people of Ontario, I am sorry for your pain, for your losses, and for the impact that these experiences must have had on your faith in this province, and in your government.

I am sorry for what you and your loved ones experienced, and for the pain you carry to this day. In the case of Huronia, some residents suffered neglect and abuse within the very system that was meant to provide them care. We broke faith with them –with you– and by doing so, we diminished ourselves.

Over a period of generations, and under various governments, too many of these men, women, children and their families were deeply harmed and continue to bear the scars and the consequences of this time.

Their humanity was undermined; they were separated from their families and robbed of their potential, their comfort, safety and their dignity.

At Huronia, some of these residents were forcibly restrained, left in unbearable seclusion, exploited for their labour and crowded into unsanitary dormitories.

And while the model of care carried out by this institution is now acknowledged to have been deeply flawed, there were also cases of unchecked physical and emotional abuse by some staff and residents.

Huronia was closed in 2009 when Ontario closed the doors to its last remaining provincial institutions for people with developmental disabilities.

Today, Mr. Speaker, we no longer see people with developmental disabilities as something "other." They are boys and girls, men and women, with hopes and dreams like all of us.

In Ontario, all individuals deserve our support, our respect and our care. We must look out for one another, take care of one another, challenge ourselves to be led by our sense of moral purpose before all else.

Today, we strive to support people with developmental disabilities so they can live as independently as possible and be more fully included in all aspects of their community.

As a society, we seek to learn from the mistakes of the past. And that process continues.

I know, Mr. Speaker, that we have more work to do.

And so we will protect the memory of all those who have suffered, help tell their stories and ensure that the lessons of this time are not lost.

Marie Slark, one of the two lead plaintiffs who represented the class of Huronia survivors, said this to the judge at the Settlement Hearing.

Most class actions are about things –or money. This one is about people –everyone who suffered at Huronia.

We have had NO power over our lives. Finally we have a voice –the government and the public are listening to us. We thank the lawyers for that. I am glad the Court is listening now.

It was really hard for me to speak up for myself. Like others, I was taught in the institution to keep quiet or else I would get hurt. It has been difficult to tell people about how I suffered and how this continues to limit my life. But I know that other class members are much less able to speak and understand than I am...

I hope other class members will get the chance I have had, to tell their stories. Some will use words, and some will find other ways to communicate.

This case brings to light serious injustice. We are asking the Court to make sure EVERYONE gets justice...

We appreciate the apology, but no amount of money will give us our lives back...

Maintaining the cemetery will honour those who died. Remembering the stories and sharing the documents will tell people this must never happen again to people with disabilities.

years of his life. The institutional mindset drives a machine for producing real poverty. It constrains and directs the attention and sense of possibility of those who work within it, mostly unaware of its influences. It shapes a social field that reproduces control by generating helpless dependency and disconnection from relationships, networks and sense of purpose. This social field has its greatest impact on people with developmental disabilities but it also depresses their family members and deprives staff of opportunities for meaningful work. Its effects diminish everyone it captures, but the weight falls most heavily on people who require the most assistance. The institutional mental model defines its inmates as being of little worth and then confirms its prophecy by withholding opportunities for development and contribution. It is critical to recognize the power a mental model has to shape patterns of behavior that are mindlessly accepted as "just the way things are". And it is vital to sense and actualize possibilities for freedom outside the institutional regime.

Tom's responses conserve his agency, his capacity to make a difference in the world, through his practice of resistance, even when all he could control was his own thinking. If you are alone and abandoned, hold relationships in memory and be forgiving. Find ways to decide, learn and make a positive difference with whatever you can control. Hold on to your story and your dreams. Sometimes you may get lost in discouragement, maybe even for years. But there are people who can rekindle hope and action by recognizing that you are a whole person with purposes that matter; be available to them.

Otto Scharmer identifies three forms of violence. Tom experienced all of them. Easiest to see is **direct violence**, caused by another person. Tom experienced abuse, neglect and punishments at the hands of staff and other institution residents. Harder to see but very powerful is **structural violence**, suffering created by oppressive economic and social structures. Tom experienced poor diet, cold, deprivation of opportunities to acquire even rudimentary literacy, poor medical care, extraction of all his teeth as a form of dental care, lack of privacy, lack of personal possessions, the rationalization of humiliation and direct violence (staff have to keep residents in line for residents' own good). All of this under cover of a culture that routinizes dehumanization as *just the way it is* and even *it doesn't affect them the way it would a normal person*. Hardest to see, but deeply wounding is **attentional violence**, the damage done when a person's higher purposes are invisible because there is no relationship that reveals them. Until he encountered staff allies who opened their hearts and woke up to the huge gap between what mattered to Tom and what they were doing to him as a client of their organization, he was seen primarily in terms of the expert prescriptions for dealing with his impairments. This perception of deficiency reduced Tom to a body broken beyond fixing, a failed character in a story of medical cure, a client in need of supervision and professionally regulated treatment in special places apart from common life.

Against this daunting history, Tom, like many institutional inmates, persevered. He concluded his autobiography in the last days of his life by bringing the dream that he identified as the source of his perseverance in the quest for freedom into the open for the first time.

> I wanted to be part of the world and wanted to leave the institution. I dreamed about the things I would do when I left. I dreamed of having a wife and children, I really wanted to have a family: my own family, my own wife and children. A happy family like we had been before my mother died. What I wanted most of all was to have a wife; a woman that I loved and who loved me back. This dream is what kept me going. It kept me alive. During times of despair I turned to it and it comforted me and gave me strength. I have held on to this dream all my life and never stopped hoping it would come true.

The road goes ever on and on

Some pathfinders return from their quest for a home or job of their own and settle in, warmed by the memories of their quest. Others, a bit more like the knights of legend's round table, rest a bit and then set out with their companions in search of the next adventure.

Barb and Larry and Tom are heroes of a generation of people with developmental disabilities who created a foundation for individualized assistance out of a personal history of deprivation. They were seen as ineducable and excluded from school. They were understood to be incompetent and unable to survive without others controlling their routines. Their families lacked support and, for Larry and Tom, this led to decades of institutional op-pression. Their journeys have brought them more interesting lives and demonstrated that having your own home and personally meaningful occupation is possible and worth pursuing.

While there is significant variation rooted in income inequality and poor accommodation by schools and services to differences in class, culture and race, this century's adults with developmental disabilities have benefited from the success of political advocacy and many professional advances. Most young adults in the US today will have had the benefit of some publicly funded support from the time that a developmental difference is identified. Advancing medical technology offers them far better chances for long life than their predecessors had. Their families are likely to have had access to mutual support groups, some benefits to cover exceptional medical expenses and other extra costs of disability, and some in-home assistance and short breaks. They will have attended school with an individual plan to guide their educational experience. While social devaluation continues to expose them to abuse, exclusion and discrimination there is growing tolerance of difference and there are organized ways to resist discrimination.[*]

In many places, pursuing the *Charter* rights to a home of your own, an ordinary job and access to inclusive opportunities for lifelong learning still demand a hero's journey. But important changes have shaped a new generation of pathfinders who can decide to find their ways in two additional fields opened in the last decades of the twentieth century. They have the challenge of figuring out new ways to use publicly funded personal assistance and the opportunity to discover bridging social roles.

Pulling together necessary assistance

As a group, today's adults with developmental disabilities have more capacities and more reasons to expect a positive future than any previous generation. They also have the challenge of working out new ways to live as adults who use publicly funded personal assistance.[†]

This challenge has two related causes. There is a growing recognition that people with developmental disabilities and their families have a right to self-direct the assistance they rely on. This in turn is influenced by the economics of publicly funded assistance in a generation where growing numbers of elders will require help.

The pattern of investment that shaped the era of deinstitutionalization assumed that administrators would, as a matter of course, take full responsibility for people with developmental disabilities by supplying residential and day services that encompassed 24 hours a day and met all of a client's assessed needs. Many parents

---

[*] For example the UK campaign against Disability Hate Crime goo.gl/9jDYyU and R-WORD: Spread the word to end the word www.r-word.org

[†] England leads in advancing this idea. The current policy heading for these efforts is Personalization. thinklocalactpersonal.org.uk.

assumed that, once they had absorbed much of the extra cost of raising a child with a disability, they could delegate responsibility for assistance and housing to publicly funded assistance. In this picture, their son or daughter would move into a residence as a young adult, moving out as their non-disabled brothers and sisters are expected to do. Growing wait lists and declining growth in public expenditures test this assumption past the breaking point. Many administrators now believe that the last century's pattern can't be sustained. In a growing number of places, most eligible people only move into publicly funded services by exception, usually in crisis situations caused by family breakdown. As well, people have to demonstrate higher levels of incompetence to be eligible for publicly funded assistance. In the US this results in more than half of adults with developmental disabilities living with family members, often into old age.

Some do the important work of campaigning for a political solution that will make good on the possibility of full publicly funded assistance for all adults labeled with developmental disability. They can record victories but progress on this front remains slow and uneven.

Others, including many campaigners for greater investment, step into the role of social inventors, searching for new paths to lives they have reason to value. By choosing this path, many people discover that they have sufficient real wealth to compose a good life by mobilizing their resources. Possibilities multiply when their assets include income from work, a flexible personal budget to purchase publicly funded assistance, benefits such as housing assistance and income support, access to technology that supports capacities, and partners willing to join on the journey. Life chances get better when a person's networks include workplaces and associations willing to negotiate necessary accommodations and people willing to exchange practical and emotional support with the person and the person's family.

Thinking about social roles*

Mother. Police officer. Boyfriend. Teacher. Coach. Social roles name the parts people play in the social settings and relationships that make up their lives. Social roles identify the different ways that people relate to one another, belong to each other, count on each other, and are responsible to each other. They point to the ways a person can contribute and make a difference in other people's lives. Some social roles describe complex and long lasting

---

* For more, see John O'Brien (2010). *SSR: Supporting Social Roles*. inclusion.com

relationships, like father and daughter; others are more circumscribed, like restaurant patron and server.

Social roles locate people in social space, structure the ways a
person who makes a particular contribution usually shows up
and acts and signal what others can expect from them in that
role. Some roles have distinctive signs: the chef's hat or the police
officer's uniform. Social roles offer cues about how to treat another person and the status they are likely to have in other's eyes.
People expect the doctor to help and she expects them to do their
best to cooperate.

This wheel suggests the great variety of social roles available to
people by identifying eight settings in which people with developmental disabilities can express their interests and capacities in
contributing roles. People can take these roles in settings identified with people with developmental disabilities and contribute to
a more closely bonded group or they can build bridging relationships by contributing in settings defined by other citizens.

For example, here are a few of the potential roles available in
home and neighborhood settings. Around the house: Tenant or
home-owner • Host, cook, house cleaner, handy-person, garden-
er, decorator, collector, hobbyist, etc. In the neighborhood: Good
neighbor, regular customer, shopper, neighborhood watch mem-

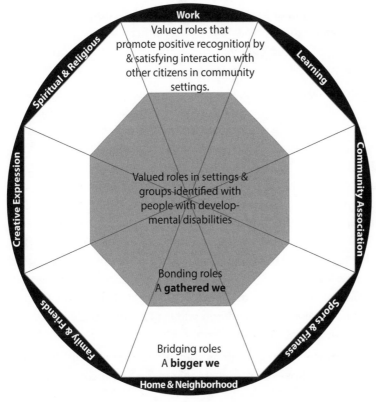

ber, participant in neighborhood clean-up or other improvement projects , etc.

On the job: Work roles are usually named by a job title: for example, receptionist, produce clerk, baker, nurse's aide, machine operator • Co-worker • Union member • Owner • Intern • Trainee, apprentice • Trainer • Supervisor • Manager • Employer

People learn social roles by watching others play them and from the spoken orientation and the unspoken cues they get from others and from the setting. Children in preschool learn the rules and practices that structure their roles from the way the teacher organizes their activities and the ways the other kids act.

Social roles are not straitjackets. There are many ways to play a role because each social setting has it's own qualities and each person brings a particular personality and capacity to their role. Different schools have different traditions and teachers have their own identities, but almost every teacher can be recognized in their role, and someone who acts outside the unspoken image of what usually goes with the role of teacher draws attention –and often generates some discomfort just because they don't fit typical expectations.

Expectations attached to social roles are powerful. A shy person often becomes more outgoing when he takes the role of greeter for his congregation or best man at his brother's wedding. Aggressive people often quiet down when a police officer arrives and asserts authority. Many fire fighters say that they do courageous things because it's expected on their job.

History shows that people with developmental disabilities can get trapped in a lifetime of roles that justify exclusion and supervision. To guide efforts to overcome the horrible institutional conditions of the mid-20th century, Wolf Wolfensberger used the idea of social roles to describe how good people could support settings that insulted people's human dignity and limited their development. The process is simple to describe and happens outside people's awareness. Those the person counts on have a perception of difference that casts the person into a devalued social role. This role shapes and is reinforced by the way that people are grouped, the physical settings that people are placed into, the activities that people are given access to, the power that people have, the terms in which people are understood and explained, and the images and symbols that surround them.

An example: A person who is seen and treated as if his developmental disability were a sickness that made him incompetent is controlled by a hierarchy of medical personnel and their assessments, prescriptions, and practices. When this regimen fails to cure, pessimism can take over and powerful people may doubt that he can have a life of quality or even that he is worth what it costs to keep him alive. This puts people with the most extensive impairments at risk of being seen and treated in an even more devaluing way, as less than human. When everyone that the person counts on relates to him in the social role of an incurably diseased person, his world can shrink to fit inside this single dead-end role.

Social roles not only provide a key to understanding how bad things happen to people with developmental disabilities, they also open a way to increase the chances that good things will happen to a person: see, treat and actively assist people as developing, contributing citizens.[*] Because people with developmental disabilities are vulnerable to being stuck in devaluing or limiting social roles, as if nothing better were possible, a good sign that the work of pushing back discrimination and exclusion is succeeding is the active presence of people with developmental disabilities in more and more different valued social roles in more and more different community settings. Supports, technology, and treatments can improve people's life chances, and a good sign that these investments are working is people showing up in contributing roles in community places.

Bonding based on developmental disability

In the last half of the 20th century, people with developmental disabilities benefited from the creation of many opportunities to play valued social roles in groups of people with developmental disabilities. People First and other organizations gathered people with developmental disabilities to strengthen their voices, build their skills, influence practice and policy and self-organize activities. Special Olympics, Very Special Arts, and a great variety of local art, music, and theatre programs gave people opportunities to develop and demonstrate their talents in ways that challenged and shifted common perceptions of developmental disability. Community recreation programs organized opportunities for groups of people with developmental disabilities to swim, bowl, and play games and sports together. Social clubs, like Gateway in Britain, held parties and dances that expanded the social life of groups of people with developmental disabilities. Best Buddies

DEVALUED
SOCIAL ROLES[*]

Wolfensberger deconstructs the structures and practices that each of these devaluing roles subject the person to.

Person as…

… sick

… subhuman organism (vegetable)

… animal

… menace

… object of pity

… burden of charity

… holy innocent

[*]Wolf Wolfensberger (1969/1975) *The Origin & Nature of Our Institutional Models.* Syracuse, NY: Human Policy Press. Copy of 1969 version online at goo. gl/QrCnSo.

---

[*] To begin study of these fundamentally important ideas, Wolf Wolfensberger (2013) *A Brief Introduction to Social Role Valorization, 4th Edition.* Valor Press. goo.gl/fDw8yf

and a variety of clubs and initiatives brought young people with developmental disabilities and young people who do not identify as disabled together for shared recreation and community service.

All of these efforts express a similar pattern. They are addressed to a group defined by shared assignment to a developmentally disabled status. They respond to something perceived missing for the group –social contact, exercise, competition, opportunities to develop artistic talent, mentoring. They offer an experience for people with developmental disabilities that is as much like the typical analogous experience as its non-disabled organizers can imagine. Many of these efforts engage volunteers who do not identify as disabled in defined helper, companion, coach or mentor roles. Social statuses and boundaries are preserved: organizers and volunteers are there to offer service; people with developmental disabilities to receive it. There is a risk that these activities will be a simulacrum, imperfectly imitating life outside services and even contributing to social distance (as when the perception that everyone in Special Olympics gets a medal fuels jokes).

Engagement with any of these activities builds real wealth. People's capacities, networks and relationships expand. Their gifts come into better focus and develop. Pride, confidence and resourcefulness grow. All of this happens within the boundaries created by bonding social action. People come together on the basis of their identity as developmentally disabled.

Many people with developmental disabilities will find these opportunities sufficient. The journey from contributing within the familiar boundaries created around people with developmental disabilities to making a difference in more diverse settings challenges established relationships, routines, rules and investments. When these challenges seem unmanageable, people will make their lives within a **gathered we**, bonded by their identification with developmental disability.

Often it is relational innovation, not intellectual that is important, because otherwise you would think that all that is needed are new ideas. New ideas are not in short supply. What is in short supply is coalition, people who are willing to work together to implement the ideas.

–Adam Kahane

Bridging action

There are more and more efforts to build bridges that reduce the challenges involved in building a **bigger, more diverse we**. As social inclusion has come into better focus social inventions have developed that create opportunities for people with developmental disabilities to experience a greater variety of roles in more diverse networks.

Paid work in an ordinary workplace offers opportunities for contribution and social connection and confronts prejudices. Many more people with developmental disabilities want a real job than administrators currently support. Their desires for employment have invited great creativity from social inventors in supported and customized employment. Innovations in finding jobs, negotiating accommodations, customizing jobs and consulting with employers to greatly improve the odds of success on the job offer the option of employment to more and more people with developmental disabilities. As the Finnish punk band Pertti Kurikan Nimipäivät demonstrate, a real job can take many forms and a bonded group can become part of a larger, more diverse network and serve as a springboard to new roles.

Other bridging actions extend or refine earlier efforts. These innovations invite non-disabled people to play more equal or more typical roles. Unified Sports, a Special Olympics initiative, joins people with and without developmental disabilities on the same teams. Very Special Arts assists artists and performers who want to develop their talent into a career. Best Buddies now actively supports people into jobs and civic involvement. Stay Up Late matches Gig Buddies, people with a common interest in night life who share their leisure time. Post-secondary education initiatives offer opportunities for people with developmental disabilities to experience aspects of college and university life. These social inventions have the potential to expand people's networks and build capacities in the context of more diverse groups organized for people with developmental disabilities.

Some people and families want even more. They know that there is a much wider space of possibility to create real wealth outside the boundaries of service world than within it. Not only do they want to benefit from good relationships with other disabled people, they also want to engage their individual interests and capacities among people who are not identified with the world of developmental disability. They want to create new bonds based on shared passion for punk rock, polka or food justice

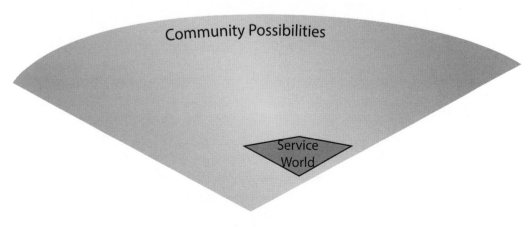

rather than waiting for those who care about people with developmental disabilities to hold a talent show, organize developmentally disabled polka lovers, or bring a group to the community garden. If they stop to think about it, they see themselves as having plural identities rather than one assigned master identity as developmentally disabled that frames every activity. Punk rocker and political activist and radio show host and disabled role model.

The pervasiveness of social exclusion means that intentional, sustained bridging action is necessary to build a **bigger we** that brings more of a community into personal involvement with itself. The work of making connections happen can be tiring and sometimes demoralizing, More than one mother has realized that she plays a much greater part in her developmentally disabled child's social life than other mothers do. More than one person has discovered that active membership in a community association they care about depends on their assistants' commitment. Growth of real wealth keeps people going.

We never know how our small activities will affect others through the invisible fabric of our connectedness. In this exquisitely connected world, it's never a question of *critical mass*. It's always about *critical connections*.

–Grace Lee Boggs

Making Art in Your Life

Pertti Kurikan Nimipäivät (PKN) represented Finland in competition with musicians from 39

other countries in the 2015 Eurovision Song Contest. Their performance of *Aina mun pitää (Always I have to)* won a nationally televised contest with 17 other performers by popular vote. This is the first time in the 60 years of Eurovision history that performers with developmental disabilities have built a bridge into the competition.

PKN has built this bridge a step at a time from a deep resonance between their group's sensibilities and the Finnish punk scene.

Four men with developmental disabilities formed PKN in 2009 around Pertti (second from left) and his 30 year passion for punk rock. Since the success of their first song –a celebration of Kallio, Kari's old home neighborhood that has been viewed 387,000 times on You Tube–they have toured in Europe and the US, released five recordings, built a follow-

ing in Finland and Germany and stared in *The Punk Syndrome*, an award winning documentary released in 2012 (goo.gl/8Ah8BW). The band and its members get assistance from Lyhty, a service that supports people with developmental disabilities in media and culture work.

Many of their songs, like their Eurovision entry, express anger at life in services, and one of their aims is to encourage other people with developmental disabilities. *People have to look at what we've done and learn from it*, says Kari (far left). *They need to get out there and do things they love. And they need to show their parents and others that Pertti Kurikan Nimipäivät has proved that you need to be alert and brave.*

In a conference presentation in 2014, Sami Helle, the bass player made these points about how anyone can make their dreams real.

- Think of acting on what matters to you as making art in your life.
- Find a scene that fits with your passions and capacities and find your framework in that scene.
- Let your emotions move your actions: bad feelings can be a source of energy –one of PKN's hit songs is *Päättäjä on pettäjä (Policymakers betray us).*
- Let things be unpolished and unfinished: take a risk and just put your work out there.
- Try things out and expand your expression.
- Success and failure happen; feel good about either.
- Listen to new people from different walks of life (journalists, artists, etc).

Sami is active in more mainstream politics. He is a founder of a self-advocacy group in Finland and made these points to a Committee of the European Parliament in 2013.

Me and my friends all over Finland think that we have not been taken into the process of designing the support that we need for equal quality of living and working. This has led into designing support that we don't need or we don't want.

Even though the services are funded by the taxpayers money, the services we get do not create equality among citizens. …Why can't we live our lives to the fullest?

I think this is because people in Finland actually do not believe that people with [developmental] disabilities should be equal, active and successful citizens. We hear that we should demand less, be quiet and happy for what we receive from the society.

Me and my friends and the new generation of people have different dreams. We have new skills and abilities and we are prepared to change the world as we know it, now.

I would like to give back to the society who has supported me a lot in various ways through my life. At the moment I think I am driving the car with the handbrake on. Even though I try, nothing much happens. I am the lucky one, I have a career and I am active. How about the great silent majority of people with [developmental]disabilities?

We should make things better. Now I think that we are returning to the 1950's and 1960's. Special schools, special group homes and special institutions for people with [developmental] disabilities. Should I always be special, a label, a person with a disability?

*We are obliged to surrender to the will of the strong. Big companies, cities and municipalities decide what is best for us. **This is about power**. Why do I feel a lack of power in my own life?*

We need more options. If people have options, they can choose.…

People should have the opportunity to develop and design services together with the service providers and together with their community. If the service is no good, things should change. We need to have the choice and opportunity to work in music, media and other professional fields. We need to have a meaningful life.

Living, daily activities and work are not the only things where we need support. We need help and support to influence things politically in our communities, in our area and in Europe. Are we prepared to include people with learning disabilities in all areas of life?

3

Partners

He who would do Good to another
must do it in Minute Particulars…
for Art and Science cannot exist but
in Minutely Organized Particulars.

–*William Blake*

Partners are people whose occupation gives them opportunities
to answer calls from people with developmental disabilities and
join them to build communities that work better for everybody.
They offer pathfinders and their allies differing gifts that help
them along their journey to social inclusion. Some accompany
the person day-to-day, offering the assistance necessary to live a
good life and sustain the quest. Some partners meet the person
along their way. They use their capacities in person-centered
planning to help pathfinders use their voice, clarify their vision,
assemble their company and keep their journey to contributing
citizenship on track. They discover local knowledge that opens a
way toward satisfying opportunities for participation. They use
their clinical skills to find useful ways to minimize the impact of
impairments on the person's choice of activities. Other partners
assist in designing the combination of technology, accommodations and assistance that will allow a person to be securely at
home, productively at work and meaningfully engaged in community life. Some perform the essential work of organizing the
journey's logistics. They help people and their allies put together
finance and meet the requirements that come along with using
public funds. They offer back-up for people and allies to recruit,
train and manage trustworthy, capable assistants and useful professional resources.

 Three threads of partnership weave through these different
contributions. Good partnerships are individualized. Good
partnerships are co-creative. Good partnerships deal openly and
creatively with inequalities and competing values.

Partnerships are individualized. Each partnership engages a particular person and is animated by sharing that person's desire to discover meaningful ways to contribute to a community that works better for everybody. In the many places where the capacity to support *Charter* rights is underdeveloped, this involves moving beyond what is usual and pulling together what is necessary to claim their choice of home, work and community roles.

Not everyone wants to be a pathfinder. Many people with developmental disabilities simply want respectful, timely and effective delivery of a standard package of assistance specified and contracted by government. There is no shortage of organizations willing to supply this assistance when funds are available. Partnership, however, expresses a shared commitment to an individual pathfinder's quest for more interesting and productive community engagement.

Partnerships are co-creative. Partnerships form because of resonance of purpose and recognition of good possibilities in shared efforts. Pathfinders and their allies want a better life that requires opportunities and a form of assistance beyond what is available to them. Partners want to develop capacities that better serve the new and more demanding expectations embodied in *The Charter*. Pathfinders want to be active in designing and directing supports tailored to their lives. Partners recognize that the way out of the trap of selling prepackaged solutions is to move outside the usual boundaries of human service administration and collaborate in social invention with willing pathfinders, allies and citizens. Co-creation is necessary when the life change that pathfinders want can't happen without partners learning new ways and learning that organizations can't stay relevant without engagement with pathfinders.

Partnerships deal openly with inequalities and competing values. The common understanding of partnership assumes equality among partners who are able to act as they see fit and free to enter or leave the partnership as they see the advantage to themselves. This picture shifts in the world of people with developmental disabilities. Here, effective partnership consciously and creatively takes account of inequalities like these.

- People with developmental disabilities depend on staff people to assist with everyday things that they are unable to do without help. Some people count on staff for assistance without which their health would deteriorate and an active life would be impossible. The best computer aided communication system in the world will leave a person mute if staff

The loyalty problem

Most of us have loyalties to the people who take care of us. They feed us, give us our medication, have control of when and where we go, help us get our employment, sit in and control our IPPs, can decide what and how much we get to eat, control where we get to shop, what we get to buy, whether we can have a pet or not; basically they become a parent who may not love you unconditionally. If you "tell" on them, they get mad at you. If they "tell" on you, you get in trouble. Either way you may get punished and lose your independence. If this happens, you will probably lose your friends, your job, and may be placed too far away for any family to visit. I know; it has happened to me several times after my safety overcame my loyalty and my fear of change. This loyalty problem kicks in even when you finally live independently because staff members are hard to find. If you can't be left alone, your fear of that overrules your concerns about your staff.

–Tina Ewing-Wilson[*]

[*] Tina Ewing-Wilson, who relies on daily personal assistance, made this statement in 2005 when she was Vice-Chair of the California Department of Developmental Services Consumer Advisory Council. The Council was discussing the limitations of consumer satisfaction surveys.

neglect to charge the battery. Others need assistance with tasks that require literacy and numeracy. Some need assistance to make sense of situations, think things through and make decisions. Others need highly personalized support to deal with episodes of physical crisis, emotional dysregulation or mental ill health. Dependency is a fact of every arrangement, even when the person employs the assistant directly.

- Staff can, and sometimes do, walk away. Organizations sometimes reject people too. But for people with developmental disabilities, exit from poor support can be difficult unless better replacement assistance is easily available (and where underfunding strains response to crises, it usually is not). The capacity to voice complaints is only as effective as staff and manager's willingness to heed and act on them. No matter how vivid the talk of empowerment, most people have little effective control or even influence unless staff agree to follow the person's lead, shift-by-shift.

- Legal tradition and regulations assign staff and their employers extraordinary responsibility for the safety of clients who are unable to protect themselves, or are seen that way. Many people with developmental disabilities have been judged incompetent to make decisions and placed under another's legal guardianship. Insurance carriers are vigilant about potential risks and there is fear that courts will base their rulings in liability cases on a tight interpretation of staff and management's duty of care.

- There can be real differences in knowledge of what is possible and how to navigate administrative structures. Some service providers rule out possibilities because they do not know the better ways that others have discovered. Some people and families trim their expectations to fit a pattern of assistance that cannot hold their purposes simply because they lack knowledge that would encourage them to imagine better.

- Organizations that provide assistance have multiple responsibilities, some of which constrain their partnerships with pathfinders. Boards of directors are responsible for protecting organizational assets, which often includes real estate designed and financed to house or occupy groups of people with developmental disabilities. Some families have entrusted organizations with responsibility for security and stability within the well defined boundaries of buildings that group and closely supervise people. Management is accountable to staff for good working conditions. Public authorities expect compliance with an increasingly complex and detailed rules and penalties. They also expect adaptation to shortfalls of money without compromise of the quality they measure.

- In more and more places, organizations are agents of a care management organization whose service coordinators specify the exact service the organization will offer a person.

No one likes the idea of inequality or commitments that compete with the idea that an organization puts people first, so it can be hard to talk about the ways that these forces shape a partnership. It helps to notice that these inequalities and constraints are structural. They are not necessarily the deeds of immoral or ignorant people but conditions that people who want to make change need to address. Anyone who offers or receives personal assistance has to deal mindfully with dependency and the emotions that dependency stirs. Anyone who accepts responsibility to manage or direct publicly funded support has to balance movement toward personalized supports with responsibility for the diverse interests the organization serves.

Partnership is a relationship aimed a co-creating better ways to assist a person to find more in their life. It is a process of traveling together on a learning journey, not a transaction in which the pathfinder demands and the partner delivers from inventory. The design and development of creative supports is a matter of thoughtfully identifying constraints and figuring out how to make progress by creatively reshaping the social space those constraints define.

Organizing for partnership

Some forms of organization are better suited to partnership
with pathfinders than others are because they can respond more
flexibly to individual opportunities and challenges. Organizations
are shaped by a fundamental choice between implementing a logic of **push** or a logic of **pull**.* The most common strategy pushes
predetermined service answers to anticipated need. As car man-
ufactures aim to push their products to meet predicted demand
by designing, manufacturing and marketing a range of standard
models, administrators anticipate need by matching their classifica-
tion of people with predetermined responses and, as funds become
available, they push the production of specified responses to that
need. This Request for Proposals (RFP) demonstrates the logic of
push: predict, standardize, produce then place people.

Request for Proposals – Level 4 Adult Residential Facilities

*[The administration] is looking to coordinate with interested parties in developing level 4 adult res-
idential facilities, serving individuals with severe behavioral challenges and severe self-care deficits.
This development would allow for individuals to reside in the least restrictive environment within
their community and with an appropriate peer group…*

*The standard for residential facilities is to provide quality care to all consumers residing in the home.
It is to be a home-like environment that focuses on the needs and interests of the individual consumer. The residential facility is to provide the least restrictive environment that promotes independence
while assuring the consumers' health and safety. Consideration will only be given to single story
homes with a maximum capacity for 4 residents. Each consumer shall have his or her own bedroom.
One non-ambulatory bed [sic]is required; wheelchair accessible preferred. All Level 4 facilities must
be prepared to have 24 hour awake staff. (Accessed 30 March 2014)*

The logic of pull organizes platforms that help people mobilize
what they need to achieve their particular purposes as opportunities arise in specific circumstances. Pull allows orchestration of a
distinctive network of resources, one person at a time.

Push predicts that four people assigned the status of "severe
behavior challenges and severe self-care deficits" will need a bed
and follows a standard procedure to produce a facility for them.
Pull starts from the fact the Edie and Gary want a good home life
for their adult sons, Doug and Brian.

Doug and Brian are brothers whose impairments and requirements for assistance would qualify them to live in a residential

---

* J. Hagel, J. Seeley Brown & L. Davison (2010). *The power of pulll: How small
moves, smartly made, can set big things in motion.* New York" Basic Books.

facility produced in response to the RFP above. But, when their parents, Edie and Gary, visited the facilities their sons were eligible to wait for the funding to move into, they found themselves in a dilemma. Doug and Brian required more support and deserved more adult space than family life could offer *and* no potential residences came close to meeting family expectations. Many families find themselves trapped by push logic and resolve the dilemma by resigning themselves to expect less. However, this situation was different. The whole family had a long standing partnership with The ARC of Rensselaer County (RARC), an organization committed to its own organizational journey to better individualize supports and customize people's living arrangements.*

Doug and Brian's living arrangements emerged from disciplined application of pull logic. Their familiarity with their neighborhood and the importance of sustaining the roles and relationships they had established, the size and configuration of the family home, and an idea from Edie's exploration of an in-law apartment for her mother combined to identify the necessary real estate. The brothers would live downstairs in the family home in an adapted space with 24 hour staff support. Their parents would live in a renovated upstairs apartment. While RARC had good relationships with state agency managers, pulling together solutions for the legal, regulatory and financial challenges in establishing a household unlike any other that the state funded at that time took clarity of purpose, tenacity and principled negotiation over many months.

After the household was set up, RARC continued to offer the family a platform for pulling in the resources necessary to meet changing circumstances. Individualized day supports emerged to meet the brothers' different interests and capabilities. Assuring household harmony, good individualized supports and fulfilling agreements with the DD administration required negotiating and renegotiating the roles and responsibilities among Doug and Brian, their parents, staff, and service managers.

While some things in this situation could be predicted, many opportunities emerged as relationships grew deeper and wider and new challenges came up. The learning that happened with Doug and Brian strengthened RARC's capacity to partner with other pathfinders and provide a capacity to orchestrate what's necessary for their particular journeys. One thing this experience

---

* Learn more from Beth Mount & Sandy VanEck (2010). *Keys to life: Creating customized homes for people with disabilities using individualized supports.* Troy, NY: The ARC of Rensselaer County. keystolife@renarc.org

The Logic of Pull Creates Tiger Lilly Seeds

Though Tiger Lilly Seeds opened for business in 2012, its source can be traced to a group of six parents of young people with developmental disabilities in Dane County, Wisconsin who gathered in 1992 to explore the future. Their sons and daughters had grown up at home with early intervention, family support and special education and they thought that the pattern of adult services shaped by the effort to move people without these benefits back from institutions might need to develop new capacities to support them well. Group members studied the system and decided that they needed to become creators of new options rather than consumers of what was already available. The county's director of developmental disabilities services agreed to work with them because they chose to prototype self-directed community opportunities for individualized supports. Each parent had a different idea about the best supports for the distinct identity and capacities of each person, but the group agreed that this four-leaf clover pattern identifies the capacities necessary to tailor support for a good life.

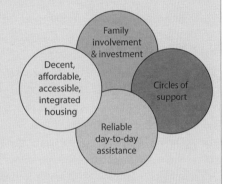

Homeownership seemed like an important, missing option in their community. At that time, the system either depended on the rental market or property owned by a service provider. The security of tenure and investment value of affordable housing owned by the person was attractive but very little was known about its feasibility. A sub-group invested about a year in building relationships in the housing finance and development sectors. They met

What people who create real wealth do is understand and emphasize the importance of relationships and personal connections to achieving their objectives.

a number of people who were interested in supporting their effort and learned that there are multiple ways to make homeownership possible for people with disabilities. They decided, with support from the Dane County Human Services Department, to form *Movin' Out* a focused organization with the mission to provide access to affordable housing for people with disabilities and their families in Wisconsin.

By 2012, *Movin' Out* had differentiated its strategies to match the varied housing interests of people with disabilities. About 1,200 people had become home owners. *Movin' Out* owned and operated community integrated rental housing for 176 households, some in partnership with other developers. Movin' Out has also undertaken a number of development projects, one of which is Elven Sted, which provides 32 affordable, accessible rental units on the banks of the Yahara River in Stoughton, a few of which are home to people with disabilities.

In addition to providing affordable, accessible, integrated housing *Movin' Out*'s development philosophy includes a commitment to sustainability and a positive impact on

the environment and the neighborhood. Elven Sted offered both opportunity and resources to reclaim a brown field site and a wetland with housing certified by Wisconsin Green Build and open community access to the river bank with walking and biking trails. They also want to encourage neighborliness and offer people with disabilities as many opportunities as possible.

True to its origins, *Movin' Out* not only provides access to housing, it purposefully generates new networks of collaboration. Elven Sted was required to provide for storm water management. *Movin' Out* chose to do this by creating a rain garden populated with indigenous prairie flowers and grasses. Curious to discover why the seeds for these plants were so expensive, Dave Porter-field, *Movin' Out*'s Housing Developer, learned that propagating, harvesting and packing seed was an exacting, labor intensive task. This led him to wonder if producing seeds in Elven Sted's rain garden might provide a micro-business opportunity for a person with a developmental disability. Collaboration with the *County Human Services Department* produced a small grant that funded a feasibility study by Leah Samson-Samuel of the *Madison Environmental Group*. The business plan was encouraging about the market for high value seeds, the potential to grow them at Elven Sted and the possibilities for generating sufficient cash flow. This led to a relationship with Corrine Daniels of *Taylor Creed Restorative Nurseries*. The nurseries provide technical assistance and pur-chase those high value seeds that meet their rigorous quality standards. *Progressive Community Services'* self-employment coordinator, Shannel Trudeau-Yancey, created a business description to help in recruiting an entrepreneur.

The search for an entrepreneur led to Brittany Romine, who lives with her family near Elven Sted and was having trouble finding a job that suited her. Brittany has a desire to improve the environment (her love and concern for the wellbeing of big cats is reflected in the name and logo of her business), loves the outdoors, enjoys working with her hands, likes detail work, is very precise, and prefers scheduling her own work to being on an employer's time.

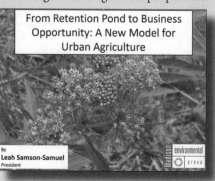

Progressive Community Services assisted Brittany and her mother to complete a self-employment plan, negotiate with *DVR* to underwrite start-up expenses, and organize the continuing personal assistance, funded by *Dane County Human Service Department*, that Brittany needs to be successful at work.

Brittany and her assistants have planted a quarter-acre of rain garden with more than 3,000 plants representing 30 varieties, many of which yield high value seeds and some of which are more popular varieties she packages for sale at garden shows. Brittany's mother does record keeping and book keeping and helps manage the business. Despite a severe drought, Tiger Lilly Seeds closed its first year with a modest profit.

Movin' Out deeded the land Brittany plants to the *City of Stough-ton* as part of the plan to develop public access to the river. The city gives Brittany the right to plant there for one dollar a year. There are other areas both locally and in other Wisconsin towns that could support seed production, so Brittany and her co-creators have opened up a new space for contribution. They have also brought a message about people with developmental disabilities to new networks by reaching across boundaries and engaging others who seek com-munities that work for everybody. This presentation to a Chicago conference on urban agriculture suggests an interesting indicator of inclusion. Inclusion is happen-ing when unexpected people tell powerful stories that include people with disabilities as important actors and the agenda has nothing directly to do with disability services or disability advocacy.

From Retention Pond to Business Opportunity: A New Model for Urban Agriculture

By
Leah Samson-Samuel
President

has not produced is a *convert-your-downstairs program model* to push to other families.

RARC developed a platform to pull necessary resources in response to what Edie and Gary wanted for their sons. As the story of Tiger Lilly Seeds shows, an organization founded on the logic of pull, like Movin' Out, builds networks that create a platform that people with developmental disabilities can choose to activate if the opportunity suits them.

Potential for partnership

People who want a secure home of their own have to find good answers to design questions like these:

- How can others in my life help me find and live securely in my own home?
- What can I afford? Am I in a position to think about owning my own home? Will I need a roommate? If I need help exploring the options, where can I get it?
- Where will I live?
- Who, if anyone, will I live with?
- What environmental adaptations and technology will help?[*]
- What personal assistance do I require?
- Who will assist me: when and how?
- How will I pay for my home and any extra costs of occupancy generated by my impairments?

People who want a satisfying job have to find good answers to design questions like these:

- What can I do or learn to do that is valuable to an employer and meaningful for me?
- How can others in my life help in getting work and succeeding?
- How will I identify a good employer and get a job (or develop my own business)?
- How will the money I earn at work affect the benefits I get and how can I work it out so I have the most possible disposable income and stay eligible for the disability assistance and other benefits I rely on?

---

[*] For a helpful resource on customizing the physical environment, see George Braddock & John Rowell (2013). *Making homes that work: Planning, design and construction of person-centered environments for families living with autism spectrum disorders*. http://goo.gl/nD9uEo The book focuses on people with autism spectrum differences but the design logic is much more widely applicable.

- What will work best for me to learn what I need to know to do a job I want?

- What environmental and social accommodations, assistive technology and customized job responsibilities will help me be successful at work and how will these be negotiated and put in place?

- Do I need personal assistance at work? If so, who will provide it, when and how?

- What needs to change in my life outside of work so that I will succeed at work? How does the assistance I get outside of work hours need to change so I can best manage my work responsibilities?

People who are looking for leisure activities that interest them, or for a post-secondary educational experience, or for a satisfying role in a civic association face similar design questions. The fewer fixed answers an organization has to these design questions before they meet a person, the more free staff are to be partners with pathfinders. The greater an organization's capacity to support social invention, the more personalized the responses to design questions can be.

History and policy can limit the potential for co-creative partnership. Many families expect to delegate primary responsibility

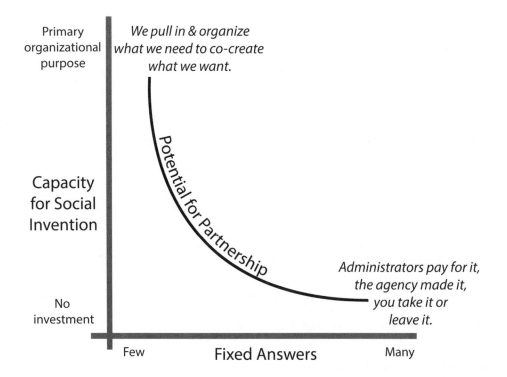

Peace

Brad's mother, Helen Jones, wrote these words for a conference on supported living shortly after he moved into his own apartment.

This I believe: Brad is fully human, living a dignified life, experiencing the inner peace that he has longed for all his life.
believe this is is due to his courage and self-determination and patience and his never holding a grudge. Brad spends all his energy on Today, creating his future.

For the first 33 years of Brad's life he lived in a totally silent world. He used his body to express his frustrations, dislikes, depressions, and anger. This brought on uncontrolled self-abusive behavior. I was on constant edge, trying to guess his needs and steer him into programs and living situations that I, and the professionals, knew were good for him. Because the school district had nothing to offer, at age 13 Brad moved to [a state institution]. There he was abused and bossed around. I spent an inordinate amount of time on the highway to be there and advocate. After 8 years of this –which Brad will tell you was SHEER HELL– I joined with 3 families to open a group home. It was a bit better in that he now had to live with only 5 other individuals he would not normally choose to live with. By now Brad was a patient of a psychiatrist with monthly appointments because his behavioral outbursts were thought to be a symptom of manic depression. He was given Lithium and suffered a horrendous reaction of profound emotional disorder. Physically, he was fragile with multiple Emergency Room visits and hospitalizations. Eventually he required a wheelchair.

I told the staff and the psychiatrist, I knew his behavior would cure itself if only he could live in a calm environment. This was ignored.

Finally, at age 33, Brad was introduced to Facilitated Communication and now he can express his frustrations, fears, dreams. It was then that he met a staff person of whom Brad repeatedly says, "He listened to me and he understood me." Brad told his brother and me that he wanted to move from the group home and find PEACE.

That became Brad's mantra as we advocated to bring about these changes. It was an uphill struggle that took many years, Brad moved into partnership with TLC [the supported living organization whose staff informed the inquiry summarized on page 87]where he began chiseling out his life, his dream of where and how he wanted to live his life. For the first time in his life, it really was all about Brad. As mom and guardian, let me tell you it was the scariest thing I have ever faced in my life. Brad set off to pioneer a lifestyle of living one person to one house. He was now responsible for hiring and firing his staff, managing his income and outgo and all the details of daily living. But when Brad sets his mind to something that is it! He was determined and therefore, we were determined to help Brad achieve the peace he longed for all his life. He led and we followed.

Let me admit from the bottom of my toes, that it has been a roller coaster ride. But Brad hung in there, matured with each crisis and never lost sight of his goal to live in a place of his choosing.

Today we can say Brad has climbed the mountain. He has not been to a psychiatrist since we began our partnership with TLC. Physically, he has never been healthier. He radiates joy for living arrangements and assistance to a service provider. They may accept that they will have to wait, especially for a residential service, but they do not see themselves as co-creators of personalized supports and most service providers accept delegation as the only way to do business. Over the past two generations family and service provider advocacy, and response to legal pressure to deinstitutionalize, has generated thousands of agency owned and operated living arrangements and day programs. Funding formulas and rules define many of the details of these service offerings, though there can be creative variation in the way a program complies. In general, social invention is presumed unnecessary because, as a condition of receiving public funds, providers assure administrators that they are able to adequately meet people's identified needs.

Some organizations were founded to co-create the individual supports people need to live a life they have good reasons to value, and some of these organizations have developed in places that value individualization and innovation.* Others, usually supporters of smaller numbers of people, have made the journey from group based assistance to individualized supports.† Still others have purposely made space for co-creation within an organization that continues to operate group based assistance, as RARC did by building their capacity for social innovation by collaborating with Doug and Brian and their parents.‡

Partnership involves making and revising big design decisions to assure people a secure home with necessary assistance, whether with family members or in a place of one's own, and meaningful roles in civic life and the labor market. Another form of partnership, just as critical to a good life, involves direct support.

Regardless of the shape that assistance takes, whether based on groups or focused on individuals, the core function of every provider organization is identifying, recruiting and developing trustworthy, capable and committed assistants and encouraging them to do meaningful direct support work over time.

---

* John O'Brien, Connie Lyle O'Brien & Gail Jacob (1998). *Celebrating the ordinary: The emergence of Options in Community Living as a thoughtful organization.* Toronto: Inclusion Press. inclusion.com

† Pat Fratangelo, Marjorie Olney & Sue Lehr (2001). *One person at a time: How one agency changed from group to individualized services for people with disabilities.* St Augustine, FL: Training Resource Network.

‡ Hanns Meissner (2013). *Creating blue space: Fostering innovative support practices for people with developmental disabilities.* Toronto: Inclusion Press. inclusion.com.

The art of direct support

The purpose of a direct support relationship is to actively assist participation and choice by amplifying a person's capacities and minimizing the impact of their impairments on their ability to act as they want to and build real wealth. For people who need assistance for much of their day, direct support is the foundation for discovering, entering and sustaining contributing community roles and making and enjoying friendships. Service providing organizations that provide good partners for pathfinders put a very high priority on cultivating the art of direct support. So do people and families who effectively self-direct their supports.

In a community-based, individualized model of supports, everything rises or falls with that key direct support person.

–Susan Yuan

Direct support workers as partners

TASH, an international association promoting equity, opportunity and inclusion for people with disabilities, recognizes exemplary direct support relationships with an award that highlights their importance to partnership.

> *The Larry J. Brumond Supportive Relationship Award honors two individuals who have maintained a mutually supportive relationship for at least five years in which the dreams and aspirations of the support recipient are supported in that person's chosen home and community. The net result when such a relationship is formed is the fulfillment of two lives: in learning and teaching each other; in discovering better who they each are; and in understanding more deeply how critical relationships are to a satisfying and valued life.*

The award is unusual because it is presented to a relationship rather than singling out the achievements of a person with a disability or the contribution of a staff member. It recognizes the interdependence at the heart of direct support. It commends people sticking with each other through the ups and downs of at least five years. It honors both the mutual benefits and the difference in the relationship. Both learn and teach and both learn better who they each are. The direct support worker chooses to place their capacities in service of the person's hopes and aspirations for a good life in their community. Although direct support workers are paid, their commitment and their choice to put the person's interests first can't be bought and sold.

The award sets a high standard, as awards should. For every assistant who reaches the five year mark, there will be many who have moved on. But no matter how long they stay most direct support workers have choices about how they show up in a

"Didn't Jason do the right thing..."

In 2103 TASH presented The Larry J. Brumond Award to Andreas Yuan and Jason Guymon, who have shared their lives for eight years. Much of their experience of community is shaped by a massive interest in connecting with other people and a common passion for music clubs and festivals and the music scene backstage. Jason is Andrea's way in to the world of musicians, soundmen, bartenders and bouncers, his guide and sometimes his protector within it. Their love of travel, and Jason's other job as a bouncer, lets them follow the music around their home state of Vermont and as far away as Florida. They operate a small business advising clubs and festivals on accessibility. Both are advocates for inclusion and the interdependence of self-determination. They present to conferences and serve together on the Board of New England's TASH Chapter.

As Susan, Andreas' mother puts it, Jason is the person who *keeps the balance, who opens up opportunities yet helps Andreas keep his exuberance within bounds... Many times, Jason says, people approach Andreas at rock festivals and concerts, and offer him a joint. Jason's answer: 'Oh, no; he comes naturally stoned!'* (The extra hands in the photo belong to Susan. Andreas intentionally positioned the appearance of her support in TASH's official picture of the award winners.)

Susan makes it clear that Andreas had to live with far less effective support before he and Jason found each other.*

> In a community-based, individualized model of supports, everything rises or falls with that key support person, and we couldn't find one...
>
> Stability came within reach as a young mother looked for a way to work and still be with her children. Andreas loved her and her babies, and she would load him and her children in her van and cruise all over northern Vermont. He watched Barney videos, but at least he was occupied, happy, and, we thought, safe. After three years, we learned that his social circle had grown to include crack addicts, pill poppers, and methamphetamine tweakers.
>
> How ironic that I worked in the field of disability, yet Andreas wasn't safe.... I felt guilty that I loved my job, and didn't want to give it up to become his permanent companion.
>
> Despair had almost taken over when Jason entered our lives...
>
> We didn't do anything to find Jason, he found us. No matter how hard we try to control life, we can't. We didn't when Andreas was born, and we don't now. But that doesn't mean that life isn't good. It may not last, but we've learned how to appreciate it while it does!

---

* Susan Yuan (2006). The ups and downs of finding a support person. *Impact: Feature Issue on Parenting Teens and Young Adults with Disabilities 19*(2).

In 2013, Jason married a woman who recognizes the importance of his commitment and chose a life that includes Andreas.

In response to the award, Andreas, who uses Facilitated Communication, typed this recognition of the power of interdependency.

If help for this life of mine means totally giving up your individuel life then didn't Jason do the right thing forming a relationship with me. There hasn't ever been someone else into giving that like he has. Sitting here typing this makes memories we have together. This is why I work so hard to say things in their special way to honor our connection with living together. Thank you.

Jason said,

Andreas and I have cared for each other for many years now, and our love and respect for each other is what makes it work for us. As I support Andreas, our friends and neighbors support me, and in the end that is what makes it work and feel so satisfying.

person's life. Much of daily life is routine: getting up and getting ready, going to bed, preparing meals, doing housekeeping chores, paying bills, moving through the daily routine at work. Most direct support time involves assisting performance of these ordinary tasks. When this assistance is understood and supported as a relationship, everydayness can provide a context to develop trust, confidence and shared practical knowledge of what helps the person get more of what matters for a good life.

The most effective assistance is founded on empathy, the desire to get better and better at seeing things from the point of view of the person who receives assistance. Even the most adventurous and creative pathfinders have to get washed and dressed in the morning. Anna, who has cerebral palsy, used her letter board to spell out the difference it makes when assistance happens in a way that attunes each to the other's experience.

> *If I could, I would give each staff person a gift. I would give them the gift of feeling what it is like for me to get up in the morning and get ready for the day. They know it from their side; they know what it's like to do the work of helping me shower and get dressed. But I want them to feel the work it takes from my side to get the help. It takes a lot of energy from me and I can tell, by the person's touch, whether they care anything about my day or not. When you matter to the person helping you, this work of getting help is not so tiring.*

When a person requires a great deal of assistance, as Anna and Andreas do, Andreas' insight is essential to understanding the person's perspective, …*help for this life of mine means totally giving up your individual life.* In a culture that prizes individuality and defines independence as do-it-for-yourself, appreciating this experience demands imaginative attention.

When empathy is missing, a personal assistant can fall into a trap that at best robs both the person with a disability and the worker of dignity and at worst degenerates into neglect and abuse. There are two common traps. The first leads assistants to show up in a mechanical way, as if the work were simply a matter of performing routine tasks on a needy body or that body's groceries, household chores or checkbook. The second trap tempts assistants into finding satisfaction in exercising control over others seen as inferior because they depend on assistance and occupy client status.

Many assistants avoid the traps and show up in people's lives as good company. They settle into a comfortable, or at least predictable, routine that often includes shared pleasures and accomplishments. If a person experiences episodes of difficult behavior, they have found ways to manage the situation that usually work out. There can be an exchange of genuine concern and affection even when things are difficult. Assistants who are good company provide safe and mostly pleasant conditions. Active partnership in social invention demands even more of direct support workers.

Direct support practices that energize partnership

Sixteen capable direct support workers from two supported living organizations participated in an Appreciative Inquiry focused on how they make a difference to the people they assist when they are at their very best.* Refection on their accounts of what makes their work effective, meaningful and sustaining for them identified six qualities of relationship that work together to provide strong companions for pathfinders' journeys.

Mindful presence. At its best, direct support flows from attention to the person's responses to what is happening and the possibilities and difficulties that arise moment by moment. As memories of these discoveries accumulate the direct support worker becomes custodian of a distinctive story about the person,

---

* Lyle Romer and Pamela Walker (2013). Offering person-centered supports on a daily basis: An initial appreciative inquiry into the relationship between personal assistants and those seeking support. *Research and Practice for Person's with Severe Disabilities 38*, 3: 186-195. We have interpreted their findings; see the original paper for their understanding. Appreciative Inquiry is an approach to investigating and transforming organizations by creating an account of the positive core of their work and the conditions under which that positive core of practices and attitudes can develop and thrive in changing environments, see appreciativeinquiry.case.edu.

Seeing through the force field

In good support relationships new and better stories become possible. Kyle describes the discovery of a new and better story. Wanda's behavior,
which challenged the people who assisted her, did not
disappear when Kyle came to a deeper appreciation
of her identity, but the story he and Wanda created made it possible for him to appreciate her more
deeply and stick with her when things got hard.

*Wanda's emotions, and the ways she could express
them were very turbulent. They could just change
on a dime, without notice. It wasn't something that
you did. It wasn't that you overstepped a line. It
was just where Wanda was at. She had emotions
that kind of ran like a rabbit, this way and that
way, moving all around. If you couldn't change with her, she would throw you for a loop.
She frustrated a lot of people. She terrified a lot of people. She went through a lot of people
who approached her in a caregiving role.*

*One thing I began to see with time was that the constant, jack-rabbit, lightening bolt
switching and changing of emotions –and the continuing shifting back to aggressive,
angry, insulting states– was really like an electrical force field that she generated around
herself. Within that force field was a human being who needed to protect herself. She had
essentially donned the bent armor and wore it through her life. But to stick around, and
to really look at her and appreciate her, you began to distinguish between the force field
and what was inside the force field. Inside the force field was an absolutely lovely person.
[When you could see that person, you] really began to develop a deep love and compassion and devotion.*

*It would sometimes amaze, or amuse, me when I'd see other people encountering that
force field and being repelled by it. I'd want to say, "that's not who this person is. You are
encountering the suit of armor, not the person inside."*

*That's one thing that Wanda really taught me. How to look for the essential person beyond
the personality and communication difficulties that might repel you.*

their interests and capacities, and what works and doesn't work to
bring out their best in different situations.

Authentic listening. At their best, direct support workers recognize the person as author of their own life story with desires they
want to satisfy and feelings and moods that shape their actions
and deserve acknowledgment and accommodation. They listen
for what matters to a person and what a person wants to accomplish in each particular time and place. They listen to the person's
whole body and to the tones that express emotion. The more limited the staff person is in understanding the person's communication,

the more disciplined the direct support worker is in learning to read whatever meaning they can understand.

Moving with. Capable direct support workers are more than witnesses to people's interests, they work out ways to join the person in bringing what matters to them alive. They are partners in the dance of daily life. Sometimes they are up front, representing the person to others or shifting barriers out of the person's way or mitigating threats. Often they are in the background, unobtrusively doing whatever will smooth those interactions or activities where the person needs assistance.

Negotiation. Many of life's routines are well served by habit. When direct service workers are at their best, they assure that routines reflect a person's preferences rather than simply imposing their own habits on the person. It usually takes only a moment to discover whether a person usually prefers a relaxing bath before bed or a brisk morning shower. Sometimes negotiation is more complex. A person wants to do something new and needs others' involvement. A person wants something that the direct support worker can't offer. Anger, disappointment or betrayal may be troubling the relationship and demand working through to avoid breakdown of the relationship. At their best in any of these situations, direct support workers choose to take the person's perspective into account and, as much as possible, to look openly and honestly for an acceptable way to help the person get what matters to them, both immediately and in the longer term.

Trust. At their best, direct support workers take personal responsibility for the impact they have on people's lives and treat their agreements as promises to be honored. They show up on time, ready to offer the assistance the person needs or give people notice of their inability to show up as expected. Their sense of integrity keeps the person whole: they thoughtfully identify and avoid even little ways in which they might exploit the person's dependency on them. They invest their trust in the person, thoughtfully finding ways to show up as themselves and share some of their own lives. As trust deepens, more and more interesting shared stories enrich their memories, offer

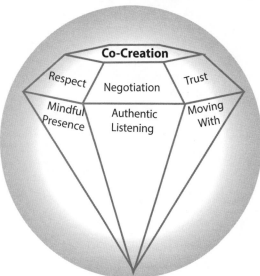

reassurance in frightening or troubled times, and provide a foundation for wider visions.

Respect. At its best direct support is a relationship in which people honor each other's purposes. The person wants to have a good life; the support worker finds meaning in assisting the emergence of that good life. The relationship is a site for compassion and forgiveness on both sides. Good direct support acknowledges differences and usually puts the person's interests first. As one participant in the inquiry put it, *[I practice] the open vessel approach. I can contain what this person is interested in even if I really don't share that interest.* The relationship includes asymmetries: the person needs help, the support worker takes direction from the person; the support worker deserves respect that sometimes a person's impairments or history of trauma make it hard for them to extend. These differences are understood as expressions of interdependency among people of equal dignity.

It's important to recognize the context in which appreciative inquiry surfaced these qualities. The direct support workers who were interviewed represented two agencies that practice the logic of pull to offer individualized support so the people they assist live in their own homes and experience meaningful days that usually include some paid work. The people these agencies support have been assessed by administrators to require intensive support. Each organization has its distinct structure and culture, but both recognize the importance of direct support and focus on cultivating relationships that reveal the six qualities that make people good partners. Continuity of relationships through time is of high value to each organization and both recognize that meaning in relationship is the key to the continuity that sustains and refreshes the relationship and the creativity that supports good experiences for people and those who assist them. Tenure demonstrates that support workers find their job meaningful. On average, the workers interviewed in this inquiry have offered direct support for an average of more than five years (7 months to 20 years) and primarily supported the same person for an average of more than four years (3 months to 20 years).

These qualities –mindful presence, respectful listening, moving with, negotiating, trust, respect– are hard to cultivate under conditions that are common in service providing organizations. Some organizations have norms and policies that shape distant and impersonal relationships. They define direct support in terms of what not to do. Don't be a friend, maintain the professional distance and objectivity appropriate to your (temporary) paid role. Don't become involved with a person's family. Don't every invite a person you support into your home or family life. Be with people only for scheduled work time, leave immediately when your shift is over.

In the right light these injunctions make sense. A growing number of providers organize their assistance on the assumption that there will be high turnover, low commitment and low competence among direct support workers. More and more public funding comes attached to timed and specified tasks designed to control costs through uniform application of standardized procedures. Increasingly stringent enforcement of labor laws heightens risk of overtime claims. Direct channels to people's families can complicate the work of those assigned to supervise or coordinate assistance. The risk that a support worker will simply take a person along as they take care of the staff member's own business is as real as the chance that a person could have an accident in a staff member's home. Relationships introduce emotion, conflict and uncertainty that make assistance hard to manage, especially assistance that assign staff to groups of people with disabilities. People do experience loss when friendly staff leave.

But there are costs to imagining that these problems can be prevented by instructing people to depersonalize the direct support relationship and perform it as an increasingly efficient transaction. Staff still spend many unsupervised hours with people. Avoiding neglect, abuse or exploitation depends more on integrity and respect for another person's dignity than on surveillance. And a relationship dominated by surveillance and protocol stifles positive experiences. The impulse to relationship remains strong enough to undermine even the sturdiest wall of professional distance. Staff's opportunities to find meaning in their work will shrink and they will see their bosses treating them as if they were interchangeable parts in a care and supervision machine. But the greatest cost is the unmeasured and unmeasurable loss of meaning and contribution from incapacity to be good partners with people who want to claim their rightful place in community life.

As the organizations involved in the appreciative inquiry well know, there are no easy answers to the concerns that fear of uncertainty, conflict or liability reveal. There is only the leadership confidence, borne of experience, that enough people find sufficient meaning in expressing the good in direct support that they will keep coming up with ways to overcome the very real problems built into direct support and the increasingly powerful trends that threaten its highest possibilities. The good these efforts serve is a form of partnership with people which reveals their dignity and strengthens their resolve to develop and contribute their gifts.

Cultivating direct support partners

Organizations with the capacity to develop trustworthy, capable partners do three things. They consistently promote a clear and challenging framework for thinking about good quality work. They organize people in teams. They invest in developing people.

Valued experiences and accomplishments

Pathfinders and their companions journey outside what is already well known. It helps to have shared language that enables those on the journey to take bearings and notice the difference between ladders worth climbing and chutes that will deposit the explorers back into more of the same old thing. Its also essential for people who choose to stay inside the boundaries of existing assistance to benefit from the work of staff who have a clear idea of what defines good support.

Our framework for thinking about good human service work begins by identifying five ordinary human experiences that are strongly influenced by the way assistance is organized.[*]

Belonging in a diverse network of relationships and memberships.

Being respected as whole people whose history, capacities and future are worthy of attention and whose capacities engage us in valued social roles.

Sharing ordinary places and activities with other citizens, neighbors, classmates, and co-workers. Living, working, learning, and playing confidently in ordinary community settings.

Contributing by discovering, developing, and giving our gifts and investing our capacities and energy in pursuits that make a positive difference to other people and build real wealth. There are gifts of being and gifts of doing: contribution can include interested presence as well as capable performance. Contributions may be freely exchanged or earn pay.

---

[*] The idea of valued experiences as ideals guiding action came from study of the pragmatist philosopher E.A. Singer as extended and applied by his students, West Churchman and Russell Ackoff. See Russell Ackoff & Fred Emery (1972). *On purposeful systems.* London: Tavistock and C. West Churchman (1972), *The design of inquiring systems.* New York: Basic Books.

A complementary framework for thinking about good human service work which has influenced us a great deal and the field considerably is Social Role Valorization (SRV)/ Normalization. For a summary of SRV, visit www.srvip.org/ overview_SRV_Osburn.pdf

Choosing what we want in everyday situations in ways that reflect our highest purpose. Having the freedom, support, information, and assistance to make the same choices as others of a similar age and learning to make wiser choices over time. Being encouraged to use and strengthen voice regardless of mode of communication, clarify what really matters, make thoughtful decisions, and learn from experience.

The valued experiences share these qualities…

… Most people would identify each of them as important in a life that they would have good reasons to value living.

… They contribute directly to the creation of real wealth and shape a set of lenses to view the conditions that will allow a particular person to build real wealth.*

… They are consistent with rights established in the *Convention on the Rights of Persons with Disabilities.*

… People with developmental disabilities are vulnerable to socially imposed limits on each of these experiences. Conscious and creative effort is necessary to establish and sustain them in their lives.

… They define ideals worth seeking through continual learning rather than objectives that can be completed and set aside.

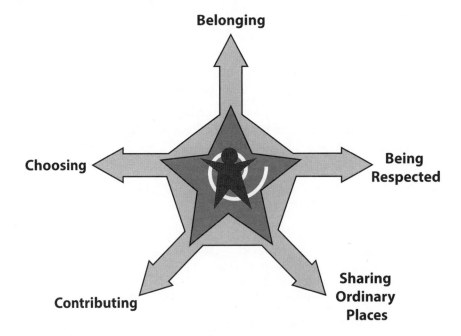

---

* Personal Futures Planning is organized to identify opportunities for constructive actions that will increase a person's access to each of these experiences.

> … As a set they relate to one another in ways that define both virtuous circles and dilemmas. For example, belonging usually increases options for choice and honoring relationships can constrain choices.
>
> … The structures and practices of human service organizations make a significant difference in the extent to which the people they serve experience them.

Valued experiences emerge from interactions among people with developmental disabilities, the other people in their lives, including assistants, and available opportunities. A service provider has influence but can't be accountable for producing these experiences as if they were countable objects. This is a good thing because it leaves room for people's freedom. Staff can not be assigned to manufacture relationships or contributing roles as "outcomes". Too many things beyond staff control are involved. Organizations can choose to be accountable for developing staff who intentionally direct their attention to discovering and creating the conditions in which the person they assist has more valued experiences.

As a set, the valued experiences indicate accomplishments* that focus continual efforts to improve the quality of publicly funded assistance. Organizations that support good partnerships keep asking themselves these design questions and so learn in action how to do their part in discovering better and better answers.

How might we better assist people to make and sustain connections, memberships and friendships? Service workers make a difference when they listen deeply and act thoughtfully to provide exactly what a person needs to build bridges to **community participation**.

How might we better assist people to occupy valued social roles? Respect comes to those who play recognizable and valued parts in everyday community stories. Service workers make a difference when they support people to identify and take up social roles that express their interests, provide needed assistance and negotiate the accommodations they need to be successful and so encourage **valued social roles**.

How might we better assist people to increase their active involvement in all aspects of community life? Service workers make a difference when they assist people to make the most of

---

* The idea of accomplishments came from Thomas Gilbert (1973) *Human competence: Engineering worthy performance.* New York: Mcgraw Hill.

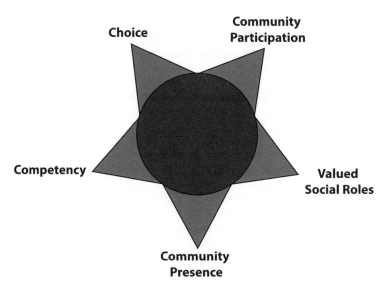

Choice

Community Participation

Competency

Valued Social Roles

Community Presence

Larry Bissonette is an artist and star of *Wretches & Jabberers*, a documentary that explores the impact of access to communication for people with autism (www. wretchesandjabberers.org.) This is what he said about increasing his capacity for self-regulation.

Working on mopping up my autistic patterns is like working on more lasting love between political parties. Ordering me to stop (my behavior) doesn't help. I need calm, reducing anxiety, patient patterning of my actions into something productive like typing.

*Larry owes his ordering of self to people around him placing words of encouragement on his partly bald head and more people like Larry potentially may live **passion driven rather than behavior pushed lives.***

the ordinary community settings that attract their interest and energy. This increases **community presence**.

How might we better assist people to develop and invest their gifts and capacities? Service workers make a difference when they focus on what each person can do to build real wealth and bring imagination and technical competence to designing and delivering what each person needs to develop **competency**.

How might we better assist people to exercise choice and control in their lives? Service workers make a difference when they honor people's rights and responsibilities and offer what works to promote their autonomy and **choice**.

The more the people responsible for designing and offering assistance attend to these questions with open minds, open hearts and willingness to join people in discovering improvements, the more real wealth people with developmental disabilities will generate. Consistently holding these questions makes a difference at every scale of action from performing everyday tasks to structuring and administering a state's publicly funded assistance.

Taking these questions seriously means being respectful of the power that socially devaluing stories about people with developmental disabilities have to hide social exclusion, control and underestimation of developmental potential under a blanket of benevolence. These stories have two insidious features. They present themselves not as stories but as facts, just the way things are, "how it is in the real world". And, devaluing stories can swallow people with developmental disabilities and their families into their account of "reality." Diagnosis can define identity. Opportunities to imagine better and do better come into view when people leave behind stories that justify low expectations and become the authors of stories of quest for new possibilities.

Our friend Marcie Brost, a skillful change maker and advocate for her son, identifies the bedrock condition for taking these questions seriously. There must be an animating belief that each person with a developmental disability is 100% there. This means:

We accept responsibility to learn how to…	rather than acting on the assumption that…
…establish communication	…"she has no language".
…create conditions for self-regulation	…"he is too violent to live outside an institution".
…actively promote wellness & engagement	…she is too medically fragile to live outside a medical setting"
…discover meaningful adult roles and activities	…he has the mind of a 3 year old in an adult body".

Because it is right to act with people rather than doing things to them, finding ways to engage people with developmental disabilities themselves with these questions matters. In their roles as board members, advisors and advocates they have much to contribute to generating better answers. As people responsible to direct their own lives, attending to these dimensions of the assistance they count on can reveal new possibilities.

Reflecting on his role as leader of a person-centered planning team in a large agency, Scott Ramsey noticed trends that concerned him.[*] The way plans had been facilitated resulted in people staying with what was most familiar or pursuing new activities they or their families though would be safe and fun. Goals were either within very easy reach or so far away as to be nearly impossible. Plans lacked any practical steps to address foreseeable obstacles. While more people spent time hanging out in familiar community places, few were included in contributing roles or making friends outside the walls of the agency. The employment rate declined because people left jobs that bored them rather than asking for assistance to find work that better fit their interests and capacities.

In Ramsey's analysis, these trends had a common cause. A particular understanding of choice had become a sacred cow. Choice had come to mean whatever a person said in the moment of the planing meeting, regardless of the information available and

---

[*] Ramsey, S. (2007). Roles Based Planning: A thoughtful approach to social inclusion and empowerment. *The SRV Journal, 2*(1), 4-12

without careful attention to exploring new possibilities. Planners acted as if respecting a person's choice meant avoiding questions, challenges or identification of obstacles to what the person said they wanted. This way of understanding choice, out of the context of other valued experiences, masked low expectations and exiled from the planning room any discussion of any real changes that might be necessary in the way staff offered assistance or in purposefully developing the person's capacities.

Ramsey's team re-designed their process based on a renewed belief in people's potential for development and filling valued community roles. The aim was to give people a stronger foundation for planning by taking time with them to explore the practical connections between self-direction and building real wealth by assuming contributing roles. Informing choice by asking people to think about the effects of being pushed by culture and society into a devalued and socially excluded status, providing opportunities to develop critical thinking skills about the ways negative stereotypes affect their imagination of a desirable future, and actively exploring the possibilities for resisting the push to social exclusion by pursuing valued roles and friendships in the community. The redesigned process, which they named Roles Based Planning, guided action that had a notable effect on the lives of 200 people over six years.

	Guided by "Whatever you say" approach	Guided by Contributing Roles Focus
Community job	35%	73%
Community friends	13%	57%
Inclusive activities	25%	90%

How might we create conditions that increase…

…belonging

…respect from contributing roles

…sharing ordinary places

…contributing

…choosing

The idealized design questions never have a final answer (although people may decide to rest for a while) because a better answer is always in the future, built on what is being accomplished now and responsive to changing circumstances. Whether it's self-directed support for a single person or an administration responsible for assisting thousands of people with developmental disabilities, an adequate organization allows people to hold the five questions in a fruitful way and support trying and learning from new practices and structures.

A geometry of partnership

Its almost automatic to think first of pyramids and policies when figuring out how to organize people's efforts. How will tasks be divided to make the most efficient use of available resources and meet demands from regulatory authorities? Who will report to whom? What policies will govern decisions and how many levels of management are necessary to assure that these policies are implemented? Organizations need some pyramid characteristics, at least to satisfy tax, labor and other authorities about their suitability to receive and handle public money and offer assistance.

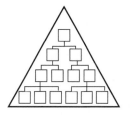

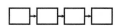

Organizations that think of themselves as pyramids limit their capacity for partnership with pathfinders. In the background of this way of thinking is the image of an organization as a well engineered machine, capable of commanding and controlling its parts to efficiently serve its owners' purposes by following clear rules and predicting, planning and implementing changes in straight lines. Teams fit inside pyramid thinking, but as one possible means to do the organization's work, not as the indispensable container for creative partnership

The trouble with this image of organization is that the work it tries to control is founded on relationships that form around efforts to serve a great variety of different human purposes, many of which require discovery of new paths. The qualities that make those relationships effective –mindful presence, respectful listening, moving with, negotiating, trust, respect– can not be produced as an inventory of parts or modules of programming. They emerge when interdependencies are carefully tended in action.

Organizations that want to cultivate good partners think and act relationally. They imagine circles and networks and U shaped processes of discovery before pyramids and linear programs. Circles include people across roles and boundaries and aim for collaboration around common purpose. The smallest unit of organization is the circle or team that forms around an individual person's desire for a life they have good reason to value living. As an organization assists more people, coordination is structured through circles of circles and shared membership among circles. Acting on circles first thinking doesn't erase lines of authority and formal accountability, it sets them in the background, as servants of the relationships that create lives that people have good reasons to value.

Life Works Flips the Script

Life Works, an organization that supports people with developmental disabilities in San Diego, is designed to customize supports for a small number of people and their allies.* The organizations founder, Beth Gallagher, had 20 years experience successfully managing an organization that exceeded the expectations of its funders and enjoyed high satisfaction ratings from the people it served and their families. Reflecting on the limitations of this success significantly influenced the design of Life Works. She noticed that her previous efforts had two blind spots. One, people were safe and their lives were good in comparison to those served by other agencies. But there was too little effective attention to the richness and fullness of life possible when people's gifts and contributions to community relationships are in focus. Two, the organization was a hierarchy that depended on Beth as hero-leader, on top of every detail. When she left, her carefully designed pyramid began to crumble.

Illuminating these blind spots has created an organization based on sustaining a culture of intentional teaming around individuals. Lines of authority and policy exist to fulfill outside requirements and provide a back up to make decisions in exceptional circumstances, but these functions are secondary to and designed to serve intentional teaming. Life Works' guide to action is *flip the script*. This applies to people with developmental disabilities. Team Tami received a script that portrayed her as "autistic, and rigid with very poor communication" and, with time and attention to the relationship between her capacities and the capacities of the rest of the team, flipped that limiting script to reveal a capable public speaker and self-advocate who has become a sushi connoisseur. It also applies to the organization's design and functioning.

Organizations in the Blind Spot		Life Works
Organized in hierarchy: authority, answers, decisions, mission identification are "up there" away from people.		• Organization is flat. • Teams form around individuals ("Team Tina", "Team Jeremy"). • People, family members, other citizens are team members. • Every employee does direct support. • People hired for individual team. • Teams have authority to decide. • Feed back, voice is key to team function. • Team fosters reciprocity -getting each other's backs (e.g. staff responsible for replacing selves on schedule). • Everyone is challenged to grow.
Staff are "caregivers", expected to do just what is in the job description.		• Team draws out & encourages every member's gifts & encourages selflessness. • Person-centered plans are for everyone. • Decision making is shared. • Creative action comes from all team members' mindfulness of the team's mission. • Team member initiative is expected & celebrated.

* Life Works' leaders share what they have learned about offering good support in Beth Gallagher & Kirk Hinkleman (2012). *Intentional teaming: Shifting organizational culture.* inclusion.com

Staff maintain "professional distance".	ℒ	• We are all team members. • We all give of ourselves. • We respect vulnerability. • We build real relationships that support the development of new relationships.
Safety is in protective staff & distance from neighbors & other, non-staff people.	ℒ	Safety is in caring relationships, knowing your neighbors & connecting our gifts.
Our job is to take care of people.	ℒ	Our job is to support people to create relationships that will increase their interdependency & work us out of our job.
Neighborhood & community don't matter.	ℒ	Connections in neighborhood & community are the heart of our work & it begins with each of us in our own neighborhoods.

A capable circle or team accepts responsibility for a shared purpose, enabling a person with a developmental disability to live a good life under conditions of uncertainty.* Because much uncertainty is created by the social devaluation and exclusion of people with developmental disabilities, these purposes make moral claims on the person's community and society as people search for recognition of their dignity, their citizenship and their right to be included in contributing social roles. Their achievement often requires social invention. The team is a consciously formed social space that supports members to…

…build a growing network of respectful relationships that result in commitment to the teams' purpose: enabling a good life for the person with a developmental disability.

…craft a new story, rooted in what team members value, that expresses the change the team wants to create and why that story matters to each member.

…work out each person's contribution to the team's work and how team members will act with one another.

…develop strategies that turn member's collective capacities into the power to sense and move into a desirable future.

…take action and critically reflect on what happened and what to do next.

---

* We have adapted this discussion from Marshall Gans' understanding of leadership in (2010) Leading change: Leadership, organization and social movements. In N. Nohria & R. Khurana (Eds.). *Handbook of leadership theory and practice*, pp. 509-550. Boston: Harvard Business Press.

It's important to recognize that team membership is not martyrdom. Enabling another person to have a better life has meaning in itself. Even more important, a good interdependent life rests on people wishing one another happiness and doing what they can to notice and offer what the other needs. Capable teams have the capability to repair breakdowns in relationships and responsibilities.

Investment in developing support workers

Good direct support is a performing art, more like acting in improvisational theatre than packing boxes for Amazon.com. It requires practical knowledge to spot, make sense of and respond to changing vulnerabilities and opportunities as they come up in the flow of daily life. It is more a matter of knowing how to make the right move than knowing that a particular policy applies.

The person with a developmental disability is the best coach for the direct support role and the relationship that a support worker builds with the person is the worker's primary source of energy and meaning. So the most important investment in development is in relationship building.

Relationships get off to a better start when…

… the person and those who know them best and have their trust play an active part in the decision to hire or assign the support worker, including the option to veto a selection.

… the person and those they trust orient and teach the assistant how to do what is necessary. Modeling the way a person wants assistance is usually very effective. It helps if a person has had a chance to consider what they want the support worker to learn. Collaboration with the person in constructing communication aids is helpful:

- One page profiles that concisely introduce the person and what works for them in positive terms.[*]

- The results of using Person Centered Thinking Tools with the person and those who know them best, especially descriptions of what is important to and important for the person, what works and what doesn't, good day/bad day, and the responsibility donut.[†]

- The graphics and other artifacts from person-centered plans and following action.

Consider the difference between a play that is scripted and an improvised performance.

A scripted play is deterministic, which significantly diminishes the scope for spontaneity and novelty. Each performance will vary in subtle ways, but in each production we know the ending in advance.

By contrast, an improvised performance allows more freedom to the actors, more room for creativity, and so has an uncertain and unpredictable path. But this is emphatically not the same as individual autonomy. On the contrary, the actors are not unbounded masters of their own destiny. Their performance will be shaped by the other actors' performances, by what happened in their lives in the lead-up to the show, by the physical setting of the theatre, the reaction of the audience and many other factors outside their control.

–Ben Lewis &
Tony Greenham

---

* See *100 One Page Profiles* onepageprofiles.wordpress.com.

† Helen Sanderson Associates, *Person-Centred Thinking Tools*. goo.gl/jhh8D2

... there is time to get to know the person in more than one place and kind of activity.

... the team makes time to help the new support worker reflect on what they are learning and the opportunities for them to grow in the relationship.

... there is intense, highly skilled, hands-on coaching to assure good performance when a person's differences in movement, communication, emotional regulation or learning require the direct support worker to act capably in stressful and uncertain situations.

It is important to encourage direct support workers to resist the social devaluation of their role in ways that do not add to the devaluation of the people they support. This devaluation shows in too little investment in learning opportunities and chances to reflect on their work. Some organizations act as if people can be trained to find the meaning and possibilities in their work with a few hours exposure to a standard curriculum mediated by a website. Support for exploration of ideas, reflective discussion of dilemmas and difficulties, and conversations linking their work to bigger social contexts go by the board.*

Investment in opportunities for learning can offer context and content for understanding the direct support workers contribution to building a community that works for everyone. Learning more about people pursing healthy community, both within the disability field and outside it, gives people a source of strength. Well guided exploration of the effects of social exclusion and social devaluation increase consciousness and encourage resistance. Developing the skills to explore the five quality questions in partnership with a person with a developmental disability offers a growth challenge that can renew, redirect and deepen a relationship.† Gathering with others who work in different organizations and communities enriches learning.

---

* We know of two usefulon-line resources for learning. *Conversations that matter,* curated by Norman Kunc and Emma Van der Klift, is a reasonably priced on-line resource that supports learning through reflection on brief, well edited conversations with a variety of resource people. It can be found at conversationsthatmatter.org.
Citizen-Centered Leadership is an intensive on-line learning opportunity, offered by Cornell University's Employment and Disability Institute and facilitated by Carol Blessing. citizencenteredleadership.org. In addition to the course, visit the site for information about on line conversations and a growing community of practice.

† For an approach to this form of action-learning see John O'Brien & Beth Mount (2005). *Make a difference: A guidebook for person-centered direct support.* inclusion.com

Detail from Onondaga Community Living *Spirit Weavers* quilt that expresses a team's sense of how a person's life is growing richer.

Opportunities to reflect on the meaning, challenges and dilemmas in the work make an important difference. Direct support workers have many capacities that can be channeled into the creation of beauty as a means to guide and express the meaning of their work. Among other expressions, direct support staff and their managers have produced original music and rap,[*] written stories and reflections,[†] performed experimental theatre,[‡] and created quilts.[§]

These investments –providing time and support for a good relationship to develop, providing a variety of opportunities for people to learn more, and encouraging reflection through creation– increase the number of capable and committed partners available to people with developmental disabilities.

In most of the US this seems utopian. Efforts to develop committed and capable staff are entangled in a web of negative forces. High rates of staff turn-over driven by low pay make it difficult for even committed workers to stick with it. Increasing pressure from cost managers to seek efficiencies by standardizing and depersonalizing assistance and minimizing staff time away from performing paid tasks cuts time for relationship building and learning. Cuts in rates for assistance and rising costs of employee benefits and insurance squeeze the potential for better pay and investment in development of workers. These worrying trends are now affecting first line supervisors and middle managers as well as direct support workers.

Until the work is more socially valued, pathfinders in the US face increasing difficulty in finding capable partners. Working around these difficulties –for example by juggling individual budgets and building in unpaid assistance from family or friends to increase direct worker's pay– demands more from people and their allies and decreases the number of pathfinders able to make the journey in search of a better life.

---

[*] See *Everyday Heroes Video* goo.gl/2pCReA

[†] John O'Brien & Connie Lyle O'Brien, Editors (1992). *Remembering the soul of our work.* Madison, WI:Options in Community Living. goo.gl/H1q6g0

[‡] *Capacity Works: Exploring Possibilities with Social Presencing Theater at Job Path* goo.gl/Pt4v2A

[§] Onondaga Community Living, *Spirit Weavers Quilt.* goo.gl/txIweN

Unless there is a significant shift in the value attached to direct support work, the most vibrant social inventions will emerge in countries that value direct support workers more than the US does. One route to increasing the social value of the work is making stronger and more visible connections between personal assistance for people with developmental disabilities and elders and successful efforts to shape communities that work better for everyone. Partnerships that assist people with developmental disabilities to show up as contributing citizens have a chance of breaking the cycle of deteriorating expectations.

Our hope is where it has always been, in the power of people with developmental disabilities to resist institutionalization in its shape-shifting forms and recruit people who care about discovering and doing the right thing to assist them. Circumstances may limit the number of these social inventors and the scope of their effort, but their spirit will continue to motivate social inventions.

Partners with clinical knowledge

Clinical know-how that reduces the impact of people's impairments on their ability to live a life they have good reasons to value continues to grow. Specialist knowledge can now make a positive difference to people who require substantially more assistance than most people do to communicate, swallow, learn new skills, increase literacy, support memory and task performance, regulate anxiety, accommodate movement differences, experience wellness, (self-)manage seizures, move and maintain a healthy posture and self-manage stress and the symptoms of mental ill health. This assistance can come in the form of a carefully tailored physical environment, well fitted equipment, personalized technology that supports alternative methods of communication, or schedule and task prompts. or practices that enable people to apply their capacities to doing what matters to them. Effective specialists attend with care to assuring that the person and those the person counts on for everyday assistance are fully competent in using and maintaining the technology and practices they recommend.

Nina's Music

Diana McCourt: My daughter, Nina, was born about 50 years ago with severe autism. She doesn't speak. She suffers from extreme anxiety which, in the past, caused her to hurt herself and kept her from experiencing new things.

What really changed things for Nina was finding her own apartment where she lives with one other person and has 24 hour support from an agency called Job Path.

There are a lot of ways to support her here that make her life better but most recently one has dramatically improved Nina's Life. Musician/soundworker Cori Bargar has designed a customized program for her. Cori's rhythmic prescriptions for Nina have slowed down her fast pace of eating and walking and his weekly visits have produced long lasting calming effects.

Cori: My work with Nina is focused on the intentional use of sound. Both playing acoustic instruments directly on the body and using recorded music that I've compiled for her.

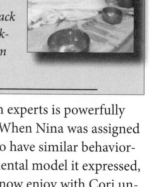

Using music and sound, specifically rhythm, to accompany Nina's daily activities adds a structure to them. I've created a series of different recordings to use at different times of the day for different activities. For instance there is a piece at 60 beats per minute that we use when Nina sits down to eat. We have music for transitioning from one space to another in the apartment, for going in and out of doors. We have music for walking. We have music for relaxation.

The idea of creating music to accompany a specific activity takes a step back from the way that we usually listen to music for entertainment… I'm looking for the way the tone, or the harmony, or the melody line or the rhythm interacts with the human body.

As *Nina's Music* shows, partnership with experts is powerfully influenced by people's living conditions. When Nina was assigned to live with a group of people perceived to have similar behavioral challenges, the group home, and the mental model it expressed, made the partnership Nina and her staff now enjoy with Cori unimaginable. Once she had her own apartment and individualized support, the stage was set for effective use of expert skill.

Experts make an important contribution to sense-making about a person's impairments. Expert stories respectfully communicate the dignity of the person with a developmental disability and frame interventions within the context developing meaningful capacities and good relationships. Effective practitioners of communication support and teaching literacy encourage the presumption of competence. Capable instructors assume that poor performance is due to inadequate instruction rather than intractable learner deficits. Good practice in customized employment calls for suspension of judgment about a person's ability to do a paid community job until a careful discovery process and a creative job development process have been exhausted. Those who understand sensory and movement differences encourage people with disabilities to develop accommodations that work for them.

Good specialist partners take a common stance. They see their task as serving the person's life journey, not prescribing its route or controlling the traveler. They like strategies that support self-management within a person's relationships. They appreciate both the promise and the limits of their knowledge. With care and discipline, improvement or sustained achievement is often possible but, at least for most developmental impairments, cure is out of reach. They understand that the opportunities and expectations afforded by a person's immediate social and physical environment are as powerful, or more powerful, as their interventions. They know that belief in a person's possibilities and support for what a person finds meaningful make a greater difference to a person's wellbeing than achievement on any abstract test of functioning..

Good experts take a critical stance toward the multiple stories current about developmental disabilities. They notice conflicts among narratives and what might be productively applied from each. They make their own choice, giving weight to the positions of the experts by experience who live inside the stories and seeking an understanding that allows the most room for action that will assist a person to build real wealth.

Finding good expert partners can be difficult. In many relevant fields, practice with people with developmental disabilities is not valued. Some of this avoidance is explained by myths that involvement with people with developmental disabilities returns little improvement. More of it reflects limits in what specialists actually do in many service settings, where much of their time is allocated to professional-bureaucratic work. In many states, policy strongly links regularly repeated expert assessment to eligibility for benefits and supports, regulatory requirements call for compilation of professionally generated information, cost control measures demand expert justifications for changes, and licensing rules impose conditions of professional oversight on some forms of assistance (for example, assisting a person to take medication or change a catheter).

Most of this bureaucratic-professional work arises from a zombie mental model that stumbles into policy and practice. It sees disability as if it were a chronic medical condition and frames assistance as if it were a delivery system for medical and paramedical procedures. On this understanding, people's relationships, living arrangements and occupations are ancillary to treatment and rehabilitation. This story shaped and maintained institutions and its residue continues to shape assistance funded as an alternative to institutionalization. Specialist physicians are very scarce on the ground, but the persistent power that the medical mental model has over the way assistance is offered casts a long shadow over the whole lives of many people.

This perspective subordinates people's citizenship and autonomy to professional authority and directs staff attention to activities that experts prescribe to remediate or cure clients' mental or physical defects and enforce restrictions dictated by experts' understanding of their duty of care to the sick, dangerous or diminished. The expert posture necessary to exert this kind of control makes it difficult to help people along a self-directed journey to social inclusion. That journey requires tenacious focus on capacity and connection.

Busting the ghosts of the medical model that continue to haunt the lives of people with developmental disabilities and making the best possible clinical assistance available in the real places that matter to a person is good if demanding work for strong partnerships. Evan's story illustrates the possibilities that open when experts accept that more of the same doesn't work, adopt a stance of co-creation, suspend their certainties and explore the consequences of new perspectives on challenging situations. The experts involved have made their best effort to join his journey rather than try to run his life.

Evan: Building a Life

I have this loving, adorable child who longs to be helpful and is thrilled when people notice him. He gives very satisfying hugs and offers to help whenever he sees a way to do that. His life, however, was not a smooth journey. He has experienced trauma in his life that has caused him problems. As a child and young adult his happy, generous demeanor would sometimes be overwhelmed by something within him that responded to unknowable stimuli: my lively son would become afraid and, as he protected himself, he seemed aggressive. He would lash out, mostly harming himself but sometimes catching others in the chaos. His anxiety landed him in the "care" of local police on many occasions, also emergency rooms, then in mental institutions and finally locked up in a state facility for people with dangerous behaviors.

A complicating factor was the psychiatric community's penchant to solve problems with medications. I never witnessed a change or improvement in Evan's situation as a result of a medication, but the "true believers" thought that finding the right "cocktail" of meds was the answer.

I am thrilled to report that ultimately we did find the right "cocktail", but there are no meds involved. What saved Evan's life is a regular diet of mindfulness practices, yoga, exercise, deep breathing and a loving, supportive staff.

While Evan was in the institutions, a team of us met weekly, over several months, to plan his homecoming. We developed a combination of strategies that we hoped would meet his needs. Luckily, the team was comprised of very creative and observant people who had experience working with Evan. We discussed what we knew about his anxiety and created a schedule of activities to help him relax and regroup whenever he needs to.

Staff were found and traveled to the institution to meet Evan and begin their work with him. The first step in his healing was to get him to participate in the strategies our team had devised, and I was amazed at how quickly he did just that! He developed trusting relationships with his staff and they are able to guide him. He has become aware of his body and he has learned that he can take care of himself and stay regulated.

When he first came out of the institution he had a schedule with a change of activity every 15 minutes. We kept him very busy as he learned the strategies that helped him build his life. As he grew, his world grew: he slowly moved from his bedroom into the living room, then the kitchen, and then out into the community. He practices breathing and relaxation exercises wherever disregulation threatens. Once we formed a "breathing circle" at the Kohl Center when he became excited at a sporting event. I imagine it looked to outsiders like a huddle of sorts. Evan now shares his ability to self regulate, teaching mindfulness practices to other people.

Today Evan works 4 days a week at a local grocery store. He participates in many community activities, competes in Special Olympics and belongs to a bowling group. Occasionally he stops by his grandmother's house to bring her lunch, he comes for dinner, and goes out with his friends and siblings regularly. He has good relationships with his neighbors: he shovels and rakes, they provide produce.

I am indeed blessed to have Evan back, healthy and whole.

–Deb Hall

4

Supporting Families

Families are people's most durable support. Enduring bonds among people, not law, delineate a wonderful variety of family forms. Family love energizes and shapes development and nurtures desire for a good life. Family knowledge and heritage forms identity. Family resourcefulness buffers crises and provides long term assistance. Family networks open opportunities. Family commitment supports educational, economic and civic involvement.

Families are imperfect. They are sites of conflict where intergenerational fallibilities interact and cause wounds that influence members' paths through life. Dramas of estrangement and reconciliation track family histories. Families in isolation are vulnerable: positive relationships outside family boundaries balance,and when necessary protect from, the consequences of misfortune or over or under attachment.

Family breakdown is catastrophic for whole communities. Exhausted and demoralized families struggle to mobilize their assets and capacities in service of family's members development. Families strained past the limit of their resourcefulness experience diminished wellbeing and contribute less to the common good. Families overwhelmed by material poverty, addiction or mental ill health can become neglectful or abusive.

The Plague of Inequality

Inequality shadows every dimension of family experience. It multiplies the difficulties families encounter when a member has developmental disabilities and limits the effectiveness of family support strategies. Summarizing a large and growing body of evidence on the causes of health inequality for the MacArthur Foundation Research Network on Socioeconomic Status and Health, Nancy Adler and her colleagues write this (get the complete summary at goo.gl/qoYFIO).

Societies are structured like ladders. The rungs of the ladder represent the resources that determine whether people can live a good life –prosperous, healthy, and secure– or a life plagued by difficulties–insufficient income, poor health, and vulnerability. People standing on the top rungs are the best educated, have the most respected jobs, ample savings, and comfortable housing. On the bottom rungs are people who are poorly educated, experience long bouts of unemployment or low wage jobs, have nothing to fall back on in the way of savings, and live in substandard homes. The people in the middle have more resources to rely on than do people at the bottom, but far less than people on the top. In reaching for health, every step up makes a difference. Your position on the ladder predicts how long you live and how healthy you are during your lifetime...

The age of death is only one outcome that varies along the ladder's rungs. Other serious health problems follow the same pattern of inequality. Those lower on the socioeconomic ladder are more likely to experience:

- *Newborn health problems like premature birth, low birth weight, birth defects.*
- *Signs of future disease like high blood pressure, obesity, weakened immune system.*
- *Chronic diseases like diabetes, heart disease, and many forms of cancer.*
- *Infectious diseases ranging from HIV/AIDS to the common flu.*
- *Disabilities like blindness, mental illness and decline of physical strength.*

A powerful cultural story of individualism makes it hard for people and policy makers in the US to connect the dots that establish the powerful negative effects of inequality on family life. The social injustice of inequality hides behind stories of hard working individuals overcoming the odds and disdain for those judged too weak and lazy to make it on minimum wages in neighborhoods where low performing schools and predatory lenders are far more plentiful than good jobs and affordable supplies of nutritious food. Evidence that citizens significantly overestimate the proportion of the population that steps up to higher rungs in a generation (goo.gl/dGxru3) does little to undermine the myth.

Families of people with developmental disabilities will benefit from polices that make life easier for every family. Workplace flexibility, paid parental leave, tax relief or subsidy for energy efficiency all will help. Policies that make life easier for people who are poor in money –like community wealth building, higher minimum wages, Earned Income Tax Credits, educational benefits and housing subsidies– improve things for families who also have developmental disabilities. The less generous and effective these measures are, the more families will have to rely on programs aimed at their family member's status as developmentally disabled. Some low income households must count on disability benefits as their most reliable source of income. Others have found the option to hire family members as personal assistants a pathway to income security. These survival strategies can limit opportunities.

> Current social policy debates are dominated by the assertion that we face levels of public expenditure which are not affordable. We need to turn this around –instead of talking about what level of public expenditure we can afford, we should be talking about what kind of economy we can afford. The kind of economy we currently have is bad for the wider health of our society because it creates great inequality, insecurity and poverty.
>
> –Jenny Morris

It is no accident that without intentional and sustained support, many more pathfinders will come from families that stand on at least the middle rungs than those on lower rungs of the ladder. Urban Innovations proves that there are many pathfinders waiting for connection in neighborhoods plagued with inequality. Making this connection is partly a question of cultural competence so that differences in race, language and traditions don't separate people from opportunities. But most of the remedy is down to finding practical ways to address the effects of inequality until society discovers a more just economics.

Everything we say in this chapter applies to all families, regardless of where they stand on the ladder. And inequality makes everything more complex and difficult for people on the lower rungs of the ladder. That so many create good lives despite inequality identifies a source of knowledge and hope that calls for respectful inquiry.

Surplus difficulty

Every family faces the challenge of developing a sustainable daily routine by weaving together family members' diverse capacities and interests. All families find this challenge easier when they have access to secure housing, meaningful and flexible employment, good quality childcare and education, good and affordable healthcare, access to good help to repair strained relationships and a vibrant civic life. Regardless of other circumstances, when a member has a developmental disability families experience surplus difficulties in orchestrating a sustainable routine. Simply put, developmental disability brings extra work on top of what it takes to raise any child. How a family deals with this extra work affects every family member and the contributions they all make to community life. While all family members are affected by the extra work involved in managing surplus difficulty, mothers and sisters typically do more of it than fathers and brothers do.

Many families make positive adaptations to surplus difficulties and find meaning in the experience. In a recent survey,[*] Alberta families identified many difficulties, most related to the availability and quality of publicly funded assistance they are eligible for. Two out of three parents said that, overall, having a family member with a disability has been positive for their family.

- More than 70% said their family is stronger because of the family member with a disability.

- Almost 90% said that wonderful people have come into their lives.

- Almost 90% said that they have learned what is really important in life.

- Over 50% said that they now laugh more and are less bothered by trivial things.

Because developmental disability refers to life long impairments difficulties change shape with life stages and changing circumstances, but they endure. Much surplus difficulty comes from the need to do necessary work for many years beyond the age that other children will become able to manage without (as much) parental help. This has special significance for the growing number of families who do not have access to the resources that would offer the choice to establish their adult sons and daughters in households independent of their own, a condition that can last for 50 years or more unless parents become incapable or die.

---

[*] David McConnell, et al. (2014) *Family Life: Children with Disabilities and the Fabric of Everyday Family Life.* goo.gl/vIigM0

Current estimates say that more than half of adults eligible for developmental disability services in the US live in their family home and count on other family members for a substantial amount of assistance.

Because developmental disability is an umbrella term each person has a distinctive constellation of impairments and the form and degree of surplus difficulty is different for each family. Those whose family member needs occasional assistance with learning new things will experience different surplus difficulties than those whose family member requires several hours of physical help each day or has frequent episodes of emotional dysregulation and self-injury.

The long term presence of surplus difficulty justifies focused public investment in supporting families with developmentally disabled members. The purpose of this investment is to offer each family assistance in living a life that they have good reasons to value, which includes strengthening family capacity to provide the conditions for all members to thrive. Developing capacities to understand and respond to each family's particular situation among those who administer and provide assistance is essential.

Extra work

Surplus difficulty comes in the form of extra physical, mental and emotional work and extra money costs. Some of many possible examples follow.

Physical and mental work. Help with washing, dressing and toileting. Help with seating and positioning. Extra laundry. Regular lost sleep to meet physical needs or deal with dangerous situations. Implementing practices that enhance development, preserve physical capacity or assist the person to regulate emotion. Protecting the person or others from harm, which may require constant monitoring. Providing rides. Scheduling and attending meetings and appointments with multiple doctors, therapists and service providers. Managing medications. Establishing and maintaining eligibility for benefits and services. Scheduling, coordinating and documenting assistance to the person. Discovering relevant services and benefits and doing the paperwork necessary to get and keep them. Recruiting, training and supervising assistants. Advocacy to protect and extend public funding or improve policy.

Emotional work. Coping with shame or guilt or desire to assign blame for the occurrence of impairments. Experiencing hurt and anger when extended family members or friends reject the person or cannot accept the person as a whole person. Facing cold, disrespectful or incompetent responses from experts or managers whose resources you need. Dealing with turnover among service coordinators and assistants. Coping with the presence of assistants in your home. Conflict over most appropriate settings and services with schools and service providers or arguments over preauthorization of funds for equipment or supplies. Experiencing embarrassment when a person has difficulties in public. Empathic pain when a person is rejected or ignored, especially when rejection comes from people and places of significance to the family, such as their church. Coping with strain on marriage. Working out how to balance attention among brothers and sisters and extended family members. Anger at the costs to dignity of getting assistance: having to tell stories of deficiency and incompetence to establish eligibility and priority on wait lists; being kept waiting; failures to call back or follow through on important matters. Fear that complaint or requests for change will lead to retaliation against the person with a developmental disability. Anxiety at points of transition: the move from preschool to school, from grade to grade, from school to adult life. Loss of personally valued activities (for example, parents often significantly decrease their own participation in sport or leisure activities they have enjoyed).

> Our disability system turns people like me into beggars. We parents call it competitive misery. The most miserable might win funding and support, but if you win the misery game, it means you are losing at life.
>
> –Sally Richards

Money costs. Lost time from work when a child is sent home from school or an adult family member is excluded from a day program or to attend appointments or when an assistant defaults or a worker can't be found. Foregone or missed promotions because of uncertain demands on time and energy. Costs of personal assistance or expert services. Specialized equipment and supplies. Equipment maintenance. Co-pays for medical treatment, drugs or equipment and supplies. Home and vehicle modifications. Unusual wear and tear on home and furnishings.

Redesigning support to families

Publicly funded help to families has grown, mostly in the form of assistance targeted at the labeled member's assessed deficiencies. In the US children are entitled to developmental supports from birth to 3 years and a free and appropriate education, defined by an individual education plan, from age 3 to 21. Most developmentally disabled people are eligible for Medicaid and Social Security benefits which can pay for a variety of services and equipment and supplies when they are deemed medically necessary. Most adults qualify for some kind of day service. Some places make some cash available to meet extra costs.

Visit From A Service Coordinator With Great News*

Service Coordinator: Great news! You have come off the waiting list and your daughter is now on the waiver [shorthand name for a more substantial funding source than the family has had access to before].

Mother: That's good. What's the next step?

Service Coordinator: You choose the services that will be best for your daughter. What disability services do you want? Do you want in-home respite? We have a couple of local agencies that do respite, so you can choose.

Mother: No, thanks. We don't need any more services in our home. What my daughter needs is opportunities to be with other kids her age and build up her friendships. She's been in a gym class at the community center for the past couple of years and I have been going with her. It gives her lots of chances to use her communication strategies and get some exercise, but for me the main thing is the social connection. Now that she is nine, it's not cool for her mom to be hanging around as her assistant. So I'd like to use the waiver money to hire a really great young woman from our neighborhood to be my daughter's assistant at the gym. My daughter already knows her and she can deal with my daughter's needs for personal assistance without making a big deal out of it.

Service Coordinator: We don't do things like that. The waiver can only pay for disability related services. Wouldn't you like some therapeutic toys?

Mother: Therapeutic toys would be for her to use at home. She doesn't need more to do at home. She needs more chances to be out with other kids and some time to be with them without her mom. That's what's most important to our family right now.

Service Coordinator: We don't do things like that. The waiver only pays for disability related services. There is a disability service provider not too far away that offers a gym class just for people with disabilities. If we place her there, she would have 1:1 support to work on the goals in her plan....

And so it goes.

---

* Paraphrased (with her approval) from a mother's contribution to a discussion of publicly funded assistance for families and their children. The funding source in question is probably flexible enough to pay for what she wants but not in the mind of the street level bureaucrat whose interpretation prevails unless parents want to add research and an appeal to her list.

Families identify many ways that publicly funded assistance could be improved. These are observations of available assistance as some families experience it.

- Service coordinators have large caseloads and frequently leave or are reassigned. They can be helpful in a crisis but seldom have time to learn about each family's situation. Families are expected to trust the judgment of people who do not know them. As budgets shrink, service coordinators more often inform families about waiting times or limits on available assistance than about new opportunities or immediate links to relevant publicly funded assistance.

- Many families feel that they are not informed of the resources available to them in a timely and useful way.

- Things that families identify as helpful in their particular circumstances are often denied or have to be adjusted to accommodate rules or staff interpretations of rules.

- Though there is talk of assistance being family-centered, assistance very often seems to be offered on others' terms. Families are expected to accommodate their routines to suit provider availability. Service planners often seem unconcerned to find out about or accommodate family routines. Those in coordinating roles often *empower* parents to make their own arrangements and locate their own resources. Planning meetings leave mothers with longer to-do lists.

- Schools and teachers are under pressure. Families can be caught in bureaucratic fights about payment for and use of equipment or services. Schools sometimes respond to difficult behavior by sending students home or shortening the student's school day.

- There are often waiting periods for access to more intensive assistance. This could deprive people, especially young children, of opportunities to develop their capacities. It can leave adults who live with their families with significant periods of time without adequate assistance.

- Definitions of available assistance seems to be growing narrower and more tightly tied to specific needs identified by computerized assessment tools. The person and the person's deficits are the focus, not the whole family and their aspirations for a good life.

- Available rates of pay limit the supply of capable direct support workers. Authorized hours of assistance go unused for lack of workers.

- There is a cost to use public funds. Families must repeat their stories of deficiencies to establish and re-establish their eligibility. Pre-authorization of payments can be time consuming and frustrating. Required planning meetings happen during work hours. Supplying required documentation and following rules takes time and energy.

- Many families of adults count on day services to make the whole family's weekly schedule work. Cuts in hours or changes in transportation arrangements can shake a family's whole routine. So can delays in getting a job through supported employment or getting another job when a person is laid off.

- The political decisions that limit access to publicly funded assistance to live outside the family home to the time when family capacity to assist breaks down seems unfair and exploitive to many families.

- Families who want their child to grow up fully included often find what is offered misaligned with their purposes. Schools may offer a form of inclusion that is far from the family vision of full participation in typical school life with accommodations and assistance. Benefits administration turns paid jobs into a minefield of bureaucratic tracking to assure that the person earns little enough to remain eligible.

It is long past time to redesign the way publicly funded assistance works for families.* Current responses were assembled a generation ago by planners who assumed that most people with developmental disabilities would move from their parent's home as young adults. Nearly everyone took it for granted that answers to developmental disability would be delivered in clinics, day centers, workshops and group residences, so in home support was either an afterthought or focused on converting family homes into sites to deliver expertly guided interventions. New offerings grew opportunistically when some distinct element of surplus difficulty, say tuition for summer camp or a supply of incontinence pads, met a new funding source, a sympathetic legislator or an administrative moment of surplus.

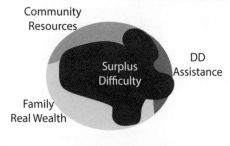

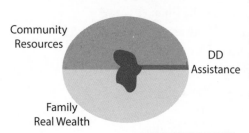

In redesign, it makes sense to take the perspective of diverse whole families. Think of each family as managing its own distinctively shaped lump of surplus difficulty as they work to maintain a context where every family member can thrive. Family real wealth, a person's impairments, stage of family life, the quality of available publicly funded assistance all affect the size and shape of the lump. Families are best positioned to decide where publicly funded assistance will make the most difference to them in dealing with the surplus difficulty that they live with.

---

* See *Building a National Agenda for Supporting Families With a Member With Intellectual Disabilities* (goo.gl/0zaXyH) and connect with The Community of Practice for Supporting Families (supportstofamilies.org).

A competent redesign considers the ways that past tries to implement a family centered approach got stuck. Burdened by a mental model that structures funding as if developmental disability were a medical condition, family aspirations are bent into pretzels of medical necessity. Family knowledge and authority is discounted on the assumption that administrators have better judgment about what will be of assistance than family members do. The stigmatizing superstition that families are typically self-serving and untrustworthy leads administrators to split hairs in defining needs and demand close scrutiny of the ways all families use assistance.

Sadly, the story that administrators disallowed a family request to purchase a tablet computer because the child might use the tablet for something other than meeting an assessed clinical need is not apocryphal. Overruling the recommendation of the communication expert and service coordinator who work with the child, administrative staff with no expert knowledge and no personal contact with the child or family required purchase of a much more expensive specialist communication device just because it only had a single purpose and was neither cool enough nor multi-functional enough to tempt the child or his brother to find non-therapeutic uses for it.

Redesign by learning from family action

A meaningful design will emerge if politicians and administrators support and learn from a new generation of family creativity. Families continually invent new ways to live good lives but their successes currently have too little impact on the way public funds flow. Following families as they integrate public funds into their lives is a better approach to design than trying to herd families into predefined answers.

In the 20th century redesign would have been managed according to a master plan engineered for implementation on a large scale with family input. Model programs would be rolled out across the country. This formula for solution is too limiting for today's re-design question, **How might we generate a sufficient range of publicly funded responses to effectively reduce the variety of ways that families experience excess difficulty?**

Family variety is the key element in designing answers to this question. There are many differences among families. Family and extended family size, composition and location. Stages of life encompassed in the family. Extent of real wealth –resourcefulness, relationships and networks, capacities, assets. Cultural heritage.

Accessible neighborhood and community resources. Health status of every family member. The constellation of impairments and accommodation and assistance required by family member(s) with developmental disability. Adequacy of other resources and their alignment with family purposes. The number of possible combinations of meaningful family differences demands a structure for publicly funded family assistance that can work in a family-centered way.

Variety burns out any scheme to plot family need onto a matrix of predefined benefits and activities. From an administrative point of view, the answer is straightforward. Learn by offering families an individual budget and then figuring out additional administrative investments that will increase the number of families able to use their allocation as an asset in living a good life.

The outline for learning the way to a better design for supporting families is easy to make.[*] Three elements are necessary for new and useful solutions to emerge family by family. First, there must be lots of **agents**, families with the authority to decide on how to use public money in combination with their own real wealth. Agents can do anything with their individual budget that is not criminal and enter into any deals that they believe will serve the family's purposes. They can modify the way they spend money as they learn. Second, there must be **some connections** among families so that they can choose to invent ways to make cooperative use of the resources available to them. Third, families must be willing to **try and tell**. This generates learning among interested families about what is possible, what works and what does not. It also defines areas for administrative investment to decrease family vulnerability or increase family effectiveness.

Examples of supports for self-direction begin on page 230.

The main difficulty with taking this approach to redesign arises because it turns the current mental model on its head. It shifts the administrative default from distrust of family integrity and capacity to trust in family resourcefulness. Instances of fraud or neglect are managed as the exceptions they are. At the same time the new mental model recognizes the necessary contribution of public funds and administrative skill to creating conditions that improve family capacity, it doesn't promise to cut costs.

This approach reopens settled questions in a new context, one of encouraging family agency. It calls for rethinking the ways that public funds are allocated and accounted for, the roles of experts and service providers, how to accommodate changing conditions

---

[*] For the reasoning behind this approach to design see John H. Holland (1996). *Hidden Order: How Adaptation Builds Complexity.* New York: Basic Books.

and insure against the bad effects of major failures of family effort, how to offer adequate assistance to parents who themselves have limited capacities, and how to respond to families who are neglectful, abusive or dishonest.

There is too much to learn to try for a whole system restart. Creating social invention zones that encourage a new era of family creativity will produce learning at a pace that administrators can absorb. Individual budgets that consolidate available public resources and ruthlessly control the temptation to attach strings to families use of public money form the foundation for redesign. Thoughtful investment in learning how to multiply and strengthen emerging family discoveries will increase the scale of redesign.

The political difficulty of untangling current administrative structures is massive enough that the most practical next step may be to pray for angels to come and make the bureaucratic changes necessary to free families to use public money as families think best. But the depth of the crisis in supporting families that is forming on the horizon may be enough to open space for social invention, at least in the form of demonstration projects.

Families as social inventors

History shows the generative power of organized families. A world wide movement grew in the middle of the last century as mothers of children with mental retardation and cerebral palsy recognized the dangers of isolation and the great possibilities of connection and collective action. Nearly simultaneously, in many places, local groups of parents came together to create new forms of assistance. Many groups were initiated with a classified ad that gathered families prepared to take civic responsibility for their disabled children's development and their family's wellbeing. As these local associations grew and found one another, family concerns moved from private troubles to public issues. Optimism about developmental potential and recognition that without assistance their children's capacities would be unnecessarily stunted animated the work. While most professional eyes were turned toward institution management and reform, self-organized family groups invented most of the first generation of community services with only limited expert partnership and few public dollars. Local volunteer efforts produced programs for children excluded from school. The most common guiding image for the earliest of these social inventions was clear for their inventors to see. The place for children excluded from public school would look and function like a school. A variety of local programs grew up with the children who founded them. Pioneering students became the pioneers of adult day programs and group residences. Charity fundraising grew and turned toward increasingly sophisticated and successful efforts to lobby state and federal legislators for funds. Expanding federal and state investment in social services and early education accelerated growth.

Mothers found their voices as advocates and policy analysts.[*] Parents led redress of the injustice of exclusion by successfully lobbying state and federal legislators and supporting lawsuits that established rights to public education. Increases investment in research and the education of experts brought new practices and new voices into the work. Activist parents of sons and daughters in institutions joined other advocates for social justice to bring on the rapid growth of expenditure and local service development driven by deinstitutionalization. Parents joined inventive service providers to pioneer supported employment and supported living. Growing numbers of parents, brothers and sisters came to work in the new organizations. Many assumed positions of influence and authority.

Today's family social inventors live in different times than their mothers and grandmothers did. The next generation of family supports will make the best of these differences.

Family life is different. Economic conditions squeeze more and more families into money insecurity. Mothers employed outside the home have less time for voluntary civic action; even less if they juggle assistance to a younger person with a disability and an older family member who needs assistance; even less if they are single and extended family members are not readily available.

Civic life is different. Local associations across the board attract fewer citizens. Many face a crisis because fewer members want to do the work of maintaining a formally constituted association. There is growing citizen investment in ad hoc actions or small group initiatives organized informally around practical responses for a few people. People are more likely to turn to the internet and social media for information and encouragement. Diagnosis specific groups, often connecting more on line than in person, offer mutual support. Large scale fund raising campaigns and lobbying efforts send powerful messages that originate from national organizations with strong media connections.

---

[*] For stories of the work of this generation by five activist mothers see Connie Lyle O'Brien and John O'Brien. *My house is covered with papers! Reflections on a Generation of Active Citizenship*. goo.gl/kHrjlV

---

jacksonwest.org

This website exemplifies the next generation of family creativity.

All we know of Jackson we have learned from the jacksonwest.org, a link we discovered on a facebook page dedicated to discussion of disability reforms in Australia.

Created by Jackson's mother, Sally Richards, an Australian family leader and advocate,* the site details the family's efforts to create the conditions for Jackson, who has multiple and complex impairments, to live a meaningful life.

Their family intention is for Jackson to build good relationships in his community through working, volunteering, and participating in n physical activities he enjoys: trampolining, swimming and bush walking. The website describes the contribution a circle of support made to planning and safeguarding Jackson's future and assisting him in his daily life. Base-camp, a web application, coordinated actions planned at in-person meetings.

Jackson works at JACKmail, a mail pickup and delivery business founded by Jackson and his parents and operated by a collaboration between Jackson and a personal assistant.

Jackson and two other young men with disabilities are founder members of Benambra Intentional Community Cooperative, an integrated co-housing development that includes 22 other households. As good neighbors in his intentional community becomes a stronger source of mutual emotional support and practical assistance, the role of a formal circle of support has decreased.

The website and a book that describes why and how the cooperative developed document his family's experience to inspire and inform other families. Sally presents her experiences as a speaker and assists other families to form circles, make good plans and act to develop the conditions for good lives.

---

*View *Creating a Meaningful Life for Jackson*, a TEDx Canberra talk at goo.gl/WBmm0T.

The environment for publicly funded assistance is different. Much of this difference results from 70 years of success in expanding public investment. With each increase in public funds, administrative structures have enclosed more of the space for family control of a fair share of public resources. Even family support organizations governed by family member boards usually operate under professional management as agents of public administrators. Key decisions about support to families are made farther from local government. Parents now occupy a few seats among *stakeholder representatives* at policy tables controlled by administrators searching for ways to manage costs and scarcities.

The political climate has changed. Influential voices for shrinking government favor individualism and charity over collective responsibility and have established a politically powerful story of necessary economic austerity and retrenchment. The public role in supports for all families is in question. Defending and incrementally increasing the budgets for publicly funded assistance and refining policies and reacting to changes in administrative practice now occupy most public policy advocacy attention from advocates for people with developmental disabilities.

As families face the limits in public funding for adult services and discover that available residential options don't suit them even if funds were available, more families become entrepreneurs. They partner with other families, responsive service providers and other actors in their communities to develop solutions tailored to their situations. Learning from these initiatives makes nonsense of bureaucratic definitions that box family support into a tightly specified list of eligible services. The demand for flexible individual budgets that take family context and contribution into account will continue to grow.

The environment for family inventiveness will continue to change. The source of that inventiveness will not. The love that family members feel for each other animates desire for a good life and energizes action. When that action expresses family commitment to a person's journey to social inclusion and self-direction, the chances for inventions that will build capacities for supporting families to live a good life grow and the design of next generation ways of supporting families will emerge.

Developing a powerful family story

Developmental disability shows up as an unfamiliar stranger, bringing uncertainties that each family will resolve, revisit, and resolve again and again at turning points in family life. These uncertainties present themselves as big questions:

> *How do we understand this person's disability and what it means for our family?*
>
> *What can we expect for our family member's future?*
>
> *Who and what will help the person with a disability and our whole family to thrive?*
>
> *What will keep this person safe and secure, especially when parents are unable to?*

A family answers these questions as members make sense of their unfolding experience of difference and surplus difficulty. The family story of disability assigns meaning to extra work and guides action. It shapes the expression of family love and concern.

Some family stories are powerful because they open possibilities for creating real wealth. Powerful stories don't come fully written. They are hard won from struggles with surplus difficulty as family members compose their life together. Sometimes the choice to act from a powerful story strains or even breaks relationships.

Better Life Chances*

People with intellectual and developmental disabilities will have better life chances when these five things are true for them and their families and allies.

They have experienced a variety of community roles that provide good opportunities for contribution, developing competence and friendship, and creating knowledge of their interests and capacities.

They have confidence, based on experience, that they can take action to make good things happen, solve problems, deal with breakdowns and difficulties, and get help that respects their dignity and competence when they need it.

They have a hopeful and positive vision for themselves as contributing citizens of their communities, including seeing themselves as workers in ordinary community jobs, active participants in civic life and occupants of ordinary housing. Their vision mobilizes action that stretches them and their allies, not just wishing.

They have an understanding of their individual experience of impairment and disability that provides practical knowledge of necessary accommodations, what works and what to avoid in providing the specific assistance they require, and how to cope resourcefully with risks, including those risks associated with prejudiced and discriminatory treatment.

They have a diverse network of personal and family relationships with people who recognize that they are "100% there", believe that they have a positive future as a contributing citizen, will contribute to the thinking and action necessary to establish and sustain good opportunities for them, and will reach out to invite more people into the network when they are needed.

None of these things need to be perfect or complete. It is never too late to start and it is important to continue to broaden and build these assets and capacities throughout life. Adults and their families can start to build these resources at any time, but the work is best begun in the early years, as parents form expectations and make decisions about how intentionally to build up their support network and how much to invest in participation in ordinary places and activities.

* John O'Brien, Connie Lyle O'Brien and Marcie Brost identified these assets by reflecting on interviews with parents of people in their 20's who experience significant impairments and are employed in integrated jobs and active in community life. Parents were asked to tell stories of what they believe makes a difference in their family's ability to make the best of changing opportunities and challenges..

Powerful stories are as distinctive as the families who live them are different from one another, but careful listeners can abstract some common themes in stories told by families who are inventing what they need to live a good life.

The person is whole. Developmental disability does not diminish the person's dignity though it does make them vulnerable to devaluing perceptions and discriminatory treatment. Love of the person expresses itself in resistance to devaluation. Even when impairments appear extreme or exceed others' capacity to understand the person's communication, the person is 100% there.

Like anyone else the person has gifts of being and doing worthy of development and expression.

The person has differences that call for extra imagination, accommodation and assistance. They are not broken and in need of fixing. They are not a source of shame. They do not suffer from an incurable disease that must subject them to medical authority; that is a matter of policy or choice. People are not pitiable or frightening victims of tragedy or causes of family tragedy. Differences become disabling when the person meets a physical or social environment unwilling to adapt to them or lacks adequate support. Differences do not justify exclusion from ordinary experiences and social settings, they call for attention to the conditions for inclusion. Expert descriptions of differences can result in helpful practices or useful equipment. Expert formulations never describe the whole person whose life contains those differences. Expert predictions describe possibilities, they do not determine a person's future unless limiting stories about labels become life defining.

Family action and knowledge matter, life long. People will have a better life if family members hold the same broad expectations for them as for any other person of their age and then work out what it takes to for them to grow up included as valued participants. Even if these efforts do not fully succeed, seeking pathways to ordinary valued experiences has much better chances of building a good life than family resignation does. It is better to presume competence and seek the conditions that will reveal it than to give up on possibilities for development. Getting stuck in feeling like a victim drains energy. Taking action to influence our life chances benefits the family, no matter how it turns out.

There are allies and partners who will respond to family invitations. Families can get caught in a binary trap: either hold responsibility alone or delegate primary responsibility for the person to publicly funded service providers. Families can avoid the trap by intentionally recruiting trustworthy others and asking them to share in defining and realizing high expectations for the person.

Good investments in supporting families

Good support offers practical, family specific help with surplus difficulty while assisting families to live in ways that give rise to powerful stories. Powerful stories grow when families can resist cultural pressures to turn inward, withdraw and build a protective barrier around a member with a developmental disability. They grow when family members attune themselves to each other's gifts and listen from infancy to the disabled person's authentic calls for more and better life, however the person's body may allow that expression. The person with a developmental disability has a clear place in a powerful family story that, as the disabled person grows older, encourages each person to author a personal story that includes family roles and extends beyond family boundaries to embrace new roles.

Relationships and networks strengthen family stories. Instead of shrinking their social networks the family expands them by reaching out to connect with other families with disabled members and adults with developmental disabilities who lead good lives. Families with powerful stories clear their senses by developing a critical perspective on still common ideas of disability as pathology whose treatment demands social exclusion and supervision. They invest some of their family assets and capacities in a search for valued, age appropriate experiences and roles. They take responsibility for speaking clearly from a positive family vision to those who represent, provide or govern publicly funded assistance: service coordinators, special educators, providers and policy makers.

Some families find ways to short circuit waiting lists for developmental disability services by inventing replacements for those services. They combine their own real wealth with resources available in their communities and their share of available public funds to assist family members to get and succeed at good jobs or move from their family home into their own place.

Competent administrators incorporate what they learn from families who live powerful stories in their responses to adaptive challenges. Family discoveries play an important part in figuring out how to mobilize sufficient resources to meet changing demand in sustainable ways and how to close gaps between current reality and the human rights articulated in *The Convention on the Rights of Person's with Disabilities*. All that's needed is willingness to give families room to innovate and invest in support for social invention without dictating details.

Room to innovate comes with the development of multiple ways to put available public money under family control. Law sets the boundaries for expenditures. Families must stay within the common understanding of rights granted by laws like *The Americans with Disabilities Act* and interpretative principles like *least restrictive, most integrated environment*.

Good investments in families as social inventors develop from family initiative to fulfill multiple functions. They assist families to develop a critical perspective on the mental models, structures and practices that shape current responses to developmental disability. This supports discernment of each person's path to a socially included, self-directed life and helps people make sense of the difficulties that go with choosing this path.

Good investments offer a variety of ways to assist families to intentionally gather a circle of support, make their own plans and take action. As service administration appropriates person-centered planning for management purposes, offering this capacity independently becomes more important.

Good investments share stories of possibility and family stories of constructive action, helpful alliances and partnerships. This supports high expectations and informs the prototypes families design for themselves.

Good investments make it easier for families to recruit and retain trustworthy, capable people to assist and advise them.

Good investments negotiate inclusion in ordinary sites of opportunity: housing, workplaces, schools and post-secondary education, civic associations.

5

Pathfinders Are Social Inventors

Realizing the ideals defined by *The Convention on the Rights of Persons with Disabilities* demands social invention. Our communities need new stories of disability. Good mental models generate individually tailored ways to support people with developmental disabilities in their own homes, in real jobs and in personally meaningful experiences of leisure, culture, learning, spiritual development and civic involvement. These social inventions can't be devised by geniuses tinkering in a garage or clever policy makers gathered around a conference table. Social inventions are co-creations of people who align their capacities in action that serves a shared sense of purpose. What is needed comes from forming new relationships that produce practical knowledge-in-action and supports people to show up in contributing community roles. Without intentional action, a person will be invisible in community life, seen only as one of them, an object of pity or client under supervision.

Knowledge-in-action emerges from an intentional shift of attention from deficiency to capacity. This shift spans boundaries and engages people and their families, neighborhoods, associations and communities, employers and the providers of mainstream services as well as providers of publicly funded assistance. It happens when people choose to listen more deeply, hold fundamental questions of potential and purpose, and act from their awareness of a future worth creating.

Social inventions depend on pathfinders recruiting committed allies among family and friends and courageous partners among providers and experts. These companions risk the journey to social inclusion. Pathfinders make stronger and more diverse alliances, reach farther into more varied spaces of community life, develop more creative designs for support, and sustain what they have gained better when they cultivate two capacities: deeper listening to reveal the highest potential in their situation and agency, a sense of responsibility for action to realize that poten-

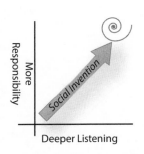

More Responsibility

Social Invention

Deeper Listening

tial. Attention to new possibilities plus belief we can make change plus some flexible resources equals social invention.

Creating social inventions – Theory U

Theory U describes a practical approach to social invention.* It provides a vocabulary and grammar to identify different possible forms of social organization, their sources and consequences. It also offers a process for designing change initiatives and a guide for doing the personal work necessary to make deep change. Otto Scharmer and Katrin Kaufer summarize Theory U this way:

> *The quality of results produced by any system depends on the quality of awareness from which the people in the system operate… The structure of awareness and attention determines the pathway along which a situation unfolds.†*

Otto Scharmer identifies the purpose that Theory U serves this way:

> *Theory U guides people to create landing strips for the emerging future by shifting individual, relational and societal awareness from ego to eco* [from a narrow focus on protecting a small sense of self to active concern for the wellbeing of the whole].‡

Two social fields: Presencing and Absencing

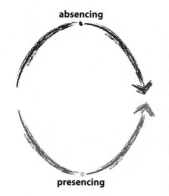

A social field is a structure of relationships that determines action and outcomes based on the quality of awareness of the people, groups and organizations composing it. Theory U understands social reality as emerging from an ongoing competition between the social fields created by two different qualities of awareness. The field of **presencing** opens us to operate from our highest future possibility, engage with diverse others to co-create beneficial responses to the challenges that face us and the disconnects that divide us, and appreciate the many

---

* The images related to Theory U in this chapter are adapted under Creative Commons License from the Presencing Institute. For in-depth discussion of the theory and its applications, see Otto Scharmer (2009), *Theory U: Leading from the future as it emerges.* San Francisco: Berrett-Koehler and Otto Scharmer and Katrin Kaufer (2013). *Leading from the emerging future: From ego-system to eco-system economies. San Francisco*: Berrett-Koehler (the quotation is from p. 18) , visit presencing.com and watch goo.gl/a78SRE. For a powerful case study to a sustained process of organizational transformation guided by Theory U see Hanns Meissner (2013). *Creating blue space: Fostering innovative support practices for people with developmental disabilities.* inclusion.com.

† *Leading from the emerging future*, p. 18.

‡ Presentation to *2014 Global Presencing Forum*, Cambridge, MA. 11 February 2014.

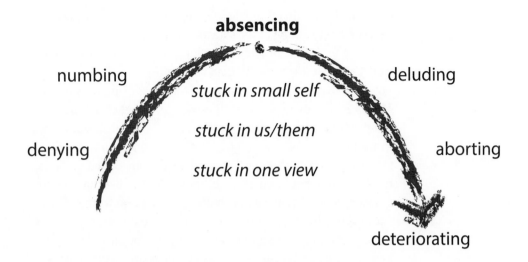

absencing

numbing   deluding

stuck in small self

stuck in us/them

denying   aborting

stuck in one view

deteriorating

sources of truth available to us. We leave behind reproducing the same unproductive patterns, explore new possibilities, open to a positive future and act to disclose that future in everyday life.

The field of **absencing** traps us in a quality of awareness that produces a deteriorating spiral of violence and destruction by restricting what we sense, narrowing the network with whom we collaborate, and shrinking the inner place of attention from which we act. Under the regime of absencing we produce more and more results that nobody wants without taking responsibility for those results. When absencing dominates, we close down into one unquestioned truth, a small US surrounded by a threatening THEM, and a single narrow and rigid identity that insistently demands to be protected and fed. We begin our discussion of Theory U with absencing because that is the social field that has dominated public response to people with developmental disabilities for most of modern history.

The absencing arc bends upwards because it attempts to escape suffering and responsible engagement in ambiguous situations by isolating a small self from the Self's whole ecology and driving defensive behavior from that abstraction. Absencing shifts awareness away from the ground of experience that includes both current reality and the emerging future. We stay stuck in confidence that we possess the single and sufficient Truth that exhausts all that it is necessary to know about our situation. We defend that confidence by denying, an active if unconscious process of not seeing anything that might disconfirm the old story we live inside. We stay stuck in a safe enclosure of those who tell and retell our old story and define that enclosing US in contrast to THEM, others cast by our old story as at the same time beneath notice and somehow a threat to US. We numb ourselves to protect our hearts from breaking at the state of current reality and the future that follows from indulging our addiction to the results of our old story. We stay stuck in our small self, telling ourselves that we can not survive outside our old story, a story that disparages the very idea of higher purpose in our life-work or a higher potential that can germinate through co-creative effort. We protect ourselves from the call of our own higher purpose and potential by manufacturing a sterile absence that deadens the bigger Self and tyrannically colonizes our energies. In the interest of maintaining the old story and its delusional promise of insulation from suffering and responsibility, we apply our capacities to delusions, reinforcing a drama that casts others as instruments of the old story, some as scapegoats and some as saviors but all as unworthy of trust. Absencing leads us to withhold the particular capacities that we might bring to building a community that works for everybody. Our capacities to create the new are obscured, even from our own awareness. We experience ourselves and others as no more than the material product of our history. The possibility that we might sense a positive emerging future and act from it is totally eclipsed. Instead of assisting at the birth of the emerging future, we abort what is positive and possible.

Lessons from a dark time

A creative sense that communities could benefit from the contributions of idiots who were given intensive, specialized education sparked the first public investments in institutions in the mid-19th century.* Small facilities founded on optimism for the improvement of idiots demonstrated exciting successes but were soon overwhelmed with growing numbers of people with increasingly diverse needs who did not improve enough to move

---

* Sensing the possibilities in a social field can benefit from an appreciative and empathic reading of history. For perspectives on the development of services to people in the US who we currently label intellectually disabled, see James Trent (1994) *Inventing the feeble mind: A history of mental retardation in the United States.* Berkeley: University of California Press; Philip Ferguson (2013). Intellectual disability in middle modern times in Michael Wehmeyer (Editor) *The story of intellectual disability: an evolution of meaning, understanding and public perception.* Baltimore: Paul Brookes Publishing and Steven Noll and James Trent (2004). *Mental retardation in America: A historical reader.* New York: NYU Press. There are a growing number of informative histories of particular institutions and efforts to reform them. Start with David Goode, Darryl Hill, Jane Reiss and Willim Bronston (2013). *A history and sociology of Willowbrook State School.* Washington, DC: AAIDD. For a sense of how life was for people with less need for assistance, who did most of the institution's work, and how they resisted the institution, see Michael D'Antonio (2007). *The state boy's rebellion.* New York: Simon and Schuster.

on to community life in the way that the institution's founders expected. Public expenditures never matched demand and maintaining sufficient numbers of trained staff remained an unfulfilled aspiration of management for more than a hundred years. More and more people were judged "incapable of improvement" and institutions turned inwards, devoting whole facilities or growing back wards to a mission of lifelong custody. Within 20 years, a story of possibility for human development was largely discarded as unrealistic and replaced by a story that fixed the causes of failure squarely within the defective bodies and minds of people with disabilities themselves. The claim to professional knowledge shifted from competence in supporting development to skill in classifying inmates by degree of incompetence or social threat and administering their confinement.

By the early 20th century, many progressives had embraced eugenics, which promised a scientific method to improve the human stock. The eugenic idea influenced many institution superintendents and distanced them and their staff even farther from appreciating the reality of people's lives under their charge. A single gene that carried feeblemindedness was postulated. The new fields of scientific charity and psychology produced studies that identified feeblemindedness as the primary cause of crime, social degeneracy and welfare dependence. Institution based experts advocated for effective remedies to prevent its transmission: forced sterilization and strict segregation and control in institutions. While many legislatures were moved to pass laws informed by eugenics, the gap continued to grow between appropriations and the rising numbers of people swept into the institution as petty crime for illiterate men or official suspicion of promiscuity for illiterate women were adopted as a diagnostic sign of feeblemindedness. More than 60,000 US citizens were sterilized in institutions and many more were admitted and placed under life long state supervision.

From a petition admonishing the Wisconsin legislature to fund an institution, submitted in 1898 by the State Medical Society, Board of Health, State Teachers Association, & Federation of Women's Organizations:

*For all these others, the blind, the deaf, and the insane, generous and ample provision has been made; while for **the feeble-minded, who are a constant menace to the good order of society, and to social and domestic safety and tranquility,** no provision whatsoever has been made.*

The scarcities of the Great Depression and the demands for defense workers in World War II fell hard on institutions. The presence of capable inmates who could do most of the institution's work, including care for less able inmates, kept the facilities functioning even as they became more crowded and the numbers waiting for admission grew. By 1967, about 200,000 Americans, more than half of them children, and a substantial number of them infants, lived in public institutions, 95% of which housed more than 500 people. High death rates kept the population of people with severe impairments in check. Beneath these statistics, a vast field of absencing.

Some people, especially the more capable and compliant, made good enough lives with what the institution could offer. Some staff and many inmates formed loving and occasionally developmentally powerful relationships. Almost every institution had specialist programs that gave them reasons to be proud and papers to present at conferences. But conditions for those who required the most assistance continued to deteriorate unregarded.

By the early 1960s a modest amount of public and political attention turned toward people with mental retardation and cerebral palsy. A variety of local programs, many founded by a growing number of local parent groups, organized and attracted support. Celebrities, including author Pearl Buck and cowboy stars Roy Rogers and Dale Evans, wrote about their daughters with mental retardation and spoke out publicly to combat the stigma and shame that left so many families closeted. State and national parent groups developed political influence. Eunice Kennedy Shriver unleashed her formidable political talents on the administration of her brother, John F. Kennedy, and a President's Panel on Mental Retardation was appointed and duly produced plans to improve services.

This moment of possibility was at risk of passing by the people at most obvious disadvantage in the current system, those diagnosed as least able and consigned to the back wards of institutions. The comprehensive and extensive report of the (renamed) President's Committee on Mental Retardation had only five brief paragraphs on institutions and these only recommended a need for more of the same with new and better designed buildings and more staff. Those who required most assistance and therefore were most isolated and dependent on others would be left on back wards with promise only of better physical conditions. The absencing cycle shaped even the enthusiasm for reform.

Burton Blatt, then a professor of special education and a widely respected leader in the field of service to people with mental deficiency, gathered a small group of friends and moved *to shatter the shell of complacency born of ignorance*. Blatt's friends, the superintendents of four institutions in the northeast, anonymous to this day, collaborated with Blatt and another friend, photographer Fred Kaplan, to create a book titled *Christmas in Purgatory* published in 1966 and abridged in *Look*, a national magazine, in

There is a wide range among the States in the cost per day spent for the care of the mentally retarded. Six States spent less than $2.50 a day per patient, while only seven States spent over $5.50 per day and no state spent more than $7.00 per day.*

–President's Panel on Mental Retardation (1964)

_____

* As a reference point: a loaf of bread cost an average of 22 cents in 1964. These costs are totals, including all staffing, housing, food and facility maintenance. Only the unpaid labor of inmates and institutional farms that permitted survival are left out of these daily rates.

1967.* The photographs on the next page are among those taken by Kaplan with an undercover camera during the Christmas holidays of 1965. The superintendents knew Blatt and Kaplan's mission; staff did not. Protection of careers was one reason for anonymity. The larger reason was to show how widespread the situation was and how deeply dehumanization was entrenched.

As Blatt notes, each of these superintendents could have shown off better parts of their institutions, but he challenged them to give the public the opportunity to sense what cried out for reform. Undoing the power of absencing, they opened parts of their facilities of which they were ashamed to the camera, the places on their campus that they were most reluctant to visit themselves and the least likely to ever take anyone on tour.

Christmas in Purgatory did shatter the shell of absencing around conditions on the back wards. It emerged at a critical moment into an environment rich with sparks of a new future for people with disabilities and at a point of rising world wide action for civil rights and against colonialism. The book, and the controversy that surrounded it, helped to energize a turning point in public services. A series of lawsuits tested inmates' right to treatment and the allocation of significant amounts of federal matching funds made the 1970's and 1980's a time of institutional reform and rapid development of local facilities to reduce the numbers in state institutions.

The images are hard to look at. People unclothed or ludicrously clothed from impersonal piles on clothing carts. Bare feet. Puddles of urine and feces. People tied to benches with cloth bands. Bodies distorted by poor diet and neglect of physical impairments. Toothless mouths. Aimless motion. A row of babies behind the bars of cribs pushed close together in what looks like an endless row.

The photographs can't support full sensation. It is almost impossible for imagination to supply the terrifying quiet of a ward full of silent infants. The pandemonium of wards overcrowded with milling adults. The infernal smell ingrained in floors and walls.†

We saw a young man who was glaring at us through the opening in the door of his solitary cell, feces splattered around this opening. He was being punished for breaking an institutional regulation.

We had a good opportunity to interview the attendant in charge and asked him what he needed most in order to provide a more adequate program. His wish was for the addition of two more solitary confinement cells, to be built adjacent to the existing two cells that, we were told, were always occupied, around the clock, day in and day out…

He was, with one assistant, responsible for the supervision of an old multilevel dormitory, housing over 100 severely retarded ambulatory adults. Almost in desperation he asked us, *What can we do with those patients who do not conform? We must lock them up, or restrain them, or sedate them, or put fear into them.*

At that point, we did not feel we had a response that would satisfy either him or us."

–*Christmas in Purgatory*

---

* A free pdf copy of *Christmas in Purgatory* can be downloaded from goo.gl/z5sTvv

† John began work for people with disabilities two years after the publication of these photographs. The reality they represent is vivid in his sense memory far beyond what the photographs convey. These memories are one source of his continuing effort to support people who co-create communities that work for everyone and modes of assistance that struggle to make institutions impossible.

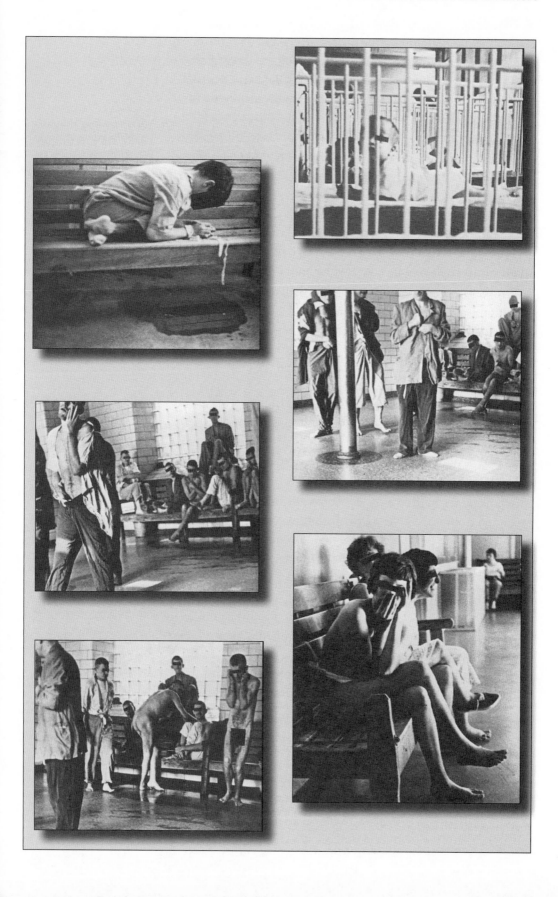

Imagine the experience of the staff who come to work here. Two or three staff for 40 or 60 or even 100 people. What is it like to tie that person to their place on the bench every day? What must you do to avoid injury to yourself and keep people from hurting each other? How do you cope with trying to keep up with so many toileting schedules and so many failures of toileting schedules. Feeding in the allocated 20 minutes? What do you tell yourself about the babies with so little trust in human contact that they stay silent when they are hungry?

Invitation to Reflection

Set a timer for 3 minutes.

With a quiet mind, absorb whatever messages the photographs on page 139 have for you in that time.

Notice the effects of what you are seeing on your awareness: feelings or thoughts that might distract you from openness to these snapshots of our history; feelings or thoughts that brought you closer to a message these images may have for you. Notice these thoughts as they arise and let them go, bringing your attention back to the photographs.

After three minutes, write down your answers to these questions:

What feelings, questions and intentions do these images activate in me?

What do I notice about the effects of these photographs on my awareness of them? What is the message for me in the way I react to these photographs?

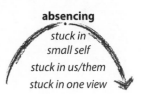

absencing

stuck in small self
stuck in us/them
stuck in one view

Many people find it easier to jump to judgment than to hold mind, heart and will open to what this sample of dreadful photographs might disclose. If we slow down and turn attention back on ourselves to reflect on this impulse to deny, we can gain a better understanding of how absencing works. Perhaps the easiest judgments create distance between US and THEM (the contemporary good guys versus the bad guys of the old days). Distance in time. That was long ago in an unenlightened time. It couldn't happen today, at least in developed countries.* Moral distance. The staff are monsters, completely unlike ourselves, a collection of ignorant, abusive, even sadistic asylum keepers. This move reinforces the idea that we now have THE TRUTH in our

---

* Anyone who wants to test this defense needs only to consider the continuing scandal of unexceptional mistreatment recently exposed at Winterbourne View in England whose well known causes remain to be remedied. See goo.gl/LX-sUxn and documentaryheaven.com/undercover-care.

current much larger money investments in structures, technologies, laws, regulations and inspections. If they knew what we know, it would never have happened. This lets us escape the demand for our own development. We only need to bring our small self to work with people with developmental disabilities. We only need to keep following the rules that we have been following. We only need to keep lobbying as we have been lobbying to get more money to do more of what we now do.

Consider the staff person at the seclusion room door who asked Blatt, *What can we do with those patients who do not conform? We must lock them up, or restrain them, or sedate them, or put fear into them.* What if we imagined that this man was a good father, a loyal husband, a good friend with a fine sense of humor and chief of the local volunteer fire department? How might he find himself, every work day, tying people up and administering sedating doses of medication with no ideas for improvement beyond doubling his ward's capacity for solitary confinement.

It is not unfair to think that, at work, this man is trapped in absencing. Day after day he reproduces a pattern of behavior that makes things steadily worse for the inmates in his charge and for himself. He has become numb to the sensory impact of his surroundings: he actually cannot hear himself think beyond reacting to threats of violence and, astonishing to any visitor, he no longer smells the place. The trap extends to his relationships. He sees people in primitive terms. Inmates either conform and he can ignore them as they enact the life depicted in the photographs or they must be frightened, sedated, restrained, or locked up. Other staff either fall in line with the coercive routines that keep him safe or they must be scared or manipulated off his ward. Any sense of higher potential in the situation or higher purpose in his work is missing. His energy is exhausted in exercising crude and often violent measures to keep a lid on pandemonium. The starkness of this worker's situation reveals the great power of absencing when it permeates the structural level of a situation. In his social psychology of evil, Phillip Zimbardo* demonstrates that a system that indulges in the occasional search for bad apples to blame and punish most often covers up the enduring social fact of bad barrels: social settings and role expectations that generate indifference to the degradation of people and encourage mindless

---

* (2007) *The Lucifer effect: Understanding how good people turn evil.* New York: Random House and www.lucifereffect.com.

perpetration of structural and attentional violence. Any impulse to notice and nurture each others' higher potential soon starves if it is not strangled at birth.

This man goes to work in a place where absencing reigns. His superiors function under the delusion that two people a shift can keep safe the 100 men that they have grouped together exactly because their responses to institutional deprivations manifest in violent and dangerous behavior. Managers have numbed themselves to life in this ward and found ways to deny that there are any means under their control that would improve the situation, which anyway is about all that can be expected of inmates diagnosed as they have labeled the men who live there. Their political masters deny the reality of these people's daily lives with a self-congratulatory sense that they are doing all they can afford. The citizens that elect them know nothing about the place beyond the vague idea that professionals are taking care of *them*. Even most of the families of the inmates of his ward are caught inside the story that this is the best, or at least the only, place for *them*.

Agency is resourcefulness in action, a practical expression of belief in the capacity to make desirable change. A setting dominated by absencing swallows agency. People are reduced to experiencing themselves as instruments of a reality beyond their control. Things can be no way other than the way things are; we are fated to reproduce current power relations and limits. Our action can make no difference. Even if we could imagine something better we are powerless to implement it.

As sparks of new possibility coalesced in the late 1960s and 1970s, structures shifted and it became easier for staff to move up the ladder of agency and take responsibility for meaningful change. In institutions, public investment grew rapidly and substantially, staff numbers increased, physical environments improved, diets and wardrobes were decent, medical care got better, and positive approaches to improving people's skills developed.

However, absencing in tactical retreat is not absencing defeated. The underlying structure and mental model of the institution remained largely unquestioned and unreformed. All too much of that structure was reproduced at a smaller scale in the local services that sprang up under the banner of deinstitutionalization.

To protect and promote agency, its a good idea to be able to notice when absencing has a grip. We can identify some signs of absencing that show up in our patterns of thought and deliberation by revisiting the question of how decent people could keep reproducing Blatt's purgatory. The great psychologist, Albert

Agency
Perceived capacity to make desirable change

4
Courage to create from resourceful relationships
We are responsible to create new possibilities

3
Active testing of assumptions about resource scarcity & authority
There is room to make some change

2
Desire for change bound by passivity in the face of complex rules & sense of scarcity
Change would be good, but they won't let us.

1
Fated to reproduce current reality
Things can only be the way they are.

Bandura,* describes moral exclusion, a set of maneuvers by which we selectively disengage our moral standards from harmful ways we behave. These eight maneuvers describe the way people, especially people in groups, enact absencing and maintain blind spots that make them mindless servants of harm.

Three maneuvers convert behavior that might otherwise attract self-blame and encourage responsible action into perceived worthy behavior.

- Describe harmful practices as a good thing. Managers called solitary confinement cells "therapeutic isolation".
- Describe harmful practices in confusing language. Forcing a person into the cell and locking them in was called "implementing a time-out protocol".
- Compare harmful practices to something much worse. Without solitary confinement cells and the authority to lock people up, staff would lose control and weaker inmates would be badly injured.

Two maneuvers absolve people of responsibility for harmful behavior.

- Displace responsibility. Staff saw themselves as doing what their jobs demand and assigned responsibility for problems to management. Managers in turn saw themselves as simply implementing the will of their state's legislators.
- Diffuse responsibility. In the institution, a complex structure of understaffed and separated professional departments each jealous of their territory and almost completely detached from those staff who spent their days with inmates gave everyone someone else to blame for anything. In the political environment, jockeying among institution superintendents and disconnection from family advocacy groups made it hard to make the case for adequate public investment. Rewards came to those who avoided scandal and made do.

Two maneuvers minimize the results of harmful behavior.

- Ignore the consequences. No feedback mechanisms tracked either the results of institutionalization or the quality of life for inmates and staff. Those responsible for managing the facility or providing professional services never or hardly ever visited the places where people lived or ate a meal with

---

* For a good introduction to Bandura's thinking on moral exclusion that is also relevant to building good communities, see (2007) Impeding ecological sustainability through selective moral disengagement. *International Journal of Innovation and sustainable development 2*, 1 pp. 8-35.goo.gl/oMexZ3

inmates. For professional servicing, or family visits, inmates were cleaned up and brought to separate buildings. On the rare occasions when inmates were subjected to research, it happens in specially resourced and furnished wards.

- Minimize or misconstrue bad effects. The normative story was that the institution is a concentration of highly specialized resources, providing the best possible care, superior to what families or local resources could offer. People and their families and communities would be far worse off without the institution.

The final maneuver is to blame and dehumanize the victims. The old story made this easy and devastating. The people on back wards are reduced to sub-human or animal status (in some places, dental procedures, routinely extractions, were conducted without anesthesia because people were assumed not to feel pain). People were portrayed as menaces, dangerous to anyone near them if not strictly disciplined and strongly contained (locked doors everywhere; high dose cocktails of psychoactive medications routinely prescribed off-label to control behavior).

> Some stories enhance life, others degrade it. So we must be careful about the stories we tell, about the ways we define ourselves & other people.
> –Burton Blatt

The stark world of *Christmas in Purgatory* shows how these common cognitive maneuvers create self-fulfilling prophecies that are self-sealing. People seen as if they are dangerous animals are caught in a structure designed as if for dangerous animals. They are treated worse than farm or zoo animals and consequently act in ways that confirm the perception of those with power over them. Fed a meager diet with no utensils and pressured to eat in a very short time people act in primitive ways, stuffing themselves and fighting over weaker inmates' food. Staff numb themselves and ignore the indignity the structure inflicts on people and act as if inmates deserve their situation. Staff inventiveness is exhausted in making the job of control easier by degrading people. Dangerous inmates are rewarded for acting as enforcers and keeping others in line. Being an insider to a group employed to enforce the institutional routine builds strong bonds and boundaries. This reinforces moral exclusion, sealing the cycle and nearly suffocating life's efforts to break through.

Noticing when these mechanisms of moral exclusion show up offers a way to become aware of absencing and choose to turn away from it. People on the outside of a group find it easier to hear these mechanisms but hard to successfully call insiders attention to them. Taking responsibility for the disconnects in our own situation is an important step out of absencing and into higher levels of agency.

We have told a story in the past tense that shows the effects of absencing at an extreme. But absencing is not a thing of the past. Its current influence is not as evident to us because our social structures are so deeply affected by absencing and we spend most of our time busy within those structures. The way forward is to intentionally shift our attention and agency to the social field of presencing. This will generate paths to good lives for all people with developmental disabilities and deliberately build communities that make institutions and today's embodiments of the institutional mental model unnecessary

Presencing

People who act violently toward themselves and others, do not communicate in ways that others understand, and do not respond to available expert interventions remain vulnerable today

to the alternatives Blatt heard in 1965: restrain, sedate or frighten. The means have become more sophisticated. Rules govern the application of physical restraints and a person may be confined and isolated as the single occupant of a highly staffed, physically hardened and locked house. More complex cocktails of psychoactive medications try to quiet violence. Elaborately designed and measured behavior plans manipulate a person's access to the smallest details of life, and sometimes threaten or deliver pain, as a way to enforce compliance. Failure usually leads to more of the same in higher doses, and sometimes to outright if surreptitious physical assaults by frustrated or frightened staff members. This generates a social field where absencing reigns.

As more effective interventions and more useful medications have become available the number of people at risk of disappearing into violence and efforts to extinguish violence decreases. Those who remain at risk benefit more than almost anyone else from intentional movement into presencing, as this chapter from Ken's life story shows.

Ken Chose Me

Gail Jacob

The Rhythms program came into my life in 2010, after many years of feeling that I was at the end of my learning curve—that I had made my contributions years before, that I had "been there, done that" in working with systems, and that I had reached the boundaries of what is possible. I was cynical about the huge amount of resources that providers felt were necessary to create the tiniest increments of quality in the lives of people with disabilities.

At the same time I didn't feel finished, thanks in large part to my friends--parents who believed in the hidden potential of their children, who were puzzling to them, as well as to the services that supported them. At that point I met Martha Leary* who opened a new world of possibility for me. Martha brought with her a view that allowed us to meet people with fresh eyes by offering a different way to see and connect, a way that opened doors of opportunity again. Martha could spend minutes with someone who seemed impenetrable and connect in ways that left no doubt that the world had missed the boat on that person for the lifetime before that very moment of connection. And it didn't just happen once. With person after person she created new openings that left me in awe and humbled at my own hubris and ignorance.

In the past five years, the Rhythms project has emerged in Dane County, Wisconsin to support collective learning about people who present the greatest challenges to our system of supports. These are people whose "behaviors" make it difficult to keep them and their supporters safe. Often these are people who physically injure themselves and others and destroy their environment in seemingly unpredictable patterns. A support model developed over time for these folks in which they live alone with 24-hour staffing in highly modified homes. Modifications often include lexan covered windows, soft minimal furnishings, reinforced walls and doors, magnetic locks on doors, and rooms where staff can retreat when they feel unsafe. People spend most of their days at home with perhaps daily outings in modified vans or walks in their neighborhoods. Some folks can only leave the house when they are accompanied by two workers. Most people have little or no communication that others can easily understand, which creates enormous difficulty in decoding what they need or want.

Martha offers a way of seeing people that presumes people's difficulties are due to sensory and movement differences that often created huge disconnects between their intentions and their bodies actions. By understanding and addressing these differences, we can create supports and accommodations that can free people to have more fulfilling lives. Martha came to consult with a person and their team and offer training in alternative ways of seeing and supporting people. By adopting the recommendations from Martha's consultations, new (to us) practices, such as social stories, sensory input and video modeling are now available to people. In addition a local learning community meets monthly to share challenges, success and new approaches.

Rhythms launched me into one of the steepest learning experiences of my life. I hadn't met anyone before who needed a modified environment to be safe. I almost never worried about my own safety in almost 40 years of my career. And to say I was frightened many times and usually at a total loss of how to be and what to do would be an understatement. I learned to observe, observe, observe!

I met Ken three years ago, a man in his mid-20's, considered one of the most challenging people in the county, when Martha and I were asked to work with him and his support team. He had been with the same agency for five years and they felt unable to make progress in creating a safe space or engaging in significant activity beyond the most basic personal care routines and occasional walks to the neighborhood park.

---

*Martha Leary & Anne Donnellan (2012). *Autism: Sensory-Movement Differences and Diversity*. Madison, WI: Cambridge Book Review Press.

The story about Ken was discouraging on every level, especially the feeling among staff that there was little hope of improvement and that Ken had no interest in anything other than food. Prior to our first visit we were told to keep our physical distance from Ken, to not make eye contact and to not speak to him, as breaking these rules would likely result in an episode of aggression. I was terrified.

We walked into a home that was entirely bare, except for large wooden pallets in each room covered with threadbare gym mats and two exercise balls. Ken was locked into the front space of the house away from the staff living room and the kitchen. A small tabletop on hinges was unfolded for meals. Upon meeting Ken, Martha proceeded to break every rule. We sat with Ken, he smiled, we smiled, we talked to him and he used his limited signs with us. He was curious, interested, and eager to connect. We walked to the neighborhood park. He climbed to the top of a jungle gym, we swung on swings and we walked back home. It was a thoroughly lovely visit.

Something magical happened on that first visit between Ken and me. I can't describe it other

words than that a powerful connection happened. It was the beginning of a journey of love, commitment, and discovery. Martha says Ken chose me. I think he really did. The past three years of getting to know Ken could fill a book.

Though the agency working with Ken was well intentioned, we never got on the same page about what is possible for him. But I had no idea how to even begin to be of help to Ken. Martha insisted I visit him weekly and would regularly give me long detailed instructions over the phone on what to try and how to engage with him. All I really did for a long time was show up. Many times he was disregulated, striking out at staff, howling for hours at a time, while I watched him through the window of the locked door. On days he was calm, I sat with him. He always seemed happy to see me. One day when he was having a hard time, I entered his space and he allowed me to be with him. I found that being tucked tight under a blanket was comforting at times when he was distressed. Then I started rubbing his feet while he was under the blanket and it seemed soothing to him.

We got into a routine of sitting together and enjoying each other's company, tucking him under covers when he needed a break. He would stick his leg out from under the covers for a foot rub every time I visited. I saw that when I came, regardless of the state he was in, he would make an effort to be in control with me. There was a lot of stress during those years of getting to know Ken. I lost a lot of sleep worrying about him, his treatment, and his obvious suffering. There was a point by the end of the first year that I realized I had no choice about being there for Ken. There were times I wanted to walk away. It felt too hard and too hopeless. But I found I was responsible for him and we belonged to each other in a deep way. It was not a great feeling to know that no matter what I did at the time, I could not impact his environment in any meaningful way. Every time I would go to his house my stomach was in knots, not knowing what state I would find him in when I walked through that door. Sometimes I would hear his loud vocalizing through the walls as I approached the house and I knew he was having a hard time. But regardless, he was always happy to see me. I had to keep showing up.

One of the things we did accomplish was to add double staffing during the week day hours. This allowed Ken to more safely leave his house. Last spring he began coming to my house once a week with staff to hang out with me. To everyone's surprise, the visits were highly successful. He

watered plants, did a bit of cooking or raking leaves and came in for a snack. That became a nice routine. What he loved most was being in my home. He would explore every room, test out every couch and especially loved resting on my king sized bed.

In June I hosted a birthday dinner at my house for Ken. About 20 people came including his mother and his aunt. I was a nervous wreck, worrying about how Ken would do with such a crowd and with family present. Staff thought he might stay 15-20 minutes. Instead the party lasted 2 hours. He had a great time, eating his favorite food, opening gifts, re-connecting with his mom and aunt. That party was a game-changer in that everyone there experienced a new story about who Ken is. As an advocate for Ken I was more confident than ever in my fight for a new start for him. Ken also seemed so much more secure in his own ability to regulate himself and, at least with me, acquired some new strategies for doing so.

It is now almost one year since the birthday party. As of 10 weeks ago, Ken is having his fresh start with a new service provider. His home is undergoing a major makeover and I am in heaven with a new decorating project. Ken has his own van and daily new experiences in community. He has supporters who celebrate every new accomplishment, a plan for increasing his communication through sign, endless ideas about the future. I'm seeing Ken laugh and smile more often. I usually see him a couple of times a week. His mom says the worry lines in his forehead are disappearing. I no longer get anxious when I approach his house or lose sleep worrying about him. Things are far from perfect, but the hard times are now moments, not days and weeks. Everyone is still in early stages of getting to know each other.

Ken changed my life and I know I changed his. He taught me about the power of caring and holding the space to discover what is necessary. I learned to hold on to a sense of urgency without letting it paralyze or defeat me. I used every resource in my power, both internally and externally, to change the circumstances of Ken's life. I'm learning what it means to be steadfast in a relationship, even when the only thing you can do for someone is to show up. Am I Ken's ally? It feels like so much more.

Ken and I are always happy to see one other. He now has other people he is getting to know and like. And I'm only a little bit jealous.

This story of action that arises from presencing slowly overcoming absencing makes it clear that presencing is an encounter of heart, mind and spirit, not a matter of formulating a concept. A deep connection between two people makes the relationship itself a third reality that others can choose to enter. In her first encounter Gail viscerally feels absencing producing Ken's world: a barren room and a story that he chooses to have it that way; staff behind an armored barrier and invitations to join them in their stories of violence, the impossibility of communication and the necessity of maintaining vigilant distance. She and Martha step outside the dominant story and inhibit the fear driven reflex to distance themselves. This creates a space in which Gail is recruit-

> Love is the only emotion that expands knowledge.
> –Humberto Maturana

ed by Ken's desire for more in this life. Gail's understanding of Ken deepens because she has the capacity to observe from a new perspective and the willingness to struggle to appreciate Ken's physiologically unique experience of the world.

Ken's journey to a more inclusive and self-directed life is frustratingly slow to start. It takes three years to gather a company of people willing to share the uncertainty of discovering effective ways to assist him. During that frustrating time, trust between Ken and Gail grows through a series of discoveries made possible by a relationship that allows Ken's interests and capacities and his efforts to regulate the anxiety that can engulf him in violence to show up. In his relationship with Gail, and then with others, a new story begins to emerge. Only the barest outline of that story has come into presence so far. Ken is a whole person who reaches out to those who recognize his dignity, enjoys the same pleasures as many other people, and works hard to regulate a body that can betray his intentions. This would seem obvious if it had not been so deeply buried in absencing.

At heart, presencing is a matter of intentional openness to possibility and purpose. The source of this openness is recognition of dignity and purpose in others –other people, our eneterprises and communities, the planet and its eco-systems. The path begins with a decision to turn aside from doing more of the same and create opportunities to observe from a position of deepening empathy and wider engagement. The path moves to a time of openness to inner knowledge of what wants to emerge and on to immediate action that embodies that possibility in a form that allows learning.

Observe
Observe
Observe

Act in
an Instant

Allow Inner Knowing
to Emerge

Ken and Gail's story can be traced as a journey through a big U that opens up new forms of assistance. It is made up of many little u's. Accommodating the unique complexities of Ken's body can demand this kind of attention on a moment by moment basis. Noticing the whole situation when anxiety is building, opening to the highest possibility in the moment, trying a move that might establish regulation. The source of meaningful action: people choosing to attend to and invest in one another's highest purposes.

The theory

As Gail and Ken practice it, the U expresses a form of natural intelligence generated by openness to potential for more of a good life. It only seems unusual in situations where absencing shapes a culture of stuckness in single truths, distrustful distance from others, and defensive control. Reflection on purposeful efforts to call on the U process in a variety of situations has produced a theory of social change that we find helpful in understanding and designing ways to make it easier for more people to make self-directed journeys to social inclusion.

There are three movements in the process of social invention, mapped on the shape of the U.

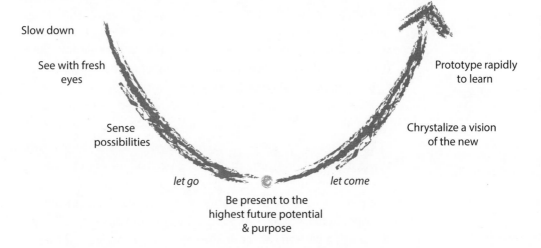

Slow down

See with fresh eyes

Sense possibilities

let go   *let come*

Be present to the highest future potential & purpose

Prototype rapidly to learn

Chrystalize a vision of the new

I. Traveling down the U: connection with people and immersion in the places with the greatest potential to reveal new possibilities.

II. Being still at the bottom of the U to retreat and reflect on these questions:

> *How can we be part of the story of a future that actualizes our highest potential rather than holding on to a story of the past that produces gaps between our action and what we value?*

> *What work activates my deepest capacity to create?*

III. Traveling up the U to animate our vision of the future we want to create, learning by rapidly trying and improving ways to live the new story.

In the context of pathfinding, presencing begins with disruption of the everyday world. Just as a computer application functions by downloading programmed routines, we can download rou-

Urban Innovations is an application of Theory U in design of a new structure for community building (page 156).

tines of control and exclusion. We are awakened by attending to the insistent desire for valued experiences and a realization that these experiences will remain out of reach as long as we keep doing more of the same thing. To find a path to a better life we need to stop moving in a straight line, turn deeper into our particular circumstances and the larger community that embeds them and cultivate the highest potential we find. To do that fully we have to intentionally create a social field of presencing.

Downloading is protective of the past. There can be a lot of activity along the straight line to more of the same, but most of it is an attempt to stay in control and avoid what we fear. Our decision to become social inventors shifts attention away from avoidance and toward what is worth bringing into reality. When the sense that change is necessary shows up, it's uncomfortable not to jump quickly to defining a technical problem and writing down action steps that assign responsibility for implementing a solution. The trouble is that obvious solutions frequently produce more of the same wrapped in different words. And quick solutions often get stuck on paper because they depend on big changes by others who act outside the effective influence of the solution prescriber.

Choosing to stop downloading and intentionally slowing down to see the situation from different perspectives allows a more fertile understanding to take shape. Discovering the different ways that other people see the situation and what is at stake for them in it, noticing the alliances that might be created, and appreciating the existing patterns of action that deserve our notice and care deepens and broadens awareness. The search will be fruitful when we notice and suspend the assumptions and certainties that lock us into downloading and open our hearts to see with fresh eyes. This allows us to sense new possibilities.

Reflecting on what we have seen, heard, thought, felt and imagined that has resonance for us and then letting go creates a space for insight to emerge. Allowing stillness opens us to consider how our engagement in this situation answers two profound questions: *Who is my Self?* and *What is my Work?* This brings us into the presence of the highest future potential that we are able to sense in our situation. The capital letters tie the questions to the source of our creativity and courage to act. Capital S, Self makes the question an inquiry into our current sense of the highest future purpose that we can serve in this situation. Capital W, Work makes the question an inquiry into our calling, the purpose that gives our life meaning. Theory U calls this alignment of will with the good that is waiting to be born presencing.

Openness to act from awareness of the highest future potential in the social field lets come a commitment to action that allows learning. Crystallizing a vision of the new imagines the form the future that wants to be born will take in our situation. Prototyping mobilizes immediate action with whatever resources are at hand and initiates a cycle of rapid tries that allow learning and improvement and create occasions to attract wider alliances and more resources.

Moving through the U

Social invention is not tinkering with things in an outside world of things an inventor can manipulate at will. It is action that intentionally influences interdependencies among people and groups, each of whom have their own perceptions and purposes. These interdependencies include and influence the inventors themselves, shaping emotions, perceptions, and action. Over time, social inventions succeed or fail based on the ways they

This type of listening focuses on the essential self of another. It's that part in the other person that is connected with his or her highest future potential that you can help to come into the present moment when you focus your attention and intention on it.

—Otto Scharmer

Listen Slow

Christine Meyer has lived for 25 years in her own home in Madison, Wisconsin with the committed support of assistants employed by Options in Community Living. Before that, since early childhood, she was shunted among 24 different institutions for people with intellectual disabilities and facilities for mental health treatment. Professionals moved her in reaction to failed attempts to fix the difficult and sometimes dangerous behavior that expresses her reaction to multiple and profoundly traumatic episodes of abuse and institutional efforts to control her. Life since moving into her community has not been easy. There have been periods when she and the people who support her have been on a painful and frightening emotional roller-coaster ride. Through all this she continues to grow and share her hard earned wisdom.

Invited to address a group of professionals on what it takes to provide good support in the difficult process of healing , Christine presented this.

> *If you are going to work with me,*
>   *you have to listen to me.*
> *And you can't just listen with your ears,*
> *because it will go to your head too fast.*
>
> *If you listen slow,*
>   *with your whole body,*
> *some of what I say will enter your heart.*

serve the highest potential in the larger whole that contains their creators.

Pathfinders and their allies and partners move through the U together by shifting the inner place of awareness from which they act. The quality of their attention structures their appreciation of the possibilities available and the actions that make sense in the situation and connects action to the source of social inventiveness. Attention can be pictured as the relationship between the boundary of the self and the focus of attention. In what follows, listening stands for all the ways of sensing a situation. Deeper levels of listening produce a more fertile social field and a deeper understanding of what is possible and how to create the good that can be.

Listener's boundary | Attention

At the downloading level of listening, **I-in-me**, attention (I) is inside the boundary (me) of the world as the listener already knows it. That boundary firmly separates the listener from what is taken to be other-than-me. Whatever might increase uncertainty is filtered out, unregistered. Difference is irrelevant if not threatening. The rules and assumptions defining current reality remain implicit and go unquestioned. The result is an echo chamber of confirmation of what the listener has already taken as true and so motivates reproduction of the past.

I-in-me

At the second level of listening, **I-in-it**, attention moves to the edge of the listener's boundary. A window opens on factual information about current reality and with new information comes the possibility of questioning what has been taken to be certain. Dis-confirmation, the recognition of facts revealing that current reality is shaped by previously unrecognized rules and assumptions that limit effectiveness and possibility, detaches the listener from downloading and allows the listener space to imagine better.

I-in-it

A social field is not just a collection of individuals. It is a web of connections among people and groups with different ways of seeing and making sense of diverse experiences. At the third level of listening, I-in-you, the listener's boundary opens to others and attention radiates from the heart, allowing an empathic view through others' eyes. Open-heartedness affirms others' dignity, the validity of their interests and the importance of their capacities. It creates a richer sense of the situation and a greater possibility of finding ground for collaboration. The listener is in a better position to reflect on the rules and assumptions that have covered up a greater good that is possible.

I-in-you

A situation is not simply the product of the linear history of interacting material elements. It also holds the highest potential future that can be born through the listener's efforts. An open boundary and capacity to sense the whole of which the listener is a creative part allows the fourth level of listening, **I-in-now**. An expanding sphere of attention creates the experience of an emerging reality that depends on the listener's creative effort. The experience can feel like being turned inside out in a way that resets awareness and action within a far larger whole. Deeper connection to multiple perspectives allows awareness of future possibility to flow through the listener. This recognition of emerging reality calls the listener to intentionally join in a creative effort to generate a future that expresses new and richer possibilities and more subtle and inclusive mental models. Shared commitment to the emerging future mobilizes collective intelligence.

I-in-now

Leadership is personal

Moving through the U calls social inventors to listen and act in ways that develop their own highest potential for leadership. This form of leadership is not a matter of motivating and directing others. It is a matter of cultivating mind, heart and will as organs of perception, sources of insight and guides to action. The social field of presencing grows stronger as the shared capacity to bring open minds, open hearts and open wills into the situation grows. An open mind suspends old habits of thought and allows seeing with fresh eyes. An open heart mobilizes emotional intelligence and grants access to different perspectives and appreciations of the situation. Redirecting attention to the perspectives and experiences of others allows a deeper appreciation of new possibilities. An open will transforms the fear of moving beyond the smaller self that clings to the false security of the old story. This openness hosts an experience of the new story that wants to be created.

The old story, automatically reproduced by downloaded rules, actively resists change. Social inventors experience these enemies of deeper listening as three voices, each protecting a gate to the next level of opening that will move them to assisting the new story to come.

The **voice of judgment** defends the listener's old story from the threat of an open mind. Attention is fixed on whether or not something matches current certainties. New information, new knowledge, new points of view, new appreciations are submerged in an obsessive internal monologue that sorts what fits the current mental model and is therefore taken as correct, true, practical, and realistic from what falls outside the old story and is therefore denied as boring, stupid, false, useless, and impossible. Social inventors intentionally open their minds by noticing and suspending the judgments that shape their current awareness, at least in the time they are noticing new differences. An open mind allows social inventors to take in the facts that connect them to current reality and its structures.

The next protector of the old story, the **voice of cynicism**, defends against the fear of failure and disappointment and a heart broken by recognition of suffering. This voice depreciates the power of trust and resourcefulness. It undermines agency by speaking of the powerful interests that will defend their stake in the old story, the uncertainties of going for something new, the vulnerability bound up with trusting other people to collaborate and the puniness of the social inventor's resources. This voice speaks from the sense of a community comprised of isolated individuals who must jealously look out for their own interests in a world dominated by scarcity and competitiveness. A hard shell and a hard heart fit us for survival. Openness is a naive invitation to shrewder others who will exploit it. Permeable boundaries tempt invasion. Social inventors intentionally create spaces in which they can soften their hearts. This lets them sense more of the depth and texture of their situation and the possibilities for creative development.

The **voice of fear** testifies to the power of the old story. It protects the gateway to letting go of a future that can be accurately predicted and reliably produced by extrapolation from the past. This space of awareness is disorienting. Things seem inside out. Negative consequences and positive possibilities that the old story hid away come forward and call for commitment to discover and realize better. These possibilities attract us because they beckon toward the expression of the highest potential in the situation and our purpose in life, but we don't quite know where our sense of them came from. The emerging future does not come with a reassuring blueprint but will have to be discovered through cycles of

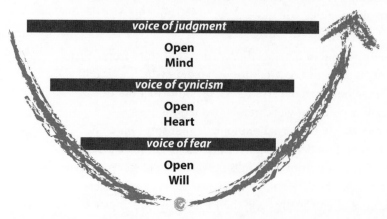

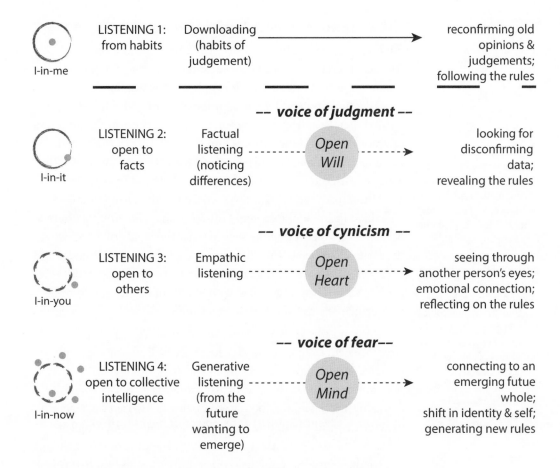

prototyping. Creative collaboration with others who are not like us is a necessary part of learning the way. Intentionally opening our will to the uncertainties of creating a new story takes courage and tests our trust in relationships and our resourcefulness.

Pathfinders, allies and partners can invest in practices that quiet these voices and build their capacities for incorporating new knowledge, practicing empathy and investing their whole Self in skillful action. Mindfulness practice increases awareness of the flow of judgments, thoughts and emotions that can inhibit movement to Level 4 Listening. Regular mindfulness practice creates an internal space of sufficient stillness, openness and freedom to sustain co-creating new and better stories.* The Presencing Institute generously provides guides to practices that support movement though the U (www.presencing.com). These practices can be arranged to support social invention.

---

*See Alan Sloan (2011). *Gentle heart, fearless mind. Discovering confidence, compassion and wellbeing through the practice of mindfulness.* inclusion.com

Urban Innovations: A Social Invention Generator

Each year for more than twenty years, Beth Mount and her friends Fredda Rosen and Carole Gothelf have accompanied a group of ten to fifteen young people as they graduated from special education and began their journey into adulthood. They refined their practices as they learned from successive generations of graduates and their families, but the structure of their work remained the same. Families from all over the city chose to join a group with other families to organize their son or daughter's transition from school. Families worked in the group to create and share individual Personal Futures Plans. The group gathered occasionally to exchange stories of what they had tried and what the results had been. The aim was for each person to discover and connect with contributing community roles, especially work roles, usually within walking or rolling distance of home. The foundation principle was "one person at a time".

Many good things came from these efforts. Young people strengthened, even discovered, their voices. Building on multiple tries at new experiences, their capacities and a vivid vision of community life came into focus, sometimes after years of enduring special education plans hopelessly focused on their deficiencies and predicting a lifetime of socially excluding services. Relationships in the group became a source of strength and knowledge. Parents challenged one another to raise their expectations and young people found others who encouraged them to discover and pursue their dreams of a whole self. Young people discovered and tried out a variety of community roles which strengthened their prospects for individual employment.

In 2013 there was a profound change. The effort had a modest budget, made up in different ways over the years, but a key investment had dried up. The three friends made the need to find a new source of funds the occasion for deeper reflection. What they had been doing made a difference, but they shared a sense that even more wants to happen at the intersection of a critical transition in young people's lives, a period of crisis in services to people with developmental disabilities, and times that demand renewal in their city. Exploring that sense of more disrupted past assumptions

> Perhaps stopping, letting go and hanging out in a space of not-knowing takes a leap of faith. Feminine principle is all about empty, open, agenda-less time and space. This approach asks us to trust that human beings individually and collectively have wisdom. In fact, we could say that people have all the wisdom they need to solve the world's problems. As change agents we therefore create situations in which this wisdom naturally comes forth. Wisdom is a high-minded word, but I am using it to indicate an ordinary intelligence that speaks for the whole. We can trust that the wisdom will come and will crystallize into insights, innovations, and fresh ideas. Intelligence that is not based on a small minded sense of self, but rather is inseparable from complete openness, is the feminine principle.
>
> –Arawana Hayashei

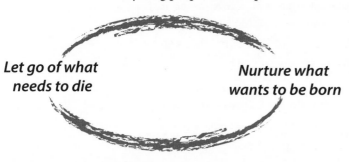

Let go of what needs to die

Nurture what wants to be born

that had flowed smoothly into practices that had served young people and their families well.

Geographic boundaries came into question. What if all the people and families came from the same part of the city? Fredda directs Job Path, an agency that assists a number of people in Harlem and plans to reorganize its services around local bases. Carole holds a senior position focused on innovation at AHRC, a large agency with a strong presence in Harlem. Harlem's art, culture and social justice issues hold a strong attraction for Beth; much of her own art is nourished by Harlem's spirit. An outline of Harlem sketched on chart paper attached to the back of Fredda"s office door soon filled with the names of enough young people already known to the two agencies to provide a focus. Kate Buncher, then Job Path's Director of Clinical Services, had recently participated in Art of Hosting Training that included community organizers and activists from Harlem. She joined in the effort because it resonated deeply with her interest in community building.

Sacred assumptions came into question. Beth was engaged in intensive study of Theory U. This expression of the theory, which guides a diverse group in social invention, spoke to her.

1
Co-initiating
uncover common intent
stop & listen to others & to
what life calls you to do

5
Co-evolving
embody the new in ecosystems
facilitate acting from
the whole

2
Co-sensing
observe, observe, observe
connect with people & places
to sense the system from the whole

4
Co-creating
prototype the new
develop living examples to
explore the new by doing

3
Presencing
connect to the source of inspiration & will
go to a place of silence &
allow inner knowing to emerge

What if young people with developmental disabilities along with direct support staff and Kate and Beth formed an association whose members were practitioners of the Theory U process, co-sensing and co-creating possibilities for engagement in their own Harlem neighborhood? Not one more version of a day

program but a membership tuned to local opportunities to make a difference who gathered for a few hours a month to share their discoveries and figure out where how they wanted to contribute as individuals or in small crews? What if they shifted the planning process, moving back and forth between joining in the work of building community and strengthening their sense of their own highest purpose and capacities? What if, instead of looking first for individual connections to established (if adapted) community roles, they became local activists, ready to partner and create new roles for themselves and other citizens who want to build a Harlem that works better for everybody?

Would repeated moves through this U process create a strong platform for each person to pull together the resources for composing a good life? The answer for many members is yes. In the first year, six of the founding group of seventeen found part-time work or paid internships that allow expression of their personal interests and capacities. Urban Innovations, as their association has come to be called, catalyzed Harlem Share in partnership with four other associations. This day long festival gave more than three hundred people the opportunity to dance, eat, make art and beautifully express their dreams for their community. Members have hung their art work in a local display space. A sub-group of poets and spoken word artists have performed in local and city-wide events. Members have joined in the work of partner community associations, mentoring children in a literacy initiative, assisting in meal preparation for a healthy food campaign, gardening in community plots. Others have joined in planting three Little Free Libraries and some have joined their neighbors in acting as stewards, keeping the libraries stocked (read the story on page 40). More and more members organize their weekly schedules and personal assistance assignments in terms of their commitment to community engagements mediated through their membership in Urban Innovations.

Each of these co-invented prototypes of social inclusion reveal and build on what works in a place where the tension between absencing and presencing is particularly strong. Partnership and local investment are guiding principles. Urban innovations always shares its work with other local associations and initiatives. For the first year, membership meetings counted on free community space and invited their hosts to tell them the stories of the host organization's work. Lunches for membership meetings are catered by local groups when the budget allows. Small groups of members gather at local coffee shops and restaurants. Individualization is a guiding principle. Members initiate and join in partnership activities based on their own interests. The purpose of the whole initiative remains clear: each young person succeeds in building real wealth through their choice of contributing community roles, particularly jobs, that strengthen their capacities, and build positive relationships in a diverse network committed to making the neighborhood work better for everyone.

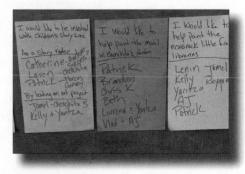

These contributions have emerged despite real difficulties. The streets and parks in the neighborhood can be and are seen by many to be unsafe. Aggressive policing exposes young men of color to stop-and-frisk, a traumatic experience for anyone. Safety concerns keep many whole families at home after dark, limiting possibilities for engagement. Some families struggle with poverty and the security of some people's homes are threatened by gentrification. Some families have multiple issues to manage and have little time and energy to actively support Urban Innovation's activities. The digital divide affects members, some of whom lack access to the internet, a significant resource for other members. The funding for Urban Innovations itself is very modest; members count for direct support on staff from the developmental disabilities programs they participate in. Many people are barred from any earnings at all by the rules that govern those programs. Continuity and engagement of direct support staff has varied and some members have been unable to participate in monthly meetings and community engagements due to unavailability or breakdowns in personal assistance. Service system rules that demand police checks of people in direct contact through Urban Innovations have limited the choice of personal assistants and restricted the contributions of potential student interns. Social exclusion shows up like the hydra, no sooner is one head amputated than another attacks.

Theory U and the practice of artistic creation guide the work of the membership. Urban Innovators activate their personal and collective capacities in service of a Harlem that works better for everybody. More and more members and associates act as conscious sensing organs for Urban Innovators. They notice possibilities for creating real wealth as they go about their daily lives and consider how to act on these opportunities in small group conversation and membership meetings. Member gatherings, about monthly, combine circle practice, a way for members to practice deep listening and share the results of their individual and small group searches, with making art. Collage, poster making, body maps, t-shirt design, spoken word, hip-hop, creating book outlines, photography and video made on smart phones all offer media that strengthen people's voices and clarify meaning and purpose. A closed Facebook page, created by members, serves as a means of coordination and a lively source for some members to exchange experiences and share opportunities that they have spotted.

After about a year and a half, Urban Innovators reached a turning point. The group grew as more young people entered the period of transition from special education. A growing number were at a place where individual focus on paid employment that makes a difference to their community takes priority. The mass of artifacts created by members grew to the point that Urban Innovators took a studio in the Dempsey Center, a community site that hosts education, arts, culture and social services.

Beth and Kate understand Urban Innovations itself as a work of artistic creation. They are inspired and guided by these words of Harlem artist and quilter Dindga McCannon.

> An artist lives on faith, the kind of faith that the image comes, the new is born with love. You fall in love with every creation and you want to see it through. If you don't fall in love, you will not stick with it. You have no idea how it will turn out, but you trust the process. You trust that what you do to create order out of the mess will heal the world, maybe not in your life time, but in some way you might never understand. Something always comes from your commitment to the process. You will have no idea what that might be... but the new is revealed through the creative process.

Thoughtfully living the process of co-creation described by Theory U has given Beth a helpful perspective on what is otherwise a very busy stream of activities. The theory underwrites the importance of practicing deeper listening and cultivating openness that allows possibilities to emerge and claim attention and commitment to action. This practice engages whole bodies, not disembodied heads. Awareness of patterns of thinking that could have closed down relationships with new partners allowed her to practice suspension, holding up deeply felt assumptions to attention in such a way that it is possible to notice them and move past them to listen to more people and observe what else is also there in the neighborhood. Here are a few of the fear-charged thoughts that Beth remembers suspending in favor of the active inquiry that turned up partners and opportunities for positive action:

> I don't know these neighborhoods. I don't live here. I can't begin to understand the culture and history of this place.

> I'm afraid of the crime rates. It's reported that 47% of Harlem residents consider their neighborhood unsafe. I worry about going to meet people in a housing project where 100 young people were just arrested on charges of gun and gang violence.

> If young people with developmental disabilities are more included and moving around in these neighborhoods there is a bigger than average chance that they could be victims of crime, exploitation or police aggression.

Only 37% of young men graduate from high school. The culture of these neighborhood is partly shaped by young men with diminished chances for employment and achievement. Even potted flowers get stolen in this neighborhood. If we plant a Little Free Library it will be vandalized and everything will be stolen.

Poverty, racism, outrage, trauma and rage all play their part in life where we have chosen to work. I can't comprehend the effects of my white privilege on my ability to cultivate good relationships. Can I deal with these issues with strength and sensitivity when they influence the work?

The developmental disability service system is so uptight and risk averse. There are more and more rules and restrictions that get in the way of people making new relationships, making a difference in their neighborhoods and working for pay.

The direct support staff who assist people are poorly paid and there is high turnover. We may not be able to consistently provide the kind of reliable and capable assistance that people need to show up.

Unless the eye catch fire
The God will not be seen.

Unless the ear catch fire
The God will not be heard.

Unless the tongue catch fire
The God will not be named.

Unless the heart catch fire
The God will not be loved.

Unless the mind catch fire
The God will not be known.

–William Blake

Suspension is not denial. It is the choice to search beyond (good) reasons to withdraw into the old story of control and social exclusion. Fears point to real aspects of the situation. The choice is to close down and withdraw or to open up to a form of attentive not knowing that leads to wider and deeper engagement. From openness it is possible to observe carefully and respectfully enough to form neighborhood relationships that will increase resilience to troubles when they occur. It takes faith to make the wager that although all these manifestations of absencing are actively at work, there are also hopeful people and groups, energized by visions of building the beloved community and available to partnership with people willing to invest their trust.

Practicing an attitude of openness sensitizes people to the pull of the good that wants to attract attention and energy. It lets members notice the cracks where something can grow in places that look to closed hearts to be barren and hardened. Calls to live in a new story arise from conversation. The effort to create a way for neighborhood people to make books came when an artist known to some members of Urban Innovators casually dropped in to a coffee shop where members were hanging their art for a show. His response to the freshness of their work led to a conversation in which the idea of making books emerged and attracted members interest. A prototyping session showed members' capacity and enthusiasm for creating short books from their experiences and imaginations.

Stopping mindless activity to be present to a new possibility can happen in a dedicated period of retreat, as masters of Theory U recommend. It can also be a matter of welcoming the new wanting to break through into what would otherwise be a passing moment or a casual conversation. Theory U points us to the ways we can use the power of our attention to disrupt the power of absencing and the short term comfort of reproducing more of the same. It indicates a space for improvisation that finds authentic moves by opening to the wisdom of the whole. By practicing many quiet moments of attention in the midst of everyday activity Kate embodies being present to highest potential, cultivating relationships that generate new possibilities.

Beth has experienced a mythic dimension of presencing in Urban Innovators. Repeated cycles through the U make her aware of an image that, for her, guides Urban Innovators growth. It is a tree. Images of trees that attracted Beth's imagination and energy came up spontaneously from several different sources in the early months of the project. The tree she imagines somehow holds the uncertainty and struggle in the work. It is a source of wisdom and consolation. The tree's desire to grow and bear fruit in Harlem is the deeper source of energy expressed in the many smaller pulls of presencing that have led Urban Innovators on their journey so far.

Mobilizing social invention

Urban Innovations generates social invention because it is designed to focus attention on the highest potential for social inclusion in the situations its members encounter and cultivate resourceful action that realizes that potential.

Freedom to invent

The chart on the next page relates attention and agency to map the degrees of freedom for social invention that people claim for themselves.

In the lower left corner (1,1), people are trapped. Fear dominates the spiral of creative energy, people have no sense of

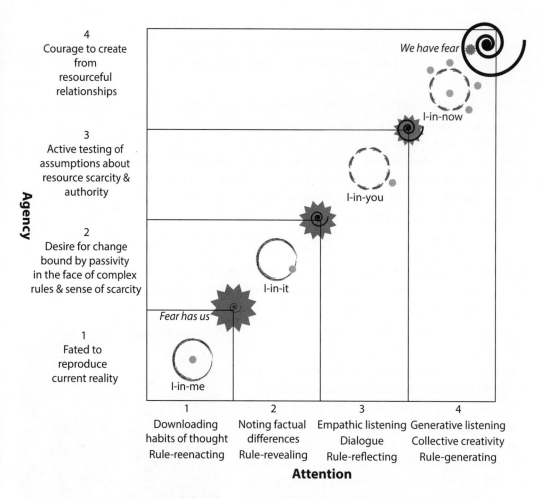

possibility for meaningful change, and attention is locked in to mindlessly following rules that reproduce the old story.

At 2,2 awareness of the situation grows but creativity is boxed in. The sense of scarcity and lack of room to grow increases along with greater awareness of the complex influence of the rules and mental models that reproduce the old story. Others look to be in control of what is needed for meaningful change.

At 3,3 a deeper appreciation of other's perceptions and capacities allows reconsideration of the old story. Relationships founded on empathic listening within a wider network of people encourage confidence in creative tests of assumptions about scarcity and availability of what's needed to make change. People begin to appreciate real possibilities for meaningful change.

At 4.4 people claim the most freedom of action. The spiral of creativity contains the fear the situation includes. There is a sense of the potentials in the whole of which people are a part and the purposes that define the meaning of their work for change. Confidence in resourceful relationships and the new story generated by listening with open minds, open hearts and open wills energizes social invention. In this space people might accurately claim that transformation is happening.

Many journeys begin at a low level of agency and awareness. There is a common idea of leadership that encourages cheer-leading, incentivizing, admonishing or guilt-tripping people into stepping up the ladder of agency. These tactics are a poor fit with social invention. When the purpose is pathfinding, it makes more sense to first move across the bottom of the chart. Shifting awareness to a generative place clarifies the situation and pulls people into prototyping in specific circumstances rather than driving them to activity aimed at escaping the undesirable by commanding more power over others. Perseverance through failures and disappointments strengthens agency. Strengthening relationships and engaging others in expanding prototypes increases resources. All that is needed for a pathfinder and their allies to begin their journey to inclusion is giving each other four gifts: time, openness to listening deeply, willingness to act resourcefully on what emerges from that listening, and trust to reach out and invite others in.

The source of social invention

Social exclusion and the devaluation of people who require publicly funded assistance give the forces of absencing plenty of room to play. Social inventors who want to contribute to a community that works better for everybody must be clear about the source of meaningful action. As they listen more deeply, multiple, mixed impulses come into awareness, discernment is necessary to crystallize a vision of the social inventions that will build a more inclusive community. The risk that the highest potential in a people's situations will be compromised increases when social inventors fail to cultivate the source of creativity.

There are many standpoints that support discernment and connection to source and many meaningful ways to articulate them. Reflection on contributions to a colloquium of pathfinders, allies and partners identifies the importance of these three commitments.[*]

Recognition of the dignity of vulnerable humanity. People whose differences call for mindful and sustained accommodation and assistance are liable to relegation to a devalued status.

---

[*] John O'Brien (2014). *Common threads: Approaches and contexts for planning everyday lives.* inclusionnetwork.ning.com

Devaluation is expressed in social exclusion, low expectations and limited investment in development, and imposed control on the devalued body of the other. Gifts and capacities are obscured and atrophy. Positive social inventions flow from simple and direct perception of a person's dignity and capacities. This plain, felt realization of dignity and capacity –once experienced, never completely lost– does not deny the person's need for assistance or diminish the accumulated scars of living-out a devalued social status. It simply grounds recognition of the gifts, personal passions and higher purpose that can open the way to flourishing if people act together with purpose and creativity.

Ubuntu, a deep appreciation for interdependency. Following Archbishop Desmond Tutu, *ubuntu* can be summarized, *I am because you are.* It expresses the aspiration to live in the generous interdependency that is the grace of human flourishing.

> *Ubuntu is the essence of being a person. It means that we are people through other people. We can't be fully human alone. We are made for interdependence, we are made for family. Indeed, my humanity is caught up in your humanity, and when your humanity is enhanced mine is enhanced as well. Likewise, when you are dehumanized, inexorably, I am dehumanized as well. As an individual, when you have ubuntu, you embrace others. You are generous, compassionate. If the world had more ubuntu, we would not have war. We would not have this huge gap between the rich and the poor. You are rich so that you can make up what is lacking for others. You are powerful so that you can help the weak. This is God's dream.* goo.gl/vMWlVc

Because their survival so obviously depends on *ubuntu*, many people with developmental disabilities have the gift of recruiting others into relationship. This runs against the grain of a dominant American culture that values individualism, independence, and making it on your own. The lives of most people with developmental disabilities set these values in a frame that is uncomfortable because they bring interdependence into the foreground. People with developmental disabilities can make choices about their lives, grow in their ability to do things for themselves and contribute to family and community life, but only with mindful interdependent support. This necessary support arises only from the active cultivation of relationships. It cannot be consumed in a business transaction or delivered as matter of correct procedure. This makes social invention a search for more resourceful and generative relationships in an increasingly diverse network. In this search people will benefit from occasions to express gratitude and ask for and receive forgiveness.

Hunger for justice. Archbishop Tutu knows as well as many people with developmental disabilities that the possibility for creative interdependence exists along with human potentials for dominance, greed, dehumanization and evil. Establishing rights in legislation and enforcing them in court does not fully satisfy hunger for justice. Legal rights and the apparatus of rules and regulations that govern bureaucracies can help only when they don't choke the intentional relationships essential to *ubuntu* or diminish dignity by imposing clienthood as a condition of assistance. Person-centered practices are small ways to build a society that makes building and rebuilding the beloved community less difficult for more and more citizens. These practices assist people to exercise their freedom to be in friendship and act in networks and associations that need their particular gifts. They are empowered by structures that give people and families effective control of sufficient funds to meet the extra costs associated with life with disability.

Cultural pressures devalue people who obviously need extra assistance, deny the necessity of cultivating creative interdependence among people and with nature, and encourage withdraw from the struggle for community and flight into individualistic consumerism, This makes **intentional resistance** necessary. Social invention resists by gathering people who will support one another to see whole situations clearly and act with courage. This denies the bureaucratic illusion that a good life could result from compliance with externally imposed and inspected rules and procedures. It means facing the real and deep vulnerability that can blight and even destroy the lives of people with developmental disabilities and acting to support the development of their freedom and their gifts with full awareness of the terrible effects of absencing. It means creating mutually supportive networks that confer strength to push through the denial, cynicism and fear that discourage many citizens from acting freely in a complex and rapidly changing world.

The salvation of this human world lies nowhere else than in the human heart, in the human power to reflect, in human meekness and human responsibility.

–Václav Havel

6

Changing the Way We Change Our System

Our system has focused on what its leaders call system change for a generation. Administrative bodies have rewritten mission statements and strategic plans to reflect the central importance of inclusion, employment, the choice of where to live and with whom, self-direction and person-centered plans and supports. Administrators make regular calls for organizational transformation.

Judgments of how successful these efforts have been depend on perspective. Some see the work as nearly done. We do not. Conditions have improved in many ways: many residential settings are smaller, make active support possible, better respect privacy and take more account of resident preferences; assistive and communication technology plays a constructive part in more people's lives; people with mobility impairments are better seated; and people spend more time in community places. More people and families direct individual budgets. The number of organizations pushing the edge of the possible has grown, and project and research funds have produced useful knowledge about reducing the impact of impairments on people's lives.

However, except in a few jurisdictions that have intentionally hosted large scale social invention, the system's center of gravity holds at about where it was set in the mid-1980s. Most public money goes to group living arrangements contracted by administrators. Employment rates, the best single indicator of the system's overall health, remain stubbornly low. Family centered assistance to the large number of families who provide housing and assistance well into people's adult years remains a peripheral investment. Those with complex needs or troubling behavior typically remain at the end of the line for access to opportunities for community participation. People, even children, continue to slip into long term placements in nursing homes, specialized facilities or prisons. Too many pathfinders' journeys set out for valued community roles but hit a wall of inflexible conditions for assistance that they cannot surmount.

System means the whole network of structures, policies and practices concerned with assistance to people with developmental disabilities. This network is reproduced and changed by the interaction of people with disabilities and their families and allies, advocacy groups, service providers, administrators charged with managing services, and legislators and courts as they take an interest in policy and resources for people with disabilities. We call it our system because we are its members, shaped by and shaping its culture.

Administration refers to the part of the system responsible for its governance and overall capacity, the body responsible for implementing law and budget decisions. **Administrators** are people responsible for the health and development of the capacity for publicly funded assistance.

It is time to change the way our system changes itself. Current approaches result in a slow growing minority of people better able to claim their *Charter* rights, usually because resourceful families make considerable effort or they have the good fortune to en-counter a service provider organized for individualization. Most people are left to find satisfaction in their life without access to the responsibilities and rewards of self-direction, personal social inclusion and a contributing role.

Creating social invention zones

Changing the way we change the system is not a matter of compelling masses of people to march in new formations. Mean-ingful change happens one person at a time. The administrators' task is to make structural changes and investments that multiply the number of people who choose a self-directed journey into inclusion in their own homes and neighborhoods, in community workplaces, in civic life. The challenge is to encourage very many more people to be that one person by vastly increasing the flexi-bility of publicly funded assistance and uprooting the devaluing mental models that justify imposed control.

The rate of multiplication depends on the quality of attention and creative investment in this design question: **How might we make it much easier for people and their families to choose self-directed journeys to inclusion?** For provider organization managers this leads to the further design question, **How might we supply good partners for those on a self-directed journey to inclusion?** For administrators this leads to the further design question, **How might we create conditions for more provider organizations to supply good partners for people who choose self-directed journeys to inclusion?**

Those who design better answers to these questions embrace the uncertainty integral to social invention and build trusting rela-tionships to do the creative and emotional work of journeying to inclusion. This involves letting go of some familiar patterns and challenging familiar assumptions and mental models. As the table on the facing page suggests, what enables the journey to freedom often runs against the grain of system structure and practices. However encouraging of self-direction and inclusion the words in strategic plans may be, habitual patterns described in the right hand column trump vision.

This is an irony that people who want to exercise leadership have to embrace and work through. At least in the US, mixed messages trap the system in a bind. There is clear call for inclusion and

	What encourages journeys to inclusion & freedom	What the current environment encourages
Organizing image	A **network of resourceful agents** continually improving their capacity to identify personally meaningful opportunities, work out how to make the best of those opportunities & connect with others to share learning.	An **efficient machine**, able to produce more publicly sanctioned outcomes with decreasing public investment & shift what it produces on command.
Logic	**Pull:** organizational partners assist people & families to draw in & organize necessary resources to co-create real wealth.	**Push:** expert assessment & plans lead to delivery of clinically appropriate, evidence-based assistance & interventions in managed settings.
Structure	**Network** of people and their circles, organized & supported by minimum necessary hierarchy & controls to supply necessary assistance.	**Multi-level hierarchies.** Policy assumption that economies of scale make bigger provider organizations efficient.
Coordination	**Based on relationship.** Promises based on shared appreciation of a person's capacities & highest purpose & commitment to embodiment of those gifts in contributing roles. Shared understanding of design questions to address & opportunities to formulate & share learning.	**Based on transactions.** Mix of authority & contractual relationship: detailed rules & performance contracts. Individual plans, vetted by system appointed professionals, specify cost effective means to meet system defined & approved needs.
Boundaries	**Open** to thoughtfully developed participation & negotiation of contributing roles & necessary accommodations with other citizens, workplaces, learning places & sites of civic and association life. Energy flows out to extend network	Assistance typically delivered in **self-contained** groups or pairs with staff. Vigilant management scrutiny of boundary crossing relationships based on distrust & fear of liability for abuse, neglect or exploitation.
Safeguards	A variety of **committed personal relationships** with negotiated authority to support the person's decisions in a way that very strongly influences the provision of assistance. Judicial intervention in criminal incidents.	**Detailed regulations**, inspections and a system of required corrections, fines or contract termination for non-compliance. Required scrutiny of & formal training & certification for staff.
Source of power	**Power from within** Contact with highest potential future & highest purpose in each person's work **Power with** Resourcefulness in committed relationships with allies, partnerships based on linked purpose, shared interests & exchange of capacities among citizens. Public funds are an asset to meet the excess costs associated with impairment & overcoming social exclusion.	**Power over** Supervision & control based on accepting full responsibility for assuring health & safety & quality through compliance with regulations. Close oversight of any public money allocated to an individual to assure that it is spent only as bureaucratically authorized.
Most influential view of person	**Citizen** with a moral claim on assistance & accommodation necessary to increase their real wealth & challenge social exclusion through personally meaningful contributing roles.	**Client** or consumer; eligible –on the basis of professionally certified deficiencies and defined needs– for specified services when public expenditure allows.

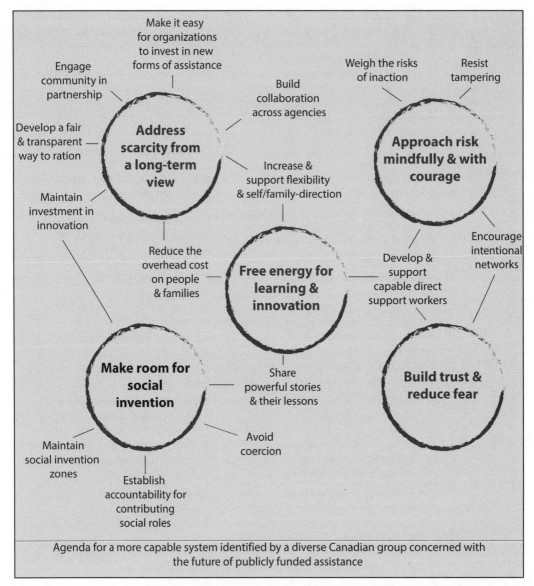

Make it easy
for organizations
to invest in new
forms of assistance

Engage
community in
partnership

Build
collaboration
across agencies

Weigh the risks
of inaction

Resist
tampering

Develop a fair
& transparent
way to ration

**Address
scarcity from
a long-term
view**

**Approach risk
mindfully & with
courage**

Increase &
support flexibility
& self/family-direction

Maintain
investment in
innovation

Encourage
intentional
networks

Reduce the
overhead cost
on people
& families

**Free energy for
learning &
innovation**

Develop &
support
capable direct
support workers

**Make room for
social
invention**

Share
powerful stories
& their lessons

**Build trust &
reduce fear**

Maintain
social invention
zones

Avoid
coercion

Establish
accountability for
contributing
social roles

Agenda for a more capable system identified by a diverse Canadian group concerned with
the future of publicly funded assistance

self-direction. And increasing preoccupation with compliance to
system imposed detail complexity –especially around managing
costs, assuring health and safety and avoiding liability– shrinks
the social space necessary for real change, diverts attention from
developing local opportunities, compromises self-direction and
drives a climate of fear that undermines people's sense of agency.
In many places, transaction costs impose a tax on learning by
trying something new that has become intolerably high.

Organizational and system change begins by taking the work seriously. Reorienting assistance at the organization and system levels requires social invention zones, spaces where there is enough
freedom and sufficient real wealth to steadily shift the numbers

of people who show up in community life as contributing citizens. Administrators committed to enabling growing numbers of people to journey to inclusion and self-direction will invest in a portfolio of these social spaces and stretch themselves to protect room for maneuver within those spaces.

There are at least five options for creating space for invention. The first two are self-organizing, created from the real wealth of the people involved; organizations and systems can build on what these pathfinders discover. The other three spaces are opened by management authority and investment.

- Some individuals and their allies have always taken action for inclusion. Partnership in performing some of the work these circles do can increase the number of these one person social invention zones. Individual budgets that people and their allies can effectively direct increase useful assets.

- Committed staff may carve out time and resources for social invention within their sphere of influence.

- Very flexible, usually small or very small, organizations driven by a desire to promote social inclusion in a particular community by supporting people in their own homes, jobs and the life of local associations. Some of these organizations are created from scratch by committed people. Others spin off from larger organizations or develop under the umbrella of a more established organization until they find their feet financially.

Life Works is one such organization, page 102

- Invention zones within a large organization. The organization creates an internal boundary and dedicates capable and influential staff who are authorized to negotiate for redirection of current organizational assets to partnership with people and families who want a real change This can happen by authorizing multiple groups of social inventors.[*]

- A cross-boundary network of mutually helpful social inventors multiplies the effects of local learning.

Support for social invention depends on the system's real priorities for change, not its administrative proclamations. We advocate expanding social invention zones because we see so many people left out of the responsibilities and benefits of citizenship. Many see the current system as capable of delivering all that people are due. Their priority is increasing the level of public investment

---

[*] For a detailed description of this option, see Hanns Meissner (2013) *Creating blue space: fostering innovative support practices for people with developmental disabilities.* Chapter 11, Developing capacity as an innovations generator. inclusion.com

enough to clear waiting lists and maintain a stable workforce. These are important issues. A fair share of public money is an important condition of system health, but simply investing in more of the same without developing new capacities would lock in the assumption that history ends with the small group home and the community experience program. Andrew Power, when President of People First in the Australian Capitol Territory, diagnosed the problem of growth without deeper change this way:

> *Things have changed, but the managers and the staff haven't caught up yet. Now they are looking at a map that has gotten all stretched and crooked. When you drive with a crooked map, you get lost. The faster you drive on a crooked map, the faster you get lost.*

We agree with Andrew that real change involves straightening out our mental maps, including the mental model and structures that shape the system's most common approach to making change.

We find four distinctions helpful in defining social invention zones: the difference between **working in** an organization and **working on** an organization,* the difference between **technical problem solving** and **meeting adaptive challenges,**† the difference between changes **done to or for** people with developmental disabilities and changes **done with** people; and the difference between **externally motivated** change and **internally motivated** change.

Working in an organization involves implementing and improving procedures to perform system defined and regulated functions that preserve current mental models, relationships and structures. **Working on** a system involves revealing, testing and reshaping unexamined assumptions and disrupting familiar structures and patterns of practice to suit new purposes. Working in a system makes sense when it reliably produces self-directed assistance to people in their own homes, jobs and contributing community roles and wants to improve processes that already work. Working on a system is necessary when the organization needs to discover new ways to partner in social invention and actively support people's journeys to social inclusion. A system that produces placements in group homes and day programs needs working on.

When the change necessary to support new purposes is a matter of correctly applying expert knowledge to a well defined prob-

---

* W. Edwards Deming. (2000). *Out of the crisis.* Cambridge, MA: The MIT Press.

† Ronald Heifetz (1998). *Leadership without easy answers.* Cambridge, MA: Harvard University Press.

lem, the change can be called **technical** even if the problem is complicated and demanding. Changing billing procedures is a technical change although it may demand extensive and skilled effort across organizational boundaries. When new ways must be found to navigate uncertain territory outside familiar boundaries and when a common understanding of purpose and ways of proceeding must be negotiated among people and organizations with different interests who face real losses, necessary change can be called **meeting an adaptive challenge**. Successfully closing a sheltered workshop and finding good community jobs for its participants is an adaptive challenge because it departs from the familiar, activates anxiety about loss, requires the creation of new patterns of relationship and practice, and renegotiates boundaries to include employers and other co-creators beyond the organization's direct control.

When a change is made by an organization's staff, it is done **for or to** people with developmental disabilities. This form of change influences transactions between the organization and the people it assists. When people with developmental disabilities are integral to the change so that the change cannot happen unless they do their share of the work, a change is done **with** people. This form of change is relational.

When a change is made to meet an external demand or earn a reward from outside it can be called **externally motivated**. Winning a new contract or passing an inspection with flying colors achieve successes that bring external reward or avoidance of punishment. When change emerges from discernment and embodiment of an organization's highest purpose, it is **internally motivated**.

A social invention zone welcomes people who are internally motivated to work on organizations and skillfully meet adaptive challenges by acting with people with developmental disabilities and their families. It contrasts with typical approaches to system change that flood the space that might be dedicated to social invention with attempts to elicit new results through instruction, inspection, incentives and technical problem solving.

How we do it now: instructions and incentives

System change efforts typically follow a pattern of issuing new instructions and implementing new incentives. Instructions come as decrees from laws and judicial proceedings. They come as targets, objectives, rules and regulations promulgated by administrative authorities and enshrined in performance contracts.

> People in positions of authority often move to find premature closure. But in an adaptive challenge they should take an experimental approach where the job of authority is to raise the tough questions and establish the processes that hold people's feet to the fire of being creative, making mistakes and learning from mistakes.
>
> This is quite different from the more common view that people in authority know what they are doing … In an adaptive challenge leaders don't know what they are doing because it's a frontier where *everyone is in over their heads*.
>
> –Ron Heifetz

They come as specifications for the deliverables a grant-maker wants produced. Experts prepare guidance, deliver training curricula and offer technical assistance to give people more detailed instructions about how to follow higher order instructions. While it would be logical to reward those who follow instructions, this seldom happens. The most common incentives are threatened penalties for non-compliance and the reward of continuing to do the work.

This pattern gains legitimacy when people with developmental disabilities and family members join as advisors or members of decision making bodies that determine what the instructions say. More and more instructions tell service providers to deliver employment, a choice of residence, or increased practical assistance from unpaid people (often administratively labeled natural support). These are identified as outcomes.

ON BUREAUCRATIZING VALUES

The issue we confront in human services is one of fundamental human values–freedom and community. Yet, our hopes and plans for securing these values for everyone are invested in government agencies and public laws, in an approach that codifies and mechanizes the "delivery" of values. In holding to our hopes, we have seriously overestimated the power of bureaucracy.

–Burton Blatt

This pattern makes common sense. Advocates for better lives for people with developmental disabilities work hard in legislatures and courthouses to win new instructions and incentives, monitor closely and complain vigorously when authorities fail to enforce compliance or meet targets. The pattern is a culturally embedded expectation of administration. Mangers are granted authority to solve problems and achieve objectives by telling people what to do. Good managers do this by involving people in specifying the instructions. Experts are hired to have the answers and teach people how to reliably and efficiently implement those answers. Media exposure of abuse by service workers demands rapid deployment of more detailed instructions, mandated training and closer inspection to enforce stiffer penalties. None but the incompetent are in over their head.

Instructions and incentives are the medium of administration and it matters that they are aligned with the changes necessary to assist people with developmental disabilities to claim full citizenship. But culture allows organizations to absorb most of these positive instructions as a need for incremental change rather than a call to suffer the disruption of an adaptive challenge. The table on the next page checks perceptions of the organizational change necessary to reliably offer person-centered assistance.

The culture that obscures adaptive challenges is shaped by two common administrative assumptions. The first is that change is a matter of using known approaches to solve technical problems. Expert knowledge sufficient to deliver new results exists and can be cheaply transferred, so it would be wasteful to invest in supporting a variety of local and individual social inventions in

Working in the system →		Working on the system
Our services are person-centered & inclusive now & most consumers are satisfied. We can always improve how we do what we are doing.	We serve most people in a person-centered way but some people would benefit from more individualized assistance. This might require adding a service we don't provide now.	To provide what people deserve, we need to fundamentally redesign the ways we offer & manage assistance. If we make deep enough change, significant improvement is possible for (almost) everyone we assist.
We know all we need to know to deliver good assistance. Our real need is for more funding and better staff. If the system administration wants a different kind of service, we are ready to provide it if they offer the right incentives & give us more money to pay for the change.	If we are expected to make changes, we need the changes specified in detail & we need access to experts who will train us in evidence-based techniques & strategies, proven to deliver individualized services & maintain our organization's financial stability. The administration has to guarantee that we are held harmless from risk.	We can only generate relevant knowledge through action focused on the capacities of the people & families we support, our communities, & ourselves. We learn by doing new things with people & reflecting on them. No matter what system managers do, offering better assistance means that we have to step up & re-purpose what we already have. We could, & probably should, fund much of the change with money we already have & we will probably have to re-negotiate interpretations of the rules.
We want some practical techniques that work with people who are difficult to manage: resistant families, non-compliant people, or people with complex needs.	We want to be taught how to work more effectively with people who challenge us & how to get more natural support & greater community acceptance.	We need to learn how to generate social inventions by working with people to discover and make the most of community opportunities. We need to grow in our ability to listen deeply, sense possibilities & co-create the assistance necessary to make the best of those possibilities.
While it may take hard work, making change is a matter of making a good plan, marketing the change to stakeholders & controlling implementation by measuring, monitoring & correcting. With good management, there is a straight line between setting a goal and achieving it.	We need technical assistance to try new approaches with the few people we assess as ready. We'll roll the change out to more people as they acquire skills & additional funding & family interest allows.	Making the vision of individualized supports real means dealing with risk, uncertainty, and loss. Leadership requires the ability to observe, interpret, & intervene in emotionally charged situations & mobilize people with different interests. This calls for more than changes in the organization; it calls for changes in our selves.
Technical change: *We do what we are paid for in the way we are told to do it.*		**Adaptive Challenge:** *We have to develop new mental models, relationships and structures. Our personal capacity for leadership must grow.*

order to negotiate adaptation to a developmental challenge. This assumption underwrites the expectation that very busy service coordinators who complete a three day training in person-centered planning will transform a system's capacity to support self-direction and inclusion.

The second assumption is that the structure that organizes the way assistance is offered makes little if any difference in the capacity to realize the system's proclaimed values. Any capably managed organization that follows the rules and avails itself of technical assistance can deliver, or learn to deliver, person-centered, self-directed, inclusive assistance in any setting recognized by the administration, regardless of size, setting, staffing or structure. This assumption includes a truth: any service setting can continually improve its staff's knowledge of and active regard for the interests and preferences of the people it assists even if assistance

---

Metaphors Capture Depth of Change

Managers involved in a learning group were invited to draw two images. The first, a visual metaphor for their organization as it currently relates to the people it assists. The second, a visual metaphor for the way they would want to organize to assist people in a positive future.

Their images have power. Current reality is expressed as painting by numbers with a small palette of two colors. The desirable future faces a blank canvas with a generous palette.

The now is a greenhouse owned operated and branded by the agency, growing uniform potted plants on tables,under glass. In a desirable future a variety of different plants in motion toward the sun have their roots in the soil of open space.

There is no straight line to follow from one image to the next. Both of these images identify a change that generates anxiety as well as excitement. Both involve a difference that implies stopping one way of working and taking up a different one. Predictability and uniformity decline and uncertainty and variety increase. Risk is real and can't be wished away.

is organized in a way that leaves staff unable to actively support self-direction or social inclusion.

The assumption that structure is irrelevant to realizing proclaimed values accommodates political reality. Existing services, including institutions, have influential and loyal constituents among staff, families and people with developmental disabilities, as well as others who benefit economically from their operation. Loyalty translates into vigorous defense of current arrangements when people anticipate loss. Distrust of the powers that be and (sometimes justified) suspicion that fine words about inclusion and self-direction mask budget cuts harden opposition. Treating the change as if it were solving a technical problem rather than meeting an adaptive challenge avoids investment in building the relationships necessary to do the emotional and creative work required. Defense of sunk costs and familiar mental models often takes its terms from the new instructions. Advocates for institutions frame their arguments as preserving choice for inmates' families. Courts defer to expert authority in determining the least restrictive environment that meets a person's needs. This cultural and political reality marks a practical limit of the instructions and incentives approach to system change. It stalls journeys by people who want to make more interesting and satisfying claims on inclusion if administrators do not balance the dues that institutional settings extract with generous investment in social invention zones.

The more varied understandings and interests a change affects and the more the people involved see a threat that they will lose something of value to them the more the work of making change is a political process. It will take time and skill to negotiate conflicts. Established interests will look for ways to divert attention from difficult long term questions to quick and easy answers. Advocates for deep change risk being scapegoated, attacked and excluded. Leadership is the personally risky process of keeping difficult questions in focus and encouraging social invention.[*] The difficult questions that leadership holds for a person concern the ways they can build real wealth; for an organization, the ways to become better partners to more pathfinders; and for a system, the ways to encourage more partnerships and encourage more pathfinders.

To better suit our ways of changing our system to the new task of assisting people with developmental disabilities to claim full and

> If a factory is torn down but the rationality which produced it is left standing, then that rationality will simply produce another factory. If a revolution destroys a government, but the systematic patterns of thought that produced that government are left intact, then those patterns will repeat themselves.… There's so much talk about the system… and so little understanding.
>
> –Robert Pirsig

> Politics is primarily a public struggle over the definition of sanity.
> –Maurice Glasman

---

[*] See Ronald Heifetz and Marty Linsky (2002). *Leadership on the line: Staying alive through the dangers of leading*. Boston: Harvard Business School Press.

active citizenship, we need a deeper understanding of the change that's required and the work necessary to make the change. That understanding includes an inquiry into the way people in the system understand key values and their implications.

What does it mean to value inclusion?

Mission and vision statements follow statements of legally established rights and embrace the value of inclusion. Its practical meaning depends on interpretation, which varies widely depending on an organization's history, current investments and structure. We have a very strong view of inclusion and we recognize that other meanings have stronger influence on today's system. Tempting as it is to imagine an authority laying down the one, single, true and correct definition (that is, ours), such fundamentalism would be a disaster. Persuasion based on arguments

Disruption

Responsibility

Influence the Public

It's up to legislation and policy makers, influenced by advocates, to shape a more inclusive community by educating the public and discouraging discrimination.

Services can play a small part in community change but are already very heavily committed to providing day-to-day support.

Q1

Invest in Social innovation

Systematically build co-creative relationships with community to open new pathways to active participation

Individualize support to valued social roles in community.

Reinvest existing service resources: deliberately move away from services that group people based on disability.

Q4

Maintain Course

Inclusion is one value among several. The higher priority now is protecting funding for existing services and meeting expanding need in a climate of fiscal restraint

The degree of inclusion a person experiences is a matter of individual choice and abilities; those for whom it is not realistic or desired need the option of good local services that provide opportunities for meaningful life among disabled peers. It's wrong to judge those who choose less inclusion.

Q2

Refine Current Practices

Work within boundaries of current service options; find ways to ease transitions among human services

Improve techniques for connecting people, one person at a time.

As new resources become available,- consider adding new options specifically designed to support inclusion.

Q3

from demonstrated benefits honors the free choice at the heart of citizenship and makes room for the necessary variety of ways that committed people will invent to assume valued community roles

The diagram identifies different practical meanings inclusion can take on, depending on perspective and organizational commitments. It maps different understandings of inclusion on two dimensions:

Responsibility – the demand for organizational action required by inclusion. Low responsibility means that, however important inclusion may be, it is primarily someone else's task. Accepting a low level of responsibility for inclusion (Q2 & Q3) often means putting higher priority on other concerns like using scarce resources to provide current services to as many people as possible or respecting people's or families' expressed choice for current arrangements, or

Inclusion is important, but it's not our job

Responsibility

Inclusion is the core purpose of our work

providing specialized interventions for under-served groups. Priority on action for inclusion might rise if funding increased to exceed perceived need for adequate pay and absorption of those who are not fully served. High responsibility (Q3 & Q4) sees inclusion as a moral and practical imperative, a matter of social justice and a measure of social responsibility. A service can't produce inclusion alone, but getting much better at the work of building relationships that cross boundaries is central to its mission and at the top of its priorities.

Disruption – the extent of social invention that inclusion demands. Low disruption (Q2 & Q3) holds that current practice is generally on track to offer as much support for inclusion as is possible and desired by people and their families. Under all but the most unusual circumstances (exceptional levels of funding or heroic levels of family effort) inclusion outside the family circle and service boundaries is unrealistic, especially for people who require high levels of assistance. On this understanding, participants in a sheltered workshop are included in community because they are performing a typical role (worker) in a building with a local address; residents of a group home who experience regular group outings in the house van are as socially included as it is realistic to expect them to be.

High disruption (Q1 & Q4) recognizes that inclusion demands deep change. In Q1, the community must change deeply but it is up to someone else to change it. In Q4 organizations shift from a mostly inward focus and learn how to engage employers, mainstream resources like post-secondary

We have just scratched the surface. We need to make deep & challenging change

We know how to support inclusion when given the necessary resources.

education settings, and community associations in ways that build collaborative support for contributing roles. Higher levels of co-creation with people and their families and far more flexible use of public funds for assistance offer personalized support to individuals as they pursue a valued pathway through life. Current funding shifts away from settings that congregate people in a marginal, special world and reinvests in social inventions that actively promote individual belonging. From this perspective, inclusion means that people fill a variety of valued social roles in typical settings, act as contributing citizens and build a more extensive and diverse network of friends, allies, memberships and contacts.

The more system administrators value Q4, the more they will invest in creating and supporting social invention zones that focus there. In the journey to Q4, commitment matters more than compliance does. Law and policy can discourage the forms of exclusion that result from identifiable discrimination on the basis of disability, and this matters. But social inclusion wants far more opportunities to create real wealth than cold toleration of a person's presence allows. It wants genuine progress toward realization of the beloved community. And the correct interpretation and accurate implementation of policy isn't enough to support the journey from exclusion to inclusion. Finding the limits of Q4 involves social inventions that creatively engage uncertainty and risk and take direction and strength from imagination and personal commitment. Beyond legislating against discrimination, it is more important for policy makers to decrease the obstacles they create to than to try to mandate journeys to inclusion. Because many people and organizations powerfully, if unconsciously, resist authoritative attempts to require what must be achieved through commitment, those who want to raise the level of inclusion will focus more on demonstrating new possibilities, building relationships, persuading and negotiating than on trying to manipulate instructions and incentives.

Deep change turns settled approaches inside out. Those who found their organizations on individualized supports are in the midst of the struggle for greater self-direction in more diverse personal networks and contributing social roles. Many well established organizations have a considerable distance to go to reach beyond their own boundaries. The demand for moral leadership and creative action in these organizations is very heavy, as the experience of JNCS shows.

The change it takes

Jay Nolan Community Services (JNCS) was founded in1975 by parents of people with autism whose neurophysiological differences manifest as challenging behavior and extreme limits in others' ability to understand their communication. This, in turn, led to their rejection or mistreatment by services available in Los Angeles before JNCS opened. By 1992 JNCS assisted 70 people in 13 group homes and a larger number in three Day Behavior Management programs. An external review by experts in assistance for people with developmental disabilities confirmed the JNCS Board's judgment that the organization, and particularly the group homes, were in crisis. Collaboration between Board leaders and review team members framed the crisis: serious problems in the relationships between staff and the people they assisted and their families were caused by the structure of the group homes. The root problem could not be solved by replacing bad staff with better staff or training ignorant staff in new techniques; in fact many staff members were committed and competent. The difficulty was not in how the group homes functioned, but in what group living arrangements can never deliver. Only radically individualized assistance could create the conditions for a violence free life and a good chance at valued experiences and roles.

Logic is the tool that is used to dig holes deeper and bigger, to make them altogether better holes. But if the hole is in the wrong place, no amount of improvement will put it in the right place.

–Edward deBono

JNCS hired one of the review team to lead the agency. The board agreed to plan with people in group homes, one person and family at a time, beginning with the Board President, who was willing to consider an individualized living arrangement for his son. The process started with one willing family who had high credibility among other parents who also wanted more for a family member with very complex requirements for assistance. Early success led other families to follow, and within a year a range of solutions to the problems of creating and supporting individualized living arrangements developed.

Initial success led to increasing momentum. Group residences closed and the buildings sold. A variety of individualized arrangements emerged. About 10% of families chose to leave JNCS to maintain a group home placement with a different agency. Today, JNCS partners with about 100 people with complex needs for assistance and their families through supported living and a number of others through a variety of customized arrangements.

The change was profound. While there were good examples of supported living for people with less complex impairments to learn from,

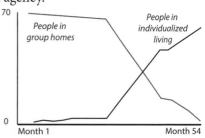

there was great uncertainty among families about how to create an adequate environment and offer and adjust capable assistance, one person at a time. There was uncertainty about the availability of secure, suitable and affordable housing. There was uncertainty about the adequacy of funds and contractual conditions from the administrative bodies involved. The stakes are high: people actually depend on moment-to-moment assistance for their safety.

There was a deep and often controversial shift in the role of people's families. Parents founded JNCS so that they could delegate day-to-day responsibility to an organization that they controlled through its Board, vigilant attention to how their son's and daughters were assisted and vigorous complaint when things were not right. The new pattern disrupted this relationship and called for active and continuing family engagement in a person's circle of support and day-to-day involvement of the circle in designing and managing the person's assistance.

The circles formed around each person apportioned uncertainty into manageable chunks. Circles held responsibility for a single person's assistance and provided a container for processing the emotion that comes up around loss of the familiar, search for new settings, routines and patterns of support, and encounters with failure and disappointment. Circles selected and directed staff, established and revised routines, planned for and took steps into a desirable future together and made decisions. Through the process the Executive Director and the Board President stayed actively in touch with each circle and guided the collective process that emerged from individual circle's actions. JNCS moved from delivering assistance through a bureaucratic structure to assisting circles to pull together, organize and re-organize the resources that will assist each person to live a good life.

Circles shared responsibility with JNCS managers for managing uncertainties around housing. JNCS managers and Board members managed negotiations with funding and regulatory authorities.

This organizational design recognizes that offering good assistance requires considerable thought. Most organizations expect management to be able to do sufficient thinking to assure good lives for big numbers of people. JNCS' design doesn't impose this cognitive overload on managers by demanding that they make judgments based on limited knowledge of people and their situations. The circle of those who know the most about one person's situation holds responsibility for most decision making. This is analogous to the architecture that allowed IBM to build Blue

Gene, then the world's fastest and most power efficient computer.
The design principle spells SMASH: Small, Many, and Self-Healing. The system gains its advantage from a very large number of
simple processors working in parallel. This allows the organization as a whole to be self-healing: if one path fails others carry on
with the work. Applied to offering personal assistance, SMASH
suggests organizing people in a circle responsible to make sense
of and respond to their own changing circumstances, act within
the smallest necessary number of externally imposed constraints
to pursue goals that they define as desirable, and connect with
other circles as they choose.

The change was exhausting for all those involved. There were
vigorous, sometimes heated debates about what is possible and
who holds responsibility. There was anxiety at leaving behind
familiar arrangements and familiar complaints about their operation. The notion of a person's own home and assistance offered an
outline, but success, even physical survival, depended on 10,000
details, many of which could only be handled while living them.
There was sometimes anger and resentment at the demand that
parents and family members play a central role in decision making through active participation in a circle. People's trust in one
another and in the organization they had invested in creating was
tested and sometimes strained past the breaking point.

Despite the great cost, no person or family who made the journey regretted the change after they made it. No one wanted to
go back to the group home. This is not because life in one's own
home and chosen neighborhood is problem free. Problems are a
constant. What people found is that individualized arrangements
create better problems and also open the gates for people to journey toward inclusion.*

The design of organizations matters

JNCS' experience has important lessons for a better understanding of deep change in the way assistance is provided. Making
the changes was not just a matter of rearranging real estate, job
descriptions and procedures. It involved turning the way JNCS
understands and organizes itself inside out. As we reflect on this
change we see consistent trust in people expressed in rigorous
application of three principles of organization.

- The principle of **co-creative relationship**. What JNCS values can only be produced if each person and those the person counts on –whether family member, ally, staff person

---

* News of Jay Nolan Community Services today at: jaynolan.org

or manager– hold the person in their trust and faithfully maintain the intention to act together to assure and improve the conditions for a good life. At JNCS the complexity of people's impairments and the need to tailor assistance to changing individual circumstances generates a circle that holds each person in trust and manages their assistance.

- The principle of **subsidiarity** means that the power to make decisions belongs as close as possible to the site where valued experiences are co-created. That is, in the day-to-day interactions of person, community, and assistance imagined and implemented by the circle. This means developing judgment by supporting circles to continually improve their capacity to understand what is valuable, sense opportunities and generate paths into them, identify problems and solve them, live through breakdowns and errors and repair or be resilient to them.

- The principle of **minimum critical specification** calls for continence that inhibits the managerial reflex to multiply general rules that drive out particular circle's judgments and circle members' desire to escape difficulties and reinforce hierarchy by delegating tough decisions upwards to managers. It is essential to invest in building a practically useful, common understanding of what the organization values and the ambiguities those values introduce. For example, in some situations the value of respecting individual choice introduces a serious question whose answer has grave consequences: *What does it mean to respect this person's choice in these specific circumstances?*. There are clear agreements about which decisions must be reviewed outside the circle and which decisions that are reserved to the organization as a whole. Within these broad and thoughtfully defined boundaries, circle members work out how to best use the organization's resources to assist the person to live a life that they and those who love them have good reasons to value.

Deep change is tough

Trouble with change initiatives is not just a human service failing. A recent survey of well-financed and intensive change initiatives in business organizations where top managers were convinced that culture change was critical to profits showed that, about half of the efforts failed.[*] The reasons for these failures

---

[*] Strategy& (2014). *The 2013 culture and change management survey.* goo. gl/4SjDal

seem familiar: key people did not understand the need for change and did not feel engaged; past failures made people skeptical of the effort; competing loyalties and priorities created change fatigue; and systems, processes and priorities did not synchronize to support change. Its is important to design any organizational change effort to minimize these four pitfalls.

Creating the social inventions necessary to competently assist self direction and inclusion takes even better leadership than these commercial change efforts do. This is because the change entangles everyone involved in three kinds of uncertainty that make it tough.

- It is **socially tough** because the purpose of system change is to multiply expression of individual difference and greatly increase the diversity of community settings that people engage and contribute to. People and their assistants cross boundaries into community settings with a variety of customs and capacities. Change intimately concerns the wellbeing of people with different purposes, different world views, different capacities, different appetites for change and different tolerance for risk. Old style services subordinate these differences to prescriptions based on professional accounts of people's deficiencies that turn them into objects of expert authority. People are classified and managed in groups bounded and controlled by managers. Some people will challenge the process by preferring not to change. People will have very different understandings of key words like self-direction, inclusion and being person centered.

- It is **generatively tough** because the bridges to community life and the means to exercise self-direction have to be designed and built for each person and place. The specifics of community access and accommodation are less complex than creating the organizational competence and flexibility necessary to try new forms for inclusion. The mental model that currently shapes assistance repeats an endless loop of tales of deficiency and malfeasance that justify social exclusion and managerial control of even the minutest details of people's lives. Getting free of devaluing stories is adaptive work for everyone, including many people with developmental disabilities and their family members. Social invention is particularly challenging because some people actually depend on assistance 24 hours a day for their physical survival. Once free of an old, fear driven story, possibilities for social invention expand but the journey to social inclusion will be one of learning from many tries.

- It is **structurally tough** because two serious disconnects generate uncertainty about capacity to negotiate social issues in an open and creative way and capacity to generate and sustain the social inventions that will assist better lives. First, the greatest share of current investment operates settings that group, socially separate and supervise people on the basis of defined deficiency. Second, most of the system's management processes weight down self-directed journeys to social inclusion with a heavy burden of detailed regulations, anxieties about liability and mechanistic approaches to managing costs.

A social invention zone is a space where people who want to generate more real wealth in their communities can engage these three uncertainties in ways that go far enough to make a real difference. It is a network of people who choose deep change and resist the pressure to grab a quick fix by tampering with policies and structures. They invest in discovery of possibilities and redesign of the system, at least around those who want to act as partners for people on a journey to inclusion. Moving deeper into change, they investigate different perspectives and possibilities and identify the limits imposed by current structures and practices. They challenge the assumptions that shape current structures. They regenerate through connection to the highest potential in the situation and commit to the highest purpose in their own work. As re-designers, they re-frame mental models and assumptions and reorganize structures and policies to realize new possibilities. The network is the medium for sharing new ways and encouraging their adoption and refinement.

Action	**React** –find quick fixes	**Create** the new
Process	**Reorganize** –structures procedures & policies	*Redesign*
	Reflect	
Thinking	**Reframe** –mindset & assumptions	
Source	**Regenerate** –sources of commitment & creativity	

The social inventors' predicament

Pathfinders' journeys are shaped by two environments: the community that offers opportunities for contribution and the administrative structure that funds and regulates organizational and professional partners.

In the last century the administration of publicly funded assistance to people with developmental disabilities had considerable autonomy in government. In the late 1990's, public officials anticipated a substantial demand for publicly funded services from the steadily increasing population who will acquire disabilities as they age. They named and began to look for ways to manage long term care, an administrative concept that lumps elders who require assistance with activities of daily living with people with physical, sensory and developmental disabilities. Autonomy for developmental disability services has steadily decreased as structures and strategies for managing long term care for a larger and diverse client population have taken precedence, shifting authority over public funds and regulation out of the hands of system administrators. Administrators with general public management experience have often replaced administrators with deep roots among people with developmental disabilities.

At least in the US, response to a predicted massive increase in demand for long term care has been strongly influenced by larger social trends. Response to fiscal crisis included austerity measures to decrease government expenditures; political decisions are influenced by a sense of distrust of public services and trust in market mechanisms. Distrust of public services extends to a sense of unease about the people who use them. These trends have informed strategies for controlling the growth of long term care costs that include these practices.

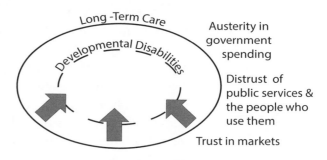

- Tie assistance tightly to assessed incompetence. This can limit assistants to delivering evidence based treatments for recognized conditions or define their job as efficient performance of well defined tasks that respond to inability to perform specific activities of daily living such as preparing meals or bathing.

- Employ objective measures to determine eligibility for services, define need for assistance and allocate funds. Repeated application of these measures assures that people remain eligible.

- Model funding for assistance on the US health insurance industry by shifting risk from government to managed care organizations that administer a capitated rate with incentives to steer eligible clients to the most cost effective means to meet their assessed needs.*

- Relying heavily on family members as providers of unpaid assistance, often for decades.

- Policing the long term care marketplace with multiple and repeated inspections to assure documentation of compliance with a growing number of requirements. Much effort goes to detecting fraud and assuring that public funds are only used for approved purchases.

- Assuming that quality can produced by a regime of setting standards and inspecting and correcting documented transactions between service providers and clients.

These strategies define a large scale social experiment to test the hypothesis that people with developmental disabilities and their families can flourish as contributing citizens under an administrative regime that makes personal assistance a closely controlled commodity delivered in conformity with standardized rules.

Pathfinders and their allies know that they can't count on this experiment to support their journey to self-direction and social inclusion, no matter what its managers believe they can promise. Partners throughout the system know that this experiment is approaching a crisis because they are at risk of being stripped of meaning in their work and turned into people they do not want to be: providers of survival level assistance and bookkeepers of transactions. Managers know that costs of compliance are rising toward the point of counter-productivity if they have not already past it. Everyone who cares about supporting people with developmental disabilities to act as contributing citizens can feel the space for social invention shrinking.

---

* If this paragraph seems written in a strange tongue, and your dictionary lacks a definition for "capitated" that fits the sentence, you understand an important point. Public services for people with developmental disabilities have reached the point where they are opaque to anyone not versed in health care finance jargon. Increasingly citizens can't understand these public functions, much less hold them accountable.

The difficulty is not with the problems administrators are trying to solve. Costs (though never care) must be managed prudently to create conditions for valued experiences. Expenditures need to be accounted. Offenses against dignity should be enjoined and disciplined whenever they occur. The difficulty is that counter-productive or unproven solutions take hold, discourage agency and become un-discussable. Failed efforts result in variations produced from the same mental model. For instance, regulations and penalties quickly become complex and overrun their benefit by distracting from or discouraging creative effort, but deficiencies revealed by close inspection justify more complex and detailed rules and sterner penalties. In this self-propelling cycle formal rationality (calculating how to follow the rules) drives out substantive rationality (figuring out how to get the most of what we value in particular circumstances).

Where people with developmental disabilities are concerned, there is a darker possibility for absencing to obliterate progress toward social inclusion. The belief that people with developmental disabilities are less than full and equal citizens because of their differences or because their impairments require publicly funded assistance remains common. Good enough for them may not include opportunities for employment outside a sheltered workshop or accommodation outside the cheapest available shelter. The assumption that segregated, professionally supervised places are where they are best off and happiest with their own kind appeals to many citizens who have had no real contact with people with developmental disabilities. *We are doing everything possible for them* locks in low expectations. Some people have an (unconscious) revulsion that reveals itself in statements like , *I'd rather be dead than be like that"* and in the still common practice of hospital staff assuming *do not resuscitate* orders for people with developmental disabilities admitted for ordinary health care.

Otto Scharmer sets this predicament in context by describing the competing forces of absencing and presencing that shape society in our moment of history.

> *We have entered a phase of increased tension between two principal sets of conflicting forces. The difference between them is that the first –the forces of fundamentalism, manipulation, and destruction–works by decreasing the degrees of freedom for the people involved. By contrast, the other set of forces increase freedom by shifting the inner place of operating and showing people*

additional ways to attend and respond to situations at hand.

The difference, simply put, is that the first looks at a human being as an object that is determined by its environment and conditioned by its past. As a consequence, it can be influenced, manipulated, and controlled through exterior mechanisms.

The second view sees human beings as subjects –carriers of a capacity to connect with a deeper source of creativity and knowing. Through this capacity, people can link with and realize a future that depends on each of us in order to come into being. The essence of the human being is to create through connecting to ones highest future possibility, one's authentic Self.

An adequate change strategy recognizes that people can only build a community that works better for everybody from their freedom. Freedom is activated when people have the opportunity to connect to their highest purpose, a purpose that engages them in realizing future possibilities that depend on their persistent and creative action in order to come into existence.

Pathfinders and their allies and partners face a struggle to claim the time and flexibility they need to begin their journey. The hero's journey to contributing citizenship takes courage and tests hope and resourcefulness. The possibilities are far greater because of the efforts of those who found the path out from under the spirit crushing weight of institutions. Today's constraints are no less daunting than those that travelers from the institution have overcome, but they are more annoying because they show up as a multitude of contradictions between administrative rhetoric of self-direction and citizenship and the reality of a space for action dominated by a swarm of no's that buzz around like the devil's flies.

People who want to build a community that works better for everyone will have more energy and better ability to find direction for the journey if they…

   … adopt practices that allow regular, even daily, renewal of connection to their highest purpose.

   … sustain membership a circle of people who can be trusted to hold one another's commitments to creating the beloved community.

   … engage the multiple intelligences of heart, head and hand as they take steps together toward inclusion and self direction.

... reach out widely to learn from, encourage and join diverse others with similar destinations.

Hope is a state of mind, not of the world. Hope, in this deep and powerful sense, is not the same as joy that things are going well, or willingness to invest in enterprises that are obviously heading for success, but rather an ability to work for something because it is good.

Hope is not the conviction that something will turn out well, but the certainty that something makes sense, regardless of how it turns out.

–Václav Havel

7

Lessons from Person-Centered Planning

For more than 30 years,[*] in one form or another, person-centered planning has been an important tactic in efforts to change organizations and systems. Under the right conditions it has also been an important support to pathfinders and their allies and partners as they journey to social inclusion and self-direction. Reflection on the ways that person-centered planning has made a difference, and failed to make a difference, offers some lessons about changing the way we try to change our system. It also shows the contribution person-centered planning can make to our preferred change strategy: multiply the number of pathfinders on a journey to social inclusion by increasing the number of organizations willing and able to be partners, and significantly expanding opportunities for self-direction.

Person-centered planning can be defined from two perspectives. Administrators and managers deploy bureaucratically defined person-centered planning as a means to improve the quality of service offerings. This is person-centered planning from the **top down**. From another point of view, person-centered planning is a multiplicity of practices that guide pathfinders and their families to imagine and move into lives that they have good reasons to value. These practices are co-inventions, adapted to individual situations. This is person-centered planning from the **outside in**.

From the top-down[†]

Person-centered planning interests reformers for at least four reasons.

---

[*] For a history, see Connie Lyle O'Brien and John O'Brien. (2002). The origins of person-centered planning in John O'Brien and Connie Lyle O'Brien, Eds. *Implementing person-centered planning: Voices of experience.* inclusion.com

[†] For an extended discussion with complete references see John O'Brien (2014). Person-centered planning and the quest for systems change. In Martin Agran (Editor). *Equity and full participation for individuals with severe disabilities: A vision for the future.* Baltimore: Paul Brookes Publishing. Pp. 57-74.

Person-centered planning enacts important values. The participation, voice and choice of people with developmental disabilities (and their families) are valued as central characteristics of good assistance. When capably done, many people and families experience person-centered planning as an accessible and engaging way to have their say about what they want from providers. Administrators and professional experts value evidence based practices. There is modest evidence that associates person-centered planning with desirable outcomes. Quality is valued. The prefix "person-centered" is sticky, all by itself it seems to express good quality in whatever it is attached to.

I call it theory-induced blindness: once you've accepted a tool and used it as a tool in your thinking, it's extraordinarily difficult to notice its flaws. If you come upon an observation that does not seem to fit the model, you assume there must be a perfectly good explanation, which you are missing.

–Daniel Kahneman

Person-centered planning can be understood in a way that fits neatly into the most common way of imagining system change: issue new instructions. In this story individual plans control the activities necessary to produce outcomes valued by the system. Person-centered planning is an incremental improvement in the construction of individual plans. It's a more interesting way to do what the system has been trying to do for half a century: assemble and coordinate packages of services that match needs.

Practices associated with person-centered planning do improve people's experience of assistance when staff attend to them in day-to-day practice. A one page profile that offers new helpers a positive introduction, a chart that identifies important relationships, a template for identifying what is important to a person and what is important for them, an expression of a person's vision– all of these instruments organize and transmit information that improves the quality of assistance when service workers pay attention to it.

Person-centered planning has figured in a number of influential accounts of change. People and families testify to positive effects; so do organization managers and system administrators.

The amount of territory covered by the words makes it hard to be precise about what people experience as person-centered planning. There are a variety of well established approaches, nine are identified on the facing page and there are many additional variations and combinations. The expected conditions for planning vary. A person might be surrounded by a thoughtfully convened planning circle and work through a well specified process with assistance from a highly trained facilitator. A person might follow an administratively defined routine with a case manager and a few support staff. Parents might work through an on-line form with their son (for example: mylifeplan.guide).

Approach	Defining features
Personal Futures Planning	Aims to generate powerful images of a rich life in community that will guide a search for opportunities for the person to take up valued social roles & develop service arrangements to support the person in those roles.
	Collects & organizes information by looking through a set of windows for change, which describe, for example, the person's relationships, important places, things that energize the person, the person's gifts & capacities, & ideas & dreams of a desirable future. goo.gl/qWJxPX
Pathfinders: Group Person-Centered Planning	A group-of-groups (5-8 focus people with their families and allies) support one another to make, implement & revise individual Personal Futures Plans. Emphasis on taking action toward a desirable future in a community setting before seeking services. Mutual support grows with shared discoveries, questions & resources. Groups do their own facilitation and recording with guidance from large group facilitator. Commonly used when people share a life transition, such as moving from school to adult life. goo.gl/h0VGFt
Make a Difference	Application of Personal Futures Planning to a way to build organizational capacity by developing individual learning partnerships between a staff member and a person the organization assists aimed at developing a contributing community role for the person. goo.gl/qWJxPX
PATH	A process that guides a person & their circle in discovering a way to mobilize their real wealth & move toward a positive and possible goal, which is rooted in life purpose, by enrolling others, building strength, & finding a workable strategy. goo.gl/aQtgBk
MAPS	A process that guides a person & their circle to clarify the person's dreams, nightmares & gifts; identify meaningful contributions; specify the necessary conditions for contribution: & make agreements that will develop opportunities for contribution. goo.gl/aQtgBk
Support Plans	A way to mobilize all available resources to support a person's citizenship. Based on six keys to citizenship: self-determination, direction, money, home, support, & community life. goo.gl/joFcMq and goo.gl/iYu4lP
Essential Lifestyle Planning (ELP)	Asks what is important to and for a person in everyday life. Specifies the support the person requires and person-specific ways to address issues of health or safety that balance what is important to the person & what is important for the person. Clearly identifies opportunities for improved assistance. Guides continuing learning about the person's supports in a way that is easily understood by those who assist the person. goo.gl/2tE32g
Person Centered Thinking Tools	A set of tools, mostly deconstructed from ELP, adopted through whole organization training, that develops the skills and behaviors necessary to think and work in a way that delivers person centered support at the direct support, agency management & system management levels. goo.gl/uUiplx
Facilitated Discovery	A systematic process for answering the question "Who is this person?" that generates a rich background for negotiating a customized employment role. Focuses particularly on people failed by typical methods for supporting employment. marcgold.com

In practice, how much benefit people with developmental disabilities experience from person-centered planning depends on four things: the real wealth available to the person through positive relationships, access to networks, assets and resourcefulness; the capacities that plan facilitators have developed to facilitate deep listening and mobilize resourcefulness; and, when the person relies on publicly funded assistance, the capacity for individualization and the actual influence person centered plans have on staff behavior. Different organizational strategies define distinct contexts for person-centered planning and have different consequences for pathfinders.

Strategy 1: Adopt new rules and procedures for individual plans to choose services and define outcomes

New rules* usually intend to strengthen the person's influence over the services they receive. They establish specifications like these. An eligible person's goals and desired outcomes have weight in the choice of appropriate and available services. The plan reflects strengths and preferences as well as clinical needs and needs for assistance. The person approves the plan. The person influences the process by shaping the agenda, deciding who to include in the meeting, when and where it is convenient to meet, choosing the person-centered planning approach and, sometimes, deciding who will facilitate the plan. In some places people can choose an independent facilitator or broker who will be paid from public funds to make the plan.

Rules may also reinforce objectives attached to a particular source of public funds. A correct plan may be required to address opportunities to seek employment, participate in community life, live in a community setting, minimize risks and assure health and safety. Person-centered planning may be expected to deliver some unpaid assistance to supplement or replace paid assistance.

This strategy imagines that person-centered plans operate like the specifications architects and engineers pass to builders to satisfy their client's requirements for a new building. The logic flows in a straight line. When people have more say in the choice of providers and in defining instructions to those providers, services will better satisfy people's needs and deliver positive outcomes.

---

* Two current examples can be reviewed in the Ontario Ministry of Community and Social Services, *Creating Good Life in Community: A Guide on Person-Directed Planning* (2013) goo.gl/YzkfUO and the January 2014 rule governing Home and Community Based Waivers (the largest source of public funding for assistance in the US) issued by CMS (The Centers for Medicare and Medicaid Services) goo.gl/AflVxs.

Plans that call for new capacities will signal organizations to develop those capacities. Better plans lead to better assistance which leads to better lives.

Adopting person-centered thinking and practices at the point of choosing a provider gives the people and their allies more voice and gives staff who assign services on behalf of the funding authority a more complete view of the person. This results in better informed decisions about the appropriate match of individual need to available assistance, managing risk, and assuring health and safety. It notifies the selected service provider of matters important to their client.

This strategy works in the system to refine the choice of service providers and the statement of desired outcomes. It addresses technical problems: definition of planning procedures, training of staff assigned to facilitate plans, capture and transfer of the information plans produce. It is done to people, at least in the sense that procedures and the rules that govern decision making are set by the administration.

To review the distinctions between working in and working on, technical and adaptive change, done to and done with see page 174

The effect of person-centered planning on people's access to their own homes, jobs and contributing community roles is limited by available organizational capacity. If the capacity to assist people to experience these benefits is already available, person-centered planning can guide people who want contributing community roles to providers who can assist them. Otherwise, there are stubborn limitations on the power of person-centered planning to deliver *Charter* values.

Simply changing expectations of individual planning does not assure negotiation of competing values in a person's favor. People's voices are amplified but can be drowned by other voices that speak up for compliance with rules designed to match assessed needs with funded assistance, control costs, manage risk and implement professional judgments about what keeps clients healthy and safe. Avoiding non-compliance can be so ingrained in organizational culture that it is not possible to negotiate creative ways to promote wellness, approach real risks with good judgment, and demonstrate the required connection between the assistance the plan specifies and the impairments that make the person eligible for publicly funded assistance.

Good assistance for valued social roles depends on grounded knowledge, created in a relationship of trust and tested in shared action. This strategy usually transmits information collected by routine under pressure. Administrators of scarce funds are seldom in a position to invest adequately in what it takes to make plans that energize action for social inclusion. Responsibility for person-centered planning is usually one among several duties assigned to case managers who are bureaucratically accountable for so many people that it is hard to build strong, trusting relationship either with people and families or among those who provide assistance to those on the caseload. This difficulty compounds when case manager turn over is high. Opportunities for learning and building capacity to listen and facilitate good plans are limited. Following the tempo of planning set by administrative rule (e.g. plan once a year; review after 6 months) doesn't respect the rhythm of reflection and revision that people trying new ways find useful. Committed case managers work hard to assure that people feel respected and heard, but time available to meet face-to-face is scarce, so deep listening, imagining better and creatively thinking through competing demands are constrained.

Under this strategy, the signal for organizational change from person-centered plans is weak. Most people who need assistance wind up selecting from the menu of currently available services, so initial expressions of desire for a different approach to assistance are damped. If people know about customized employment but no available provider offers it, placement in a community experience program is the option most likely recorded as the person's choice. Moreover, the means to convert ideas for new forms of assistance into action are usually under-resourced and over-committed.

Under this strategy, those who come into the process with sufficient real wealth and want to make the journey to social inclusion have a reasonable chance to line up some of the assistance they need. People with fewer assets, weaker networks and less resourcefulness will have to settle for less.

Strategy 2: Guide organizational reform with person-centered planning

This strategy assigns person-centered planning an important role in a larger, intentional effort to transform the system. Change is supported by administrative authority and dedicated resources. The stories on the facing page describe an initiative that employed, and researched, person-centered planning to achieve deinstitutionalization for people judged by available providers to be too difficult to serve.

From time to time, assistance to people with developmental disabilities becomes visible on the political agenda. In 2001, after wide consultation with people with developmental disabilities,

Two Perspectives on Person-Centered Planning

Here are summaries of two stories of person-centered planning written by the same authors from different perspectives. The first story,[*] published in a well respected journal, reports one of the few careful studies of the effectiveness of person-centered planning conducted and reported in proper social science form. The second story[†] is told about one study participant, written from the perspective of those who facilitated a meaningful change for him. It describes the substantial amount of work it took to disrupt the system's pull toward group based assistance and away from honoring the knowledge and choices of the person and his family.

The Willowbrook Futures Project involved 40 people who remained in state institutions because the extent of their challenging behavior exceeded the willingness of service providers to provide the supports they required despite their membership in a class entitled by court order to community placement. The study divided the group in half to contrast the effects of person-centered planning with traditional interdisciplinary team planning and assessed participants' quality of life at eight month intervals for almost three years. Compared to those receiving traditional Individual Service Plans (ISPs), person-centered planning participants were significantly more likely to move into a community living arrangement designed specifically for them; their teams were more strongly motivated to identify opportunities and solve problems than the ISP Planning teams were; and measures of autonomy, choice making, daily activities, and satisfaction showed greater improvement.

The second story from the Willowbrook Futures Project documents the perspective of those planning with Hal, one of its participants. Those involved in person-centered planning with Hal had to go far beyond making a good plan to deliver on the desired results of a home chosen by Hal's parents and taking steps toward community employment. Power shifted as Hal's parents were actively engaged in problem solving and decision making about where and with whom he would live and from whom he would receive assistance. Risks grew and subsided as safe ways for Hal to be present in family and community life were tested in action. An understanding of Hal's identity, interests and relationships framed the application of technical expertise in behavior analysis to support activities and relationships that mattered to Hal. Social inventions emerged: a community bridge builder, selected by Hal's parents, assisted him to try out a number of community roles in his new neighborhood before he moved from the institution; personalized funding for day services allowed him to escape long term placement in a disability-group space and routine that did not suit him when he tried it in favor of community activities that reflected his interests, engaged his competencies and setting him on course for a real job.

This took persistence and sustained commitment to values-guided problem solving and skillful advocacy. Despite legal advocacy for the move, a high level of flexibility and cooperation from system authorities, additional funding to support social invention, and an unusually high level of competence in team members and consultants there were significant delays. It took two years from the time Hal's father located a suitable house until the house satisfied administrative requirements and Hal could move in. There were strong pulls away from the more individualized, person-directed supports identified through person-centered planning into typical facility-based services. Hal gained access to a community life because his allies chose to use their power and competencies to partner with him.

[*] Holburn, S., Jacobson, J., Schwartz, A., Flory, M., & Vietze, P. (2004). The Willowbrook futures project: A longitudinal analysis of person-centered planning. *American Journal on Mental Retardation, 109*, 63–76.

[†] Holburn, S., & Vietze, P. (2002). A better life for Hal: Five years of person-centered planning and applied behavior analysis. In S. Holburn & P. Vietze (Eds.), *Person-centered planning: Research, practice, and future directions* (pp. 291–314). Baltimore: Brookes.

family members, service providers and professional experts, the English government adopted *Valuing People*, a policy that calls for transformational change in the nation's service delivery.[*] The policy goal is to assure that people exercise their rights, experience independence, have the power of choice in the services and supports they receive, and are included as active participants in their communities through employment in community jobs and other valued roles.

The change effort included new governance structures that provided people with disabilities and their families a key role in planning and decision making, carefully developed and authoritative guidance, a cadre of change agents and trainers, funds dedicated to the change, money for social invention and research and evaluation.

By design, person-centered planning plays a central role in the transformation process. It gives people the means to exercise their right to choose how they will be assisted and specify the ways they want to be active in community life. Person-centered plans steer local change efforts by making individual demands clear and available to local groups empowered to plan.

This is a strategy intended to work on the system by identifying and solving technical problems. Both person-centered planning and the local and national groups responsible for steering the change were designed with the intention of active collaboration with people and their families.

A centralized strategy, pushed from the top, has real advantages. Authority drives the change. There are dedicated investments of money and administrative attention to support the change. The change agenda focuses attention and increases openness to negotiation across organizational boundaries. Especially in the early stages, there can be opportunities for people with developmental disabilities and their families to influence the agenda and the structures that will manage the change and shape the resulting reorganization. In this context, person-centered planning can offer people real leverage on assistance for a better life. These are significant advantages, but they have limits, as a closer look at short and intermediate-term results show.

The initiative to implement person-centered planning to guide and energize the implementation of *Valuing People* included a

---

[*] Martin Routledge, Helen Sanderson & Rob Greig (2002). Planning with people: Development of guidance on person-centered planning from the English Department of Health. In John O'Brien and Connie Lyle O'Brien, Eds. *Implementing person-centered planning: Voices of experience.* inclusion.com.

longitudinal study that followed 93 people from four diverse localities that demonstrated a common approach to person-centered planning in a way that allowed an assessment of the impact of person-centered planning on their lives.[*] Large-scale training exposed a broad cross-section of people in each locality to the values and purposes of person-centered planning. Over two years, expert external consultants supported local organizations to develop policies, procedures and practices necessary to implement person-centered planning and provided intensive training (85-100 hours) and support to assigned local person-centered planning facilitators and local managers.

The measured impact over three years was meaningful but modest. Person-centered planning demonstrated positive impact on measures of contact with friends and family, choice of activities, and an increase in the number, variety and extent of community activities. Negative outcomes included greater staff perceived risk, more identified health needs, and more identified emotional and behavioral needs. These negative outcomes are probably the result of greater attention to health and mental health needs and staff perception that greater community presence is risky. Evidence of positive impact on inclusive social relationships or paid employment was lacking.

In the years since the study finished the *Valuing People* policy has been re-vitalized. Person-centered planning remains an important element of the reform and people's use of personal budgets has grown significantly, but delivery on key objectives remains modest. In 2011 about 15% of people in England funded for residential services lived in their own home and about 7% of adults with any degree of developmental disability worked regularly in either paid or unpaid jobs (the range across 152 local authorities is from 1% to 30% rate of employment among people served).[†] *Valuing People* has created many positive changes, but the tipping point to people's access to their own homes and jobs is yet to come.

There are many reasons for the limits on what *Valuing People* has accomplished so far. Some are circumstantial, others are built-in to the strategy. Many limits are the result of changing cir-

---

[*] J. Robertson, et al. (2006). Longitudinal analysis of the impact and cost of person-centered planning for people with intellectual disabilities in England. *American Journal on Mental Retardation* 111, 6: 400-416.

[†] E. Emerson, et al. (2012). *People with learning disabilities in England 2011: Services and supports.* Lancaster: Improving Health and Lives: Learning Disability Observatory.

cumstances. Local mangers responsible for implementing *Valuing People* were on the receiving end of repeated reorganizations and multiple targets driven by central government in addition to those specified by *Valuing People*. Reforms to long-term assistance to elders shifted attention away from people with developmental disabilities. Financial crisis reduced public investment and, after a change of government, local managers have had to deal with growing cuts to service budgets and benefits that fall heavily on people who require publicly funded assistance.

Some limits come with the design of the strategy. To make a big change in their short time in the political spotlight, strategists counted on mandates, expert assistance (including expert protocols for change management) and confidence in an unmet demand for employment and individualized supported living from people with developmental disabilities. These are good bets as far as they go, and political support is likely to depend on conviction in claiming that transformation is manageable and deliverable without much disruption or resistance.

Covering the rest of the distance to widespread self-directed and individualized support for contributing citizenship requires more room for addressing adaptive challenges and generating social inventions than *Valuing People* has been able to count on. Adaptive challenges arise when people who have to work together have real and important differences in what they value and how they understand their shared situations. When real loss is involved, people need opportunities to work through questions of fairness and the emotions stirred by shifting loyalties and attachments. When progress requires personal commitment and creativity rather than compliance and following instructions, people need ways to work out how their own purposes connect them to the effort. When expert knowledge can provide useful guidance but delivering on what reformers value depends on creating new capacities and figuring out how to open choice and valued social roles to specific people in particular communities, investing in space for social invention is critical.

Strategy 3: Person-centered planning as a medium for co-creating personal and organizational change

This strategy multiplies the numbers of pathfinders who find partners in a provider organizations. The context for person-centered planning is an organizational space or system supported network that invests in developing knowledge and encouraging action through a process of co-sensing opportunities and capacities, letting the highest potential in a situation come into presence, and learning through action. This social invention zone offers pathfinders flexibility in use of the system's assets.

Creating this space is largely a matter of what administrators and managers refrain from doing as a condition of their investment of trust, time and money. They don't flee uncertainty into a demand for plans that assure production of well defined outcomes deliverable on certain future dates. They don't require uniformity and premature standardization. They don't presume to fill the space by imposing their ideas of helpful training and technical assistance.

The journey is the living center of this strategy, not the plan. Person-centered planning serves a person's journey by convening those who support and assist, serving as a forum for negotiating adaptive challenges, encouraging deeper listening and finding purpose and potential in the knowledge that emerges, and organizing the recurrent process of learning by trying and improving creative actions. It is a process of working on the system to make adaptive change through co-created social inventions.

Administrators and managers are generous in support of social inventors connecting with each other for the exchange of knowledge, sharing skills and deepening understanding.

This strategy for person-centered planning depends on the free choice of people with different capacities who find a bond in the confluence of their sense of the difference they want to make in the world. This bond underwrites relationships of trust and forgiveness that grow with shared experience to create a *yes* space. A *yes* space supports deep listening and the emergence of creative action from diverse perspectives and capacities. Sometimes this *yes* space can feel like a tiny life raft navigating a stormy sea of *no*.

People can't be coerced or manipulated into this form of person-centered planning. The metaphor of consumer and supplier is exactly wrong for a relationship in which people of equal dignity choose to join their different capacities to discover new paths to contributing community roles. So are metaphors for system change wrong when they suggest that the work must be extrinsically motivated, like "driving" or "selling" transformation, or mechanistic metaphors for the process, like "technical assistance or training" that obscure the necessary source of creative action in people's co-discovery of a way to make some progress on the very difficult issues of social inclusion and self directed lives.

The schematic on the facing page shows the sequence of moves that Beth has refined from guiding many organizations to implement this third strategy.[*]

I. **Innovate**. The organization's managers take responsibility for social invention. A design team is composed and authorized to spend a budget of staff time and money. A way to negotiate for necessary flexibility in organizational rules and assistance routines is defined. The design team forms its vision of person-centered work by taking learning journeys to places that demonstrate potential and offer opportunities to study the nature of person-centered work and explore the implications of supporting contributing experiences and valued roles. They explore hopeful alternatives, crystallize their vision and engage pathfinders.

II. **Amplify**. The design team builds and deepens partnership with pathfinders and their allies. They begin to discover pathfinder's interests and connect to community places and associations. Initial involvements in community roles expand and deepen appreciation of capacities in pathfinders, support staff and community members. New ways to assist pathfinders emerge and begin to stretch and develop the organization's ability to individualize assistance.

III. **Activate**. Work in the first two quadrants builds capacity for social invention and individualization of assistance in community settings. In this quadrant the field of attention expands to sense opportunities for service to the whole community through meaningful engagement of pathfinders' strengths. The work includes creating possibilities for contribution, sensing opportunities by exploring local intelligence, getting involved and making a difference, crystallizing shared vision, and telling the story of a community that includes and benefits from pathfinder's contributions.

IV. **Associate**. Possibilities to inspire new partnerships and new initiatives will emerge. Pathfinders and their partners join other active citizens in co-initiating a partnership circle that engages collective will to create something together. This expands citizen's real wealth and makes local history.

Movement through the four quadrants is generated by following the celebration of each move with the question, *What more is possible if we act in a wider context?* The answers shift action into

---

[*] This process is described in detail in Beth Mount (2014) *The Imaginative Journey: Pathways to Citizenship.* www.capacityworks2.com

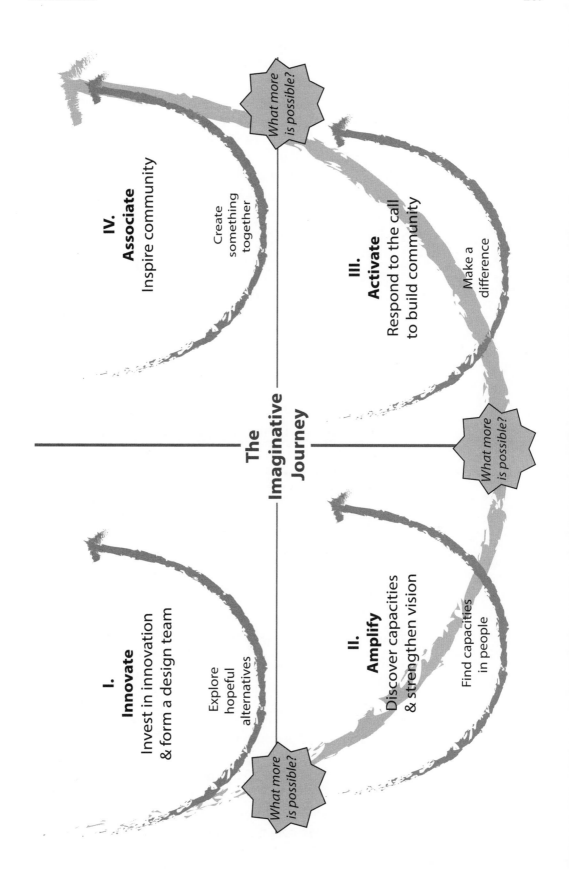

The Imaginative Journey

I.
Innovate
Invest in innovation
& form a design team

Explore hopeful
alternatives

II.
Amplify
Discover capacities
& strengthen vision

Find capacities
in people

III.
Activate
Respond to the call
to build community

Make a
difference

IV.
Associate
Inspire community

Create
something
together

What more is possible?

new, wider social fields that broaden and build capacities. Instead of jumping to tinker with structure and policies, the design team learns in action by freeing resources to identify and partner with people who want more in their lives. People's desire to make a difference challenges current structures of assistance and reshapes them to support individual participation in community life. Opportunities to build real wealth grow with the discovery of possibilities for building community and inspiring partnership.

Employing person-centered planning as a medium for partnership has characteristics that distinguish it from the other two top down strategies.

- It is a process of discovery. People's initial accounts of their preferences, interests and capacities are not taken as fixed. They are a point of departure for a search for community opportunities with the expectation that the journey will clarify and extend what people want.

- It crosses boundaries by design. Reforms to the way assistance is structured and offered come in response to providing what it takes for each person to contribute in a particular community place.

- The focus is on trying things in community places and sustaining and building on what works there. Meetings are opportunities to check-in, reflect, and renew direction; they are not the point of the process.

- Relative to the other two strategies it costs more in staff time, demands more organizational flexibility and entails more risk.

- It rests on a foundation of trust in people's capacity for development and in community members willingness to welcome.

From the outside-in

While most people today experience person-centered planning as it is defined and delivered top-down, there is a vibrant fringe where a mixture of people concerned with community building and system reform continue to practice and develop person-centered planning and person-centered work. The earliest approaches to person-centered planning originated from the outside in spaces where administrators were indifferent. These approaches developed to self-organize people to make institutions unnecessary for anyone, to include all students as active learners in neighborhood schools, to support community employment and secure homes, to assist young people to move into contributing roles, and to enable self and family direction of system resources.

Variations continue to develop from the diverse biographies, gifts and particular situations of practitioners. So the term person-centered planning applies to so many different practices that its easy to feel lost in a confusion of tongues.

It's easy to wonder, like Alice in *Through the Looking Glass*, how two words, person centered, can name so many very different things and still make sense.

> *'When I use a word,' Humpty Dumpty said, in rather a scornful tone, 'it means just what I choose it to mean – neither more nor less.'*
>
> *'The question is,' said Alice, 'whether you can make words mean so many different things.'*
>
> *'The question is,' said Humpty Dumpty, 'which is to be master -that's all.'*
>
> *Alice was too much puzzled to say anything; so after a minute Humpty Dumpty began again. 'They've a temper, some of them –particularly verbs: they're the proudest– adjectives you can do anything with, but not verbs…*
>
> *−Lewis Carroll*

It's also easy to identify with Humpty Dumpty and demand that someone decide what is "really" person-centered and what is counterfeit.

If system administrators tolerate ambiguity and refrain from enforcing definition by regulation, Humpty Dumpty provides two clues to sorting the rich variety of practices labeled person-centered. First, be clear about who is master of resources. The most common rationale for person-centered planning is to increase the person's control of their life, but the extent of self-direction depends on a person's everyday environment far more than discussions at planning meetings. In some settings a person can effectively direct no more than exactly what the staff present at the moment are willing to allow. Even an individual budget can have so many attached strings that a person has little autonomy. When methods of funding, regulating and inspecting do not open easily to principled negotiation, very little of what a person or family member says has effective force. A service structure that unilaterally defines what's available to people or regulates funds and the supply of assistance in ways that predetermine a person's options has a less than generous understanding of person-centered work.

Second, pay attention to the verbs. *Adjectives you can do anything with, but not verbs.* What can people say they do as a result of person-centered practices:

> *I'm an usher at church. I greet people and help take up the offering.*
>
> *I'm growing vegetables in the community garden.*
>
> *I'm using my new communication device to take on more responsibility at work.*
>
> *I decided to learn to read.*
>
> *Now I open the front door to my own home with my own key.*
>
> *I go to Choir! Choir! Choir! almost every time.*
>
> *I'm saving to buy an engagement ring.*
>
> *I had to fire a staff person I liked because he just couldn't get here on time.*
>
> *I'm working with my nurse to self-manage my diabetes.*

These are expressions of agency, a person's exercise of freedom to engage in experiences that have meaning for them.

The positive core of person-centered planning

Another set of verbs express the co-creative heart of person-centered practices. They are simple words: gather, listen, plan, act. Each entails the others in a process that repeats. The amount of effort these verbs demand depends on the nature of the change desired. Changes that make life better without stretching rules or routines too much, creating difficult conflicts or requiring new resources will usually demand less than changes that develop new capacities, stretch people outside their comfort zones and demand negotiation of emotionally charged differences among key people.

Gather. No one makes their life alone. A reasonable balance between what is important to a person and what is important for them, the confidence that hopeful action matters, the power to imagine better, the connections that open doors, the social models who demonstrate possibilities, the support to be resilient to disappointment or loss, all are the fruit of relationships with trusted people. When people occupy a devalued social status and have experienced exclusion, co-creation is all the more vital because they are vulnerable to a diminished, negative and hardened story about who they are and who they might become; a story that they might have difficulty resisting without the support of others who believe in a better future for them.

Sometimes it's hard to face how few people there are to gather with a person or how sure a person or family has become that no one else could have a genuine interest in their future. It's tempting to dodge this by just having a meeting and calling it person-centered. It's better to face the issue in a creative way. Richard Ruston a Canadian leader of advocates with developmental disabilities, pulled together the resources necessary to offer workshops in which people became one another's support group. The groups considered videos of hockey great Wayne Gretzky and other public figures as models of ambitious goal setting and persistent effort, shared the ways they exercise choice in their lives, practiced picturing and sharing their dreams and coached one another to take next steps in a positive direction.

Listen. Many practitioners use the metaphor of depth to distinguish the forms that listening can take. Listening can be a matter of getting down the words or images necessary to fill up a template, maybe in a rush to get to the familiar ground of an action plan or in a hurry to beat the clock running on the annually required person-centered planning meeting. Deeper listening supports a person to draw more of the threads of their story together and feel a greater clarity about what is possible and desirable. It also tends to increase trust, draw people closer and align their energies. Deeper listening creates a space in which more authentic dreams can emerge and be shared. More than a step toward change, this form of listening itself can develop capacity.

> Our job is to hear people into speech.
> –Nelle Morton

Plan. Planning is the form of conversation that gathers up what a group knows about a person's purpose and the capacities available to them, sets direction, sketches at least a first approximation of the way a desired change can happen, and encourages group members to commit themselves to making specific changes. If the way to what is desired is well known and the resources necessary are available, a plan can look like a blueprint and be produced routinely. When the way is less familiar and capacities and resources must be developed, a plan will set direction for a journey into new territory. When people have need of good individualized support on a daily basis there will be very frequent back-of-a-napkin plans to guide a week's explorations or make adjustments that increase the chances of a good day.

Act. This is the time when conversation flows into trying new things in new ways. If the intention is to make a significant change, it is a time of risk taking and boundary crossing, of victories and disappointments, of commitments honored and defaulted. Prototypes are designed, tested and revised.

How Are We Listening?*

The way we listen is fateful. It makes the difference between a person-centered planning meeting that just re-cycles old news while it does the service system's business and a process that reveals new possibilities and energizes commitment to action that will change the lives of every one in the planning circle in good ways.

Level of Listening	Experience	Result
LISTENING 1 *downloading*	Everything happened just as I expected.	No change. Nothing new. Small changes; mostly more of the same.
LISTENING 2 *debating*	I became aware of some new facts and ideas that challenged my assumptions and shifted the way I make sense of the situation.	Taking account of new realities; better informed. More aware of assumptions and alternative ways to understand current reality.
LISTENING 3 *dialogue*	I have seen the situation, and my place in it, through the eyes of someone whose experience is different from mine. I have a new sense of how another person experiences the situation and how they feel it. My own feelings resonate with those of another.	Awareness of real differences; deeper understanding of aspects of the situation that have been hidden or avoided.
LISTENING 4 *collective creativity*	I am not the same person now that I was when I entered this conversation. Together, we generated possibilities that did not exist when the conversation started. I have sensed something new that calls to be born through our action.	Renewed sense of my identity and life work. Energy and commitment for action to realize the highest potential that has been revealed.

*The table is based on an video on listening presented by Otto Scharmer in the edX course, *U.Lab: Transforming Business, Society & Self*, 21 January 2015. For more information: www.presencing.com.

Authentic person-centered practices invest time and creative energy in gathering people, opening a listening space that allows appreciation of an important part of person's story and emergence of ideas about a better future, making a plan for moving into that better future, and generating action that results in new capacities. As a result, people will experience greater effective control over their lives, do more as valued members of their community and build real wealth.

Differing gifts, different purposes

Person-centered planning is dynamic.* People with different gifts and interests have developed a wonderful variety of practices, as Judith McGill's story of the origins of LifePath Planning on the following pages illustrates.

Different approaches have developed in response to different life circumstances.

- Assuring that helpers and professionals appreciate the person's value and know what accommodations and assistance the person needs in order to have a productive interaction or a good day.

- Going to school in an inclusive way.

- Making a transition from school into young adulthood.

- Finding and succeeding in a job or civic role.

- Supporting families to develop their particular answer to the question, "What will happen for my son or daughter when we are no longer able to be in his or her life?"

- Moving from the family home into a home of one's own.

- Feeling it's time for a change, sensing a turning point, a desire for something better.

- Moving from an institution.

- Being served by an organization or system engaged in a change that involves the adoption of person-centered practices.

- Experiencing breakdowns in assistance that lead family or service staff to acknowledge that current arrangements are not working and there is great risk without substantial change.

---

* Read interviews with some of the originators of different approaches that explore the development of their work in John O'Brien and Carol Blessing, Editors. *Conversations on citizenship and person centered work.* www..inclusion.com

Origins of LifePath Planning

Judith McGill

When I was a young girl, I was given the opportunity to be a peer tutor in the classroom way down the hall on the other side of the school called the "trainably mentally retarded" class. I was given a pocket full of jelly beans to motivate a young boy who had autism. This experience shaped the rest of my life. I learned that relationships meant a whole lot more than jelly beans.

In the early eighties, while I was in university, I had two co-op placements that cracked me wide open. I worked in two large institutions. One was built for people with developmental disabilities. I was drawn to those who were placed in the back wards of that institution. The other was built for those they then called juvenile delinquents. I was told on my first day that these kids were the worst of the worst and the bottom of the barrel. They were between 12 years of age and 16. Many of them have been on the street since they were 10 and found themselves in correctional services at the age of 12. This was a place where they formed deep identities of being criminals.

I found both of these institutions dehumanizing places for those that lived there and for the staff. I witnessed people feeling abandoned. Their stories were hardened into labels and dead ends. The children released from the correctional center conspired to commit another crime so that they could return back. The prison had become home. Their identity relied on staying in prison.

Then I was hired at Ceci's Homes, an initiative that had set about to bring children who had spent the first part of their lives in a children's institution to a place they can call home. All of these children had complex labels, most considered medically fragile. I learned mostly that people want to belong and that the longing is for relationships. It helped them to understand that change emanates from that desire.

In 1983 when I graduated from university I was hired by the National Institute on Mental Retardation (NIMR) which became the G. Allan Roeher Institute (GARI) to promote a book written by John Lord, entitled *Participation: Supporting People with Severe Disabilities in Community*.

Only 10 days later I was given the opportunity to attend a 10 day course led by Wolf Wolfensberger. Wolfensberger altered the course of my life. He began the course with an elaborate critique of the wounds that people who have a disability are typically exposed to. He was singing my song – that is all I can say. His analysis rang true. I had been living it all my life. First as a child with a life threatening illness that made it difficult for me to walk. And secondly as a sister whose brother was born with cerebral palsy.

Wolfensberger helped me to more deeply understand why my brother had begged me to take him home when we arrived mid-session to the summer camp for the family visit. His disorientation and confusion rattled me. *Judith, why am I here? What is wrong with me? What is wrong with them? Who do I have to get them dressed? Why am I the only one in my cabin that can walk?* At the age of 9 he was struggling with the incongruity of roles and the injustice of walking between two worlds. One where he was valued and pretty much accepted in a regular class and another where he was sent off to a segregated camp with others who had one thing in common with him- his cerebral palsy. I was 21 at the time. I realized that he was trying to put together a coherent picture of who he was. He was searching not only for his identity but also for his own story. As a family we had taken that from him by telling his story for him.

The Wolfensberger workshop on Personal Moral Coherency set a course for the rest of my life. I became taken up with how we form and reform our personal identity, our sense of self. What gives us access to the good things in life and what keeps us from being marginalized?

At the GARI, I did a lot of assessments based on Wolfensberger's theory and appreciated the depth of striving to come to know folks through their life experience. I began writing about the power of leisure identities for people to find their place in community.

After leaving the GARI I worked for 8 years with the People First movement. This dramatically influenced how I came to listen and support folks. I became aware that what was really missing in peoples lives were initiation rites. Coming of age gatherings that help us make meaning that help us re-story our lives. That help us see the progress we are making and give us collective acknowledgment of key milestones and thresholds in our lives. This is why the formal part of LifePath planning helps create initiatory experiences that provide a turning point in peoples lives. A moment that signals "that was then and this is now, and you were all here when a change began."

I realized that those people who inspired me most had a felt sense that *I can do it*. They would tell me that they know this to be true because they had someone who believed in them. I realized then that it only took one other person who told a different story about who I was and what I was capable of to embolden me to carry the same story, even when it is at odds with the story everyone else tells about me.

I became committed to formal planning events where the alternative story gets told and heard. Where Champions can stand by the person and deepen their connection and commitment and consider if they want to be part of a longer standing support circle. LifePath planning events model what a support circle would be like and then scaffold the group to consider forming a support circle.

I have learned that we can excite people and whet their appetite for taking charge of their life. However if there are others who carry the decisions in their life, they need to be engaged and on board or sabotage can occur. We change together.

In 2000 I co-founded Families for a Secure Future because I realized that people need to find ways to be heard and balance out the negative stories people were telling about them. I learned to help people find ways to…

… contend with their will and how crushed their will forces were. Reactivate their will and their willingness to risk once again.

… have models for change.

… co-inspire one another to act differently.

… develop a broader scope of action by practicing change.

… develop a context for supported decision making by having others help them consider things differently.

… feel they can trust again.

… create a story space where there was enough time to develop a story and be heard –a space where voice emerges.

… have time to piece together what happened to me since I was labeled.

… make the silences draw forth story.

… take thin, meager stories and develop some richness and thickness.

… have others witness my life, my story

… work against the narcissistic viewpoint that "since I have the disability it is all about me" by hearing my parents' and siblings' stories and other's stories so that I can understand my own in the context of their stories and learn to hold other peoples' dreams as well as my own.

LifePath planning is directed at doing just that. (More at www.lifepathtraining.ca)

Approaches have differentiated as people gather to support change in different ways. Some practices match the structure of service organizations; others emerge from the self-organization of families and people with developmental disabilities. Some gatherings are ad-hoc and others have lasted for years.

- Influencing the way teams of service providers think about and offer assistance by providing tools and practices to guide team performance.

- Reshaping assistance with a person who challenges their assistance beyond its current limits.

- Coming together as self-advocates to support one another in reaching for new goals and opportunities.

- Meeting as a planning circle with a person who is on an important threshold in their life.

- Guiding action with a continuing circle of support for a person (some people prefer to call this a personal network or support network).

- Offering mutual support and organizing collective responses to members' concerns in a circle of circles or Family Group.

Each way of gathering creates a different locus of power. People who belong to a Family Group of strong and diverse circles have more capacity for action than people whose future is primarily determined within service world, by the disposition of system resources. When people and families depend primarily on developmental disability services, their influence depends on what the system grants in the way of funding, the flexibility and competence with which service organizations choose to individualize supports, and the willingness of system decision makers, including direct support workers, to heed their voices. While environments organized to support power-with are most hospitable to person-centered planning, practitioners have found ways to do good work under any distribution of power.

Broadly common values link different approaches:

- People with developmental disabilities should enjoy the rights and responsibilities of citizenship and exercise choice.

- Services should honor people's preferences about how they want to be assisted and support them to accomplish goals that have meaning for them

- People should be accorded the dignity of risk

- A variety of friendships and relationships are important to well being and engagement in activities that encourage relationships deserve active support
- People should be included in community life in ways that matter to them
- People should have the assistance necessary to develop to the full extent of their potential.

These values shape resistance to pressures that impoverish the lives of people with developmental disabilities by confining them in service provider controlled, segregated settings preoccupied with avoiding risk and liability and busy assuring compliance with the demands of bureaucracies that presume to know best what is good for people and what is possible for them.

These values find different expressions among practitioners. The various forms of person-centered practice emphasize distinct inquiries, shaped by the kinds of action their designers particularly want to invite. For example…

…to give people and families a tool that will personalize their interactions, focus on positive markers of the person's identity and what others should know about what works best to assure the person's success.

…to make sure that professional interventions and technology have real relevance, to be specific about what the intervention will enable a person to do.

…to change the culture and practices of service organizations by encouraging careful consideration of a person's human needs and how they are optimally met or by training the whole organization in the use of person centered thinking tools as part of an organization or system development initiative.

…to assist people's active participation in valued social roles and act from a rich and coherent story of oneself as resourceful; inventory capacities, imagine and reach out to make the social connections through which they can develop; make a space for people to tell and re-tell their story and listen for cracks in stories that have become hardened around diminished expectations; encourage expression of dreams and nightmares and identification of gifts; support the person to clarify a sense of highest purpose.

Approaches also reflect practitioners' interests and gifts. Some practitioners are deeply committed to people who have no one to count on but service workers; others are called to organize families or self-advocates. Some frame person-centered practices as a form of community organizing; others set them in the context of service reform. Some are interested in systematically improving the broad mainstream of service provision; others want to work at the very edge of social invention; still others want to support people to thrive with only the necessary minimum of service involvement. Some want to create tools that are easily accessible so many people can benefit; others offer practices that demand that facilitators commit to substantial personal development. Some find rational change management models helpful; others are attracted to non-linear ways of hosting emergent development. Some inquire and record in straightforward entries into forms; others work in narrative, image and metaphor through graphic and artistic media. Some draw on well elaborated theories such as social role valorization to gauge the worth of their efforts; others look to participant's expressions of satisfaction to validate their work.

The diagram on the next page summarizes some the differences that account for the variety of authentic approaches to person-centered planning.

The range of ways to guide better fit between people and publicly funded assistance and journeys to social inclusion and self-direction shows the depth of inventiveness that commitment to good lives generates. The bureaucratic functions of the system have framed their own concept of person centered planning to serve administrative purposes. This risks losing ground for commitment and creativity to compliance and standardization.

Review social invention zones on page 170

Social invention zones are critical in managing this risk. A system that invests generously in open space for partnership and invention will develop ever better forms of assistance and the multiple approaches to person-centered planning that can steer discovery and change. Even more important are self-organized groups that preserve freedom of action by emerging outside bureaucratic boundaries from commitments to inclusion and self-direction that transcend people's system roles and lead them to invest their own real wealth.

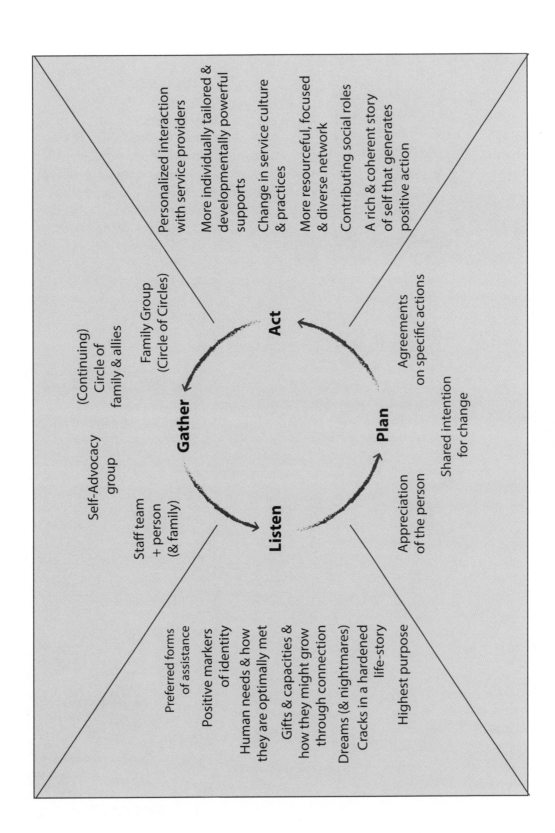

Gather

Listen

Plan

Act

(Continuing) Circle of family & allies

Family Group (Circle of Circles)

Self-Advocacy group

Staff team + person (& family)

Agreements on specific actions

Shared intention for change

Appreciation of the person

Personalized interaction with service providers

More individually tailored & developmentally powerful supports

Change in service culture & practices

More resourceful, focused & diverse network

Contributing social roles

A rich & coherent story of self that generates positive action

Preferred forms of assistance

Positive markers of identity

Human needs & how they are optimally met

Gifts & capacities & how they might grow through connection

Dreams (& nightmares)

Cracks in a hardened life-story

Highest purpose

Dismissing the Old and Letting the New Emerge

New ways of planning and working together call for new designs for learning. Typical training methods can't hold the work that people need to do to become capable facilitators of real change. Andreas Oechsner, Lisa Wimmler and Angelika Pichler, (with Beth Mount in the picture) of Zentrum für Kompetenzen Zeit für Veränderung in Austria form a team that searches for authentic ways to call person-centered planning facilitators to their highest potential based on Theory U. They form learning circles of about 30 people –people with developmental disabilities, family members, workers, administrators– who gather as equals. Circles meet six times over nine months.

Angelika says, *Change happens when people get talking and connect. Change is a lot about deep listening with a beginner's mind and above all listening with an open heart. The circles exist to give people an experience of what it really means to see and listen with the heart.*

Cultivating relationships is the heart of their work. Circles gather in the presence of Lotto, a statue of a turtle, who symbolizes slow and steady movement through phases of the U Process at the core of person-centered work. Observe, observe, observe; listen for the highest potential in people and communities; act in an instant by taking the next step toward ideals. Lotto represents quiet sensing of each person's longing and potential. Imaginatively speaking, Lotto trusts that deep wisdom will come if we go slowly and listen not only to the highest potential in each person but also to the suffering that complicates the lives of people with disabilities and their allies. A history of exclusion can create a taboo zone of undiscussable possibility that cuts people off from their highest potential. Lotto knows that people can't move deep into possibility without the care and courage to live into the ordeals that come to life when people reach for more in life. Through deep listening and steady efforts to explore new possibilities every circle member discovers their next edge and finds support from the group to step out.

Lisa summarizes her learning from this process:

- *If we manage to remain open for what people bring in and if we trust that every person has something to contribute, we strengthen people, we connect and eventually something wonderful will emerge.*

- *The taboo zone is the place where you find real stories and wisdom.*

- *When we start to strengthen people in what they really want to do, they'll achieve the impossible.*

- *I am always part of change. My social role changed from a passive learner to an active creator and learner in a team.*

- *We have to think about ourselves and we need to sense a field and dive into it in order to be able to accompany the people we encounter.*

In the learning circle Lotto is surrounded by beautiful hand made posters, carefully designed to guide each conversation. The circle encloses colorful felt boards with movable elements that remind people of the phases of the U process and the four levels of listening. While the trio has a plan for each segment of group work, they also improvise, checking in and changing course along the way in response to what matters most to participants. This models good facilitation of the process of person-centered planning.

Reflecting on the circle's learning from Theory U, Andreas says, *To me change is all about seeing our very individual images: of situations, of people, of myself. Letting go of images that do not take us to the next step or that just pursue more of the same is the core element of change. Not only dismissing old images by just replacing them by new images like a slide show, it means the flow of dismissing the old and letting the new emerge. Theory U is not a technique that can be carried out step by step. It's an ongoing movement of observing, becoming present and trying. Exploring people's capacities and finding places that need these capacities is the foundation of change.*

8

An Ecology For Self-Direction

*The absence of freedom is the imposition of restraint on my delib-
eration as to what I shall do, where I shall live, how much I shall
earn, the kinds of tasks I shall pursue. I am robbed of the basic
quality of [hu]man-ness. When I cannot choose what I shall do
or where I shall live or how I shall survive, it means in fact that
some system has already made these a priori decisions for me,
and I am reduced to an animal. I do not live; I merely exist. The
only resemblances I have to real life are the motor responses and
function that are akin to human-kind. I cannot adequately assume responsibility as a person because I have been made a party
to a decision in which I played no part in making.*

–Martin Luther King

Self-direction is a form of interdependence that expresses
agency –a person's capacity to reveal and develop their identity,
purposes, and capacities in relationships and community roles.
Strength of agency depends on the real wealth a person can mobilize, their community's openness to inclusion, and the adapt-
ability of the assistance necessary to their success.

Real Wealth page 24

   In elemental form, people with developmental disabilities
demand that others respect their dignity, take their purposes
seriously and act as allies to support their choices. Tia Nellis,
then president of Self-Advocates Becoming Empowered (SABE),
addressed an international audience of reformers with this call to
interdependent agency, *We are going to live self-directed lives and
we need all of you to help us do it!* This cry originates in the deep
human desire to live one's own life rather than adapting to a life
prescribed and programmed by staff charged to supervise clients.
Many people with developmental disabilities understand self-direction as being responsible for their own lives without carrying
the burden of paternalistic overseers who demand obedience
because they can enforce a claim to know best. Resonance with
this desire draws allies and partners to join pathfinder's journeys
toward self-direction and social inclusion.

We choose to say self-direction. Others say self-determination. We see the terms as
interchangeable.

It is helpful to distinguish self-direction in life from self-direction of the publicly funded assistance a person requires. In life, self-direction is the capacity to steer one's situation in matters large and small, to decide what really matters. Where to live. What to do for work. Whether to marry. Whether to have and raise children. When to go to bed. What to have for breakfast. To choose a direction and move toward it does not guarantee success. Wishing for a driver's license isn't enough, the first step requires studying the manual and passing a test. Self-direction is the choice to work toward the license or to give up. To realize a dream doesn't guarantee lasting satisfaction. Intimate relationships sometimes break up and cause hurt. A person can make better or worse decisions, work hard or slack off. Self-direction is having choices to make and taking responsibility for those choices. Self-direction isn't the act of an isolated individual imposing their will on the world. *Self* is best understood as a relational term. Others matter as partners and sources of support and opposition. Effective self-direction emerges from constructive interdependence.

Self-direction takes a particular focus when a person relies on publicly funded assistance. In this context it refers to the capacity to align the assistance a person requires with the life that they want to live. This matters because service structures and practices have presumed control of people's life decisions. A person who lives with a roommate in a group home under policies that discourage sexual expression will find it hard to pursue a close relationship. Settings can constrain the pursuit of life goals by design. A person who wants a career in child development will find little relevant help if trapped in a day program that packages fishing lures. Compounding these limits, many people with developmental disabilities are judged to lack mental capacity. This extinguishes their status as persons before the law and subordinates them to the will of guardians charged to act in their best interest. A legal guardian can decide that pay for a real job will threaten a person's benefits and retain them in a day program. Because the form that publicly funded assistance takes shapes so much of so many people's lives, attention to self-direction of assistance matters. Progress depends on developing ways to co-create flexible and personalized assistance. This requires mindful interdependence.

The idea of self-direction as a form of interdependence sits uneasily with common understandings of independence. A mental model, common and usually unquestioned in the US, sees self-direction as autonomy and autonomy as the rational choices made by separate individuals in pursuit their self-interest by asserting

It is our ability to be in relationships with others rather than our ability to be self-sufficient that should anchor our understanding of what it means to be a person. We do not become a person without the engagement of other persons –their care, as well as their recognition of the uniqueness and connectedness of our human agency, and the distinctiveness of our particularly human relations to others and of the world we fashion.

–Eva Kittay

their individual preferences. This understanding highlights the separate individual and celebrates individual effort. Agency is earned in proportion to capacities. The greater a person's ability to do for themselves and impose their will, the more power they deserve. This individualistic story generates dichotomies. The light switch is either set on independence and agency or flipped to dependence and obedience. Those who can't act without assistance are assigned to a dependent status, which diminishes their dignity and restricts the choices available to them. This story is so strong that it obscures all the helpers that powerful people depend on to get through their day.

This is a mental model so thin as to be a completely false guide. It denies the lived reality of free people with substantial impairments and traps them in a story of devalued dependence. If all people with intellectual and developmental disabilities bear equal rights with other citizens, as *The UN Charter on the Rights of Persons with Disabilities* says that they do, our communities need social inventions that dignify the interdependence of all humans and offer a variety of practical ways to determine and honor each person's will and preferences.

> We never have the foggiest idea what people need until we give them those unique resources that allow them to be an active part of the community making their own choices. Then we'll see what they need of us.
>
> –John McKnight

This story of isolated choosers misdirects attention in another way. It takes power-over others as a condition for successfully asserting self-interest and self-interest as an individual matter. The alternative to being on the bottom is being on top. Others impose limits on my will, and concern for common wealth penalizes me. Pursuing self-interest means competing with others who have little regard for me other than as an instrument for their ends. This story fits the situation of people with developmental disabilities poorly. They do need assistance, sometimes a great deal of assistance funded with public money, and, at present, many have much less real wealth than others do. Advocates who draw inspiration from civil rights struggles often say that power cannot be given, it must be taken. But in a struggle to take power over the structures that assist them, people with developmental disabilities and their families are at a distinct disadvantage. Even if they did become kings and queens of the mountain, most people with developmental disabilities would need a substantial amount of cognitive and intimate physical assistance to hold their throne.

> Independence is not about being able to do things for yourself. It is having whatever support you need to do what really matters in your life.
>
> –Ed Roberts

To invent the form of assistance that promotes self-direction, we need a better story about self-direction. A better story recognizes equal dignity among citizens who require different kinds and amounts of assistance. It is founded on Ed Robert's insight that agency grows from having the support necessary to do what really matters to you, not on the tasks you can do alone. (Ed was a founder of the Independent Living Movement.) A better story values power-with. It celebrates interdependency and values the struggle of people with diverse and unequal resources to co-create the conditions for all people, including those who depend on publicly funded assistance, to live their lives in ways that they and those who love them have good reasons to value.

Self-direction boxed-in

[A management consulting firm was] looking for people who had the talent to think outside the box. It never occurred to them that, if everyone had to think outside the box, maybe it was the box that needed fixing.

–Malcolm Gladwell

Service administrators transpose concerns for human rights and freedom into professional tools and administrative mechanisms. When this is successful service resources align with the substance of the concern. Less successful transpositions leave tools and terms loose to float away from substance.

Within the boundaries of services, effective control of publicly funded assistance by the person and family who rely on those resources defines the substance of self-direction. People and their allies hold responsibility for aligning their share of public resources with their own purposes and preferences. This understanding deeply disrupts a culture permeated with supervision through paternalistic and bureaucratic control. It's no wonder that less radical ways to understand self-directed services have grown influential.

Self-direction shows up in service-world contexts as…

…a purpose given for policies and practices that increase the choices given to people in provider controlled settings. For example, residential service staff may grant the choice of bedtime and wardrobe, a voice in choosing activities and menus, a say in who attends a person-centered planning meeting, access to intimate privacy.

…skills for people with developmental disabilities to achieve, perhaps through a curriculum for special (adult) education that teaches skills of goal setting, decision making, assertiveness, planning and problem solving, and grit in pursuit of goals.

…an intervention among the practices that provide positive behavior support to people with challenging behavior.

In capable hands these are worthwhile measures that improve everyday life in a service setting and increase real wealth by building capacities and resourcefulness. They strengthen the person exercising self-direction. But in themselves these measures don't necessarily increase a person's influence over their living conditions, the roles available to them or the form of assistance they receive. Control remains in the hands of those with responsibility to supervise, instruct and intervene. Staff who granted a choice can withdraw it, perhaps after negotiating administrative permission to implement a restrictive measure. A person whose dream is a home of their own may find it hard to enroll their corporate guardian in disrupting a stable nursing home placement. Some self-direction classes proceed in segregated settings that offer only a few of the most successful student real options for contributing community roles.

Self-direction also names a financing method that offers people the option of directing an individual budget. In this context, self-direction...

> ...grants people (and their families) consumer status by allowing them to direct an individual budget to choose among administratively approved service providers to meet assessed need defined in the way defined by a support plan. The consumer's role is to negotiate the terms and get approved assistance in the most cost-effective form available.

> ...grants people (and their families) service manager status through an individual budget and the authority to meet system assessed and approved needs and recruit, train, schedule, supervise and fire assistants according to an agreed support plan, administrative rules and labor laws.

These measures have merit and they box self-direction firmly within administrative boundaries. They are the gift of administrators who define peoples' zone of agency and specify conditions for use of their grant of an individual budget. Policy and the structure of assistance is shaped by the mental model that administrators act from. Their mindset defines the dimensions of self-direction.

Understanding the boxes that limit the power of self-direction begins the search for ways to make publicly funded resources available to pathfinders and their allies in more flexible, generous and challenging ways. Getting taken-for-granted mental models that shape people's agency into the light where they can be examined and tested begins the struggle to unlock the boxes constraining self-direction. Some mental models reproduce more of the same because they lack a reminder to renew purpose and revise themselves. Without mindful reconsideration a mental model gets taken as the whole story of the way things are rather than one story among many about how things can be. One way to surface mental models asks,

A good theory is one that holds together long enough to get you to a better theory.
–D.O. Hebb

Free to Live His Life as He Wants To

Muriel Grace, Vici Clarke and Rob Clarke

Person centered self directed support gives Rob the freedom to live his life as he wants to. He is not shackled by services. Supports are controlled by Rob and our family which provides Rob with what he needs. We learned early in our journey that how support is arranged and how funding is delivered is critical. Between 1967 and 1973, Rob went to 3 different institutions. Since 1979, all of Rob's support has been in his own home.

In 1979 we decided that the best way to support Rob would be for us to know who would be coming through our door to work with him. This requires that we control the funding and therefore who is hired to work with Rob. This was a significant change in how agencies supported people. At that time the funding for people was for groups not for individuals and hiring was done by agencies.

Ontario implemented *Special Services at Home*: (SSAH) an innovation that gave families control in defining supports and hiring of staff. The mechanism was right but there was not enough funding available to meet Rob's need for support. Until 1987 we were able to pull together funding by piecing together short term grants to add to SSAH funds.

After a long and drawn out battle that included filing a complaint with the Ontario Human Rights Commission, a complaint with the Ombudsman of Ontario and two appeals with tribunals, and annoying some service providers, on December 22nd, 1988 a bureaucrat left a message on our answering machine, *Merry Christmas Muriel, Rob has his funding*. That funding continues today.

In 1989 as there was no mechanism in legislation for individualized arrangements,so an agency was needed to transfer government funds to Rob. A number of people including some benevolent bureaucrats, worked together to set up a small transfer payment agency to manage funds for five people, Limestone Family Support Group Inc, Board members are family members and people who know a person being supported by Limestone.

Limestone is recognized by the Ontario Government. it is legally incorporated and follows all the requirements that agencies that support hundreds do while Limestone supports five. The goal was, and is, straight forward: the person and their family controls who comes through the door.

Limestone Family Support Group Inc, provides a mechanism for families to sustain four interrelated pillars which create the platform for good support.

1 **Authority** for hiring and firing is with the person and their family. Limestone has no agenda other than supporting the person and respecting family authority. Authority is around the person and their family's kitchen table. We decide who crosses the threshold to join us at that table, that is where it starts and ends. Our understanding of authority is simple: we have total control of hiring , training and firing. We make decisions about what Rob is going to do. We hire a Co-ordinator who assists us in carrying out our decisions. There is no office; all our attention and resources focus on supporting good lives.

2 **Natural Settings**. We have learned from Normalization and then Social Role Valorization. Our understanding of what segregation, congregation and isolation do to people focuses support in the real world, not the human service world. People's own homes and communities offer what

they really need.

3 **Relationship and Community Building:** The role of support workers is to help people build relationships that result from being present and participating in their community, which in turn builds our Kingston community. Supporters have the freedom to transcend their roles. Some support workers come to deeply care and love the person they are working with. Former supporters sometimes maintain lasting personal involvement. Three former supporters have known Rob for over 25 years and another for 14 years. He visits with them almost weekly. We can't organize this; but our family creates a context that makes lasting personal commitments possible.

4 **No Sharing of Staff.** There is no sharing of staff between people who are supported by Limestone. The developing relationship between each person and their supporter is paramount. Rob and his supporters like each other! They are not assigned to each other. It is Rob, himself, who invites people into his life and our family. The supporter's values and personality need to blend with our family. Technical skills can be taught. We clearly articulate who we are and who Rob is in the context of his family so they understand Rob's role and can decide if this is a place they want to work We hire supporters who are flexible, able to roll with things and mold themselves and their schedules to Rob's life. When there is a good match the relationship is good for both.

What we have learned so far about self-direction in our journey of 42 years

- Individualized self-directed funding is just the beginning. Controlling the money is not the end but a means to an end. The end –our living, breathing ever-evolving goal– is that Rob have a good life and have the opportunity to be the person he wants to be, a contributing member of his family and community.

- Parents, families and friends can do it. It requires attention and care; however this is not difficult or onerous. We let people know that doing what's necessary to maintain Rob's freedom experience of a good life makes the effort worthwhile.

- Allies, friends and people we trust who share our vision are important for moral and practical support. We need to speak the truth about our journey. It is not all smooth. There are times when things go well and times when they don't. Rob has people he can talk to who are neither family nor staff. Muriel and Vici need support in order to support Rob. There are people who offer to listen and walk with us on this journey. People who will ask *What do you need?* and will do it. A phone call, even with friends at a distance is comforting. From time to time, people are needed to act as a shield, a barrier, between Rob and changing government rules and regulations. There are some bureaucrats and people in service world who understand and believe that the person and family know best what should be done. They help navigate the rules.

- It is important to keep our values up-front and clear. All supporters have Social Role Valorization training. We need opportunities to connect with and learn from others we trust so we can think deeply and continue learning about assisting people to be part of their communities.

Rob makes it abundantly clear that he wants his support to be the way it is and not like it was before Limestone.

Rob attended a segregated school, lived in institutions and experienced a revolving door of staff selected and sent by provider agencies. Now he makes decisions about his life with support from people who know and love him. The more decisions he makes the more he takes control over his life. The opportunity for real decision making begins with power over this critical choice, *Who do I want to be with me to help me in my life?*

What story could we be telling ourselves that makes this practice or structure seem like the best or the only way?

What draws and shapes our attention such that this happens rather than something better?

Once it is visible, social inventors can break out of a dominant mental model and test new policies and structures based on a different sense of purpose and possibility. Pathfinders who want greater control as a means to better lives have been bending group funding structures to increase their control for many years, as the experience of Rob Clarke and his family shows.

Self-direction break-out 1: in Control

A ruling [story] does not so much combat alternative ideas as thrust them beyond the very bounds of the thinkable.

– Terry Eagleton

Simon Duffy expanded the boundaries of the thinkable by reflecting on the difference between typical practice and the assistance developed with people and families through Individual Service Funds.[*] It seemed to him morally right in principle that people and their families have control of the assistance they rely on and right in practice that putting control of public funds in their hands was a means to being in control. His commitment to assisting people to experience the rights and duties of full citizenship produced a graphic contrast between assistance as a professional gift and assistance as a support to citizenship.

In England, administration of publicly funded assistance (called social care) is the primary responsibility of 152 local governments. The central government sets targets and inspects local services. Services are funded by a combination of a share of general revenue support and some specific grants from central government, local finance, and fees.

Local authorities have considerable discretion in how they meet the duty to provide social care. They have far more freedom to innovate than US states do under Medicaid funding arrangements.

The National Health Service also provides or funds assistance for some people who are assessed to require specialist services.

The professional gift story and structure dominates the field and constrains efforts to increase self-direction. Communities delegate responsibility for assisting people and their families to governments and pay taxes to fund assistance. Governments set the terms of eligibility and the conditions for payment and delegate responsibility for assessment and assistance to specialist organizations and their professional workers. People who need assistance are served in the ways that professionals specify.

The citizenship story and structure see the person as a citizen first and recognize the community as a primary source of support and opportunity for contribution. Based on a fair and transparent allocation process, government transfers tax money to the person and the person organizes the assistance that they need and want. Providers of assistance and expertise negotiate with citizens to arrive at mutually suitable arrangements.

---

[*] For more on Individual Service Funds as a facilitator of self-direction, see Animate (2014). *Individual Service Funds: Learning from Inclusion's 18 years of practice.* The Centre on Welfare Reform. goo.gl/7qkyQx

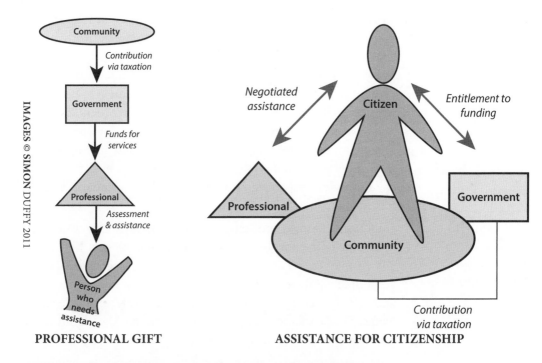

PROFESSIONAL GIFT   ASSISTANCE FOR CITIZENSHIP

The assistance for citizenship story appeals to those who want to increase self-direction, but without progress on practical answers the many HOW questions it remains no more than an appealing idea. With Simon Duffy's leadership, a small team developed a growing network to surface questions and prototype answers good enough to keep the change moving forward and spreading across England.

In Control became an effective network of social inventors who refined practices and structures that give the citizenship story wheels.* A small core group supported committed people from innovating local authorities, service providers, consultation and training initiatives, self-advocacy and family groups. The image of an open-source operating system guided the network. An operating system puts resources at the service of human purposes whether this involves harnessing a computer's processing power to a person's desire to write a message or organizing public money into assistance for a meaningful day. Anyone interested had access to what the network created. In exchange they shared their learning and any improvements they made. An Editorial Board assured consistency of new and adapted solutions with assistance to citizenship.

---

* This section focuses on the first phases of in Control's development of the means to self directed support. There is much more to learn from in Control and its development. Reports on the first three phases of its work can be found at goo.gl/tcfNm2.

The network structure allowed a very small team to support many innovators. This built commitment because network members were responsible for developing locally relevant solutions rather than being customers for technical assistance or training that claimed to offer answers. Active engagement of people with disabilities, family members, and service providers assured that local administrators took account of multiple perspectives. Those committed to change could draw on a mutually supportive network of people across the country. Progress in places where conditions for deeper change were favorable set standards and provided inspiration for the whole network.

Solutions emerged and were improved for many administrative issues, including how to determine individual budgets, how to give people control of the money for their assistance in legal and accountable ways, how to assist people and families in planning and putting their plans to work, and how to evaluate effectiveness. None of these solutions approached perfection but each moved the assistance to citizenship story along.

In Control anchored the network with a clear purpose, defining principles, a logic, a system of functions and design guidance. These ideals and ideas set boundaries and direction for social inventors.

The **purpose** of self-directed support is to offer people these six keys to citizenship.*

- **Self-determination** –making our own decisions, in control of our life.
- **Direction** –having a meaningful life that suits us and the kind of unique person that we are.
- **Money** –being able to pay our way and to decide how we will meet our own needs.
- **Home** –having a place of our own where we are safe, where we belong.
- **Support** –getting help when we need it to do the things we really want to do.
- **Community life** –playing an active part in our family, our circle of friends and our community.

The **principles** on the next page govern any effort that claims to offer self-directed support for citizenship. They define commitments that apply to any resources a decision-maker controls. Capacity can be limited by political victories yet to be won that will establish entitlement to money that assures access to assistance for everyone who needs it; by the stickiness of the professional gift story in the culture; and by difficulties in individual situations.

* This important list has been expanded and refined with experience. For Simon Duffy's current understanding of seven keys to citizenship, see *Keys to Citizenship* at goo.gl/YZw4ff. And read Simon Duffy and Wendy Perez (2014). *Citizenship for all: An accessible guide.* Centre for Welfare Reform. goo.gl/nmOQdZ

Principles	Meaning
1. Right to Independent Living - I can get the support I need to be an independent citizen.	If someone has an impairment which means they need help to fulfill their role as a citizen, then they should get the help they need.
2. Right to a Personalized Budget - I know how much money I can use for my support.	If someone needs on-going paid help as part of their life they should be able to decide how the money that pays for that help is used.
3. Right to Self-Determination - I have the authority, support or representation to make my own decisions.	If someone needs help to make decisions then decision-making should be made as close to the person as possible, reflecting the person's own interests & preferences.
4. Right to Accessibility - I can understand the rules and systems & am able to get help easily.	The system of rules within which people have to work must be clear and open in order to maximize the ability of the disabled person to take control of their own support.
5. Right to Flexible Funding - I can use my money flexibly and creatively.	When someone is using their personalized budget they should be free to spend their funds in the way that makes best sense to them, without unnecessary restrictions.
6. Accountability Principle - I should tell people how I used my money and anything I've learned.	The disabled person and the government both have a responsibility to each other to explain their decisions & to share what they have learned.
7. Capacity Principle - Give me enough help, but not too much; I've got something to contribute too.	Disabled people, their families & their communities must not be assumed to be incapable of managing their own support, learning skills & making a contribution.

The **logic** (diagrammed below) made it clear that an individual budget serves people's freedom to arrange assistance in a way that puts them in charge of their lives and allows them to act as contributing citizens. It set the administrative default at trust in people and their family's capacity to make good use of public funds.

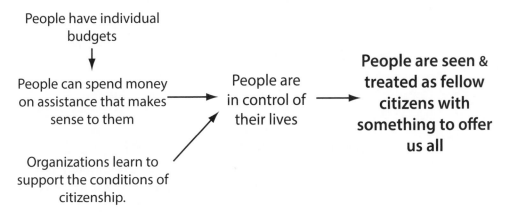

Seven steps to being in control defined the sequence of functions necessary to deliver self-directed support. Each function marked a site for invention and learning by every network member.

1. Set personalized budget	The person can find out how much money they are likely to receive.
2. Plan support	The person can work out how they can use that money to meet their needs in a way that suits them best.
3. Agree plan	The person checks out their support plan with the provider of funding.
4. Manage personalized budget	The person decides on the best way to manage their personalized budget
5. Organize support	The person organizes the housing, help, equipment or other kinds of help they want.
6. Live life	The person uses support to live a full life with family & friends in their community.
7. Review and learn	The person along with a representative of the funder checks how things are going & makes changes if needed.

Design guidance included the idea of multiplying options to encourage the greatest possible flexibility and therefore the greatest scope for people's choice and creativity. It remains common for administrators to lock onto a single way to perform each of the Seven Steps. This creates a condition that people who might benefit from an alternative have to adjust to fit. For example, a service broker might fit some people very well but poorly suit someone who feels capable of managing their own budget and organizing their own support. Positioning a case manager employed by the system's administration as the necessary source for plans and management of assistance almost alway assures that their case loads will be to large to allow them to develop an effective relationship with more than a minority of their clients. Case managers who deal with relatively few complex situations develop and use their expertise.

The menu that in Control identified for managing a personal budget provides an example of offering multiple options. A personalized budget can be managed by…

… the person or their family.

… a representative who agrees to manage the budget on the person's behalf.

… a trust, legally set up to act for the person.

… a broker whom the person pays to manage the budget and coordinate the services they want on their behalf.

... a service provider who agrees to manage the money through an Individual Service Fund –an arrangement in which the personal budget can only be spent on the person and management fees are negotiated.

... a case manager employed by the administration that funds individual budgets.

The framework created through the early work of in Control remains the best starting point we know for administrators who are serious about self-direction. Because the framework encourages learning, specific practices and concepts have been thoughtfully refined through experience and debate[*]. More experience within this framework continues to generate a deeper appreciation of citizenship, social inclusion and self-direction and so a better framework.[†]

Partly through in Control's influence, in late 2007 the Government called for large scale implementation of personal budgets under a policy titled personalization. Availability of personal budgets also grows in health care and special education.

Rapid growth in the scale and scope of personal budgets in response to central government direction has challenged administrators. Since 2010, deep cuts in funding and tightening benefits, justified as austerity measures required by economic crisis, have further stressed people and families and the whole structure of publicly funded assistance. Rising uncertainty and priority on the struggle to maintain sufficient public funding have intensified the stress of implementing personal budgets.

Even when implemented by structures under stress, personal budgets make a positive difference to most of the people who have them.[‡] However, applying the lens of in Control's approach to self-direction brings challenges into focus.

- There can be a substitution of purposes if in Control's logic collapses. Dispensing personal budgets can become the goal in itself rather than a means to self-directed supports for active citizenship.

In 2007, UK central government called for 30% of the almost 1.8 million recipients of social care to have a personal budget by 2011. The Care Act 2014 requires that all eligible people have a personal budget.

---

[*] For current resources from in Control, go to www.in-control.org.uk

[†] For Simon Duffy's 2012 update of the principles and steps, see goo.gl/OApwK3. Lessons he has learned are reported in Simon Duffy (2013) *Traveling Hopefully: Best Practice in Self-Directed Support*. Centre for Welfare Reform goo.gl/TRpol2

[‡] More than two-thirds of people surveyed said that personal budgets made things better or a lot better in 11 life areas. See *POET (Personal Outcomes Evaluation Tool) Third National Personal Budget Survey* (2014) goo.gl/k2N7aM for a detailed account of people's reported experiences with personal budgets.

- Principles can fade, weakening the moral foundation of the reform.

  - Law does not yet recognize an unambiguous entitlement to assistance or self-direction of a personal budget. Unless the principles are embodied in local policy and practice they will have no meaningful effect.

  - There is a preoccupation with technical matters. Resource allocation, which can be a common sense process, has become increasingly complex.

  - Those who receive a personal budget are treated as if they were contractors of the administration. The money is not see as theirs. Restrictions on how money can be spent and demands for accounting can accumulate to a point that decreases flexibility, compromises people's right to self-direction, sends double messages about control of public funds, needlessly complicates the use of funds and stresses people and families.

Organizations of all kinds are cluttered with control mechanisms that paralyze employees and leaders alike... We never effectively control people with these systems, but we certainly stop a lot of good work from getting done.

–Margaret Wheatley

- The rush to hit numerical targets can draw administrators attention to the technical details of compliance with rules and guidance and drive demand for answers from external sources. The whole health and welfare structure functions as an institution in too many people's lives. Multiple structures and policies limit the effectiveness of personal budgets for assistance. Disharmony with benefits and other sources of assistance artificially depress the number of people employed. Despite much relevant knowledge, people remain stuck in institutional settings for lack of competent alternatives.

Complying with external direction and advice can distract from the slow and difficult adaptive work of deconstructing a culture infused with the professional gift story and constructing a culture of support for contributing citizenship. The professional gift story hangs on because of distrust of disabled people and families. Those who use publicly funded assistance are seen as incompetent and vulnerable unless guided and protected by professionals. Duty of care becomes responsibility to eliminate risk of accident or misfortune. Stigma attaches and the belief that cheating irresistibly tempts many people and families clouds policy and practice. Hunger for stories of fraud and abuse of funds inflates perception well beyond actual incidence of misuse. Classifying mistakes in compliance with reporting requirements as misuse of funds produces an epidemic that must be treated with enhanced scrutiny.

All this obscures the good sense, creativity and resourcefulness encouraged by following in Control principles.

The professional gift story can grip people with disabilities and their families too. Poor quality assistance, too long a wait for needed assistance, isolation and lack of social support, professional disparagement of capacities and resourcefulness, and complex procedures can bring people to internalize the story that they can only survive by winning the professional gift. The desire to completely delegate responsibility for assistance to case managers and service providers grows as confidence wanes. The opportunity to self-direct and organize assistance may frustrate people and families who have come to this point. Their likely choice assigns as much responsibility as possible for their personal budget and assistance to others.

Without deepening local roots, self-direction for citizenship floats off the ground like a slowly deflating balloon, one among many programmatic targets blown around by occasional administrative attention until the demands of another government target becalm it. Bureaucratic structures under stress can't root self-direction that assists citizenship. Local alliances grow necessary roots, animated by the shared work of disabled people and families and their allies among service providers and administrators.

Growing moral and political roots for citizenship shapes the work of in Control since personalization became policy. A small team continues to serve a network of committed innovators, work in alliance with other groups, and offer expert advice and advocacy on policy affecting personalization.

The focus of in Control's attention has widened based on two realizations. One, a self-determined life includes but is larger than effective control of necessary assistance; it is a matter for whole communities. Two, social service and health structures function in an environment too unsettled and unsettling to count on to create a culture of self-directed support for citizenship without the strong engagement of disabled people, their families and their allies with one another. A community level movement for inclusion is needed and government can't deliver on its own.

Five of the principles of self-direction are asserted as rights. Law and regulation offer only a limited guarantee of these rights, even when they are definite, enforceable and adequately resourced. If disabled people and their families and allies do not experience these principles as natural rights they will not assert them. If citizens, service providers and officials do not recognize the right to independent living as a matter of common decency it will have no force in their lives and people with developmental disabilities will remain excluded..

This active recognition of common rights results from social movement, not bureaucratic rule or professional action. Accordingly in Control invests in a variety of ways to engage diverse people to connect and cultivate the conditions for citizenship in their locality. These investments include building a network of local networks through intensive learning events and support to cross country connections among allies for real change. A variety of these events give depth to understanding of full citizenship and encourage confidence in taking action that engages local resources in opening the way to social inclusion and self-direction.

Self-direction break-out 2: Dane County, Wisconsin

Dane County, with a population of about 500,000, chooses to administer services to people with developmental disabilities and their families locally rather than delegating responsibility to a managed care organization. Medicaid funds matched with state money and a substantial contribution from local taxes have been invested in developing and providing individualized supports for more than 40 years. The results of these investments demonstrate the way that options multiply when individual budgets can support partnership with a variety of providers of individualized supports.

Brittany (page 81), Christine (page 151), Wanda (page 91), Evan (page 111), and Ken (page 145) are citizens of Dane County.

- No one from the county is a long-term institution resident and the invention of intensive, individualized living and crisis assistance have steadily reduced short-term placements in psychiatric facilities and institutions for people with developmental disabilities.

- Families benefit from intensive, flexible support. Since 1980 the County has been committed to permanency for every child with a developmental disability: every child grows up in a family, their birth family with support; an adoptive family; permanent foster care or a co-parenting arrangement.

- The County's schools, especially in Madison, the largest school district, have been leaders in inclusive education.

- A variety of individualized supported living arrangements have replaced group homes and small specialized facilities. A number of people own their own homes, usually with family investment. A number of people self-manage much of their time at home with assistance from Sound Response, a technology that gives people reliable access to assistance if they need it.

- More than 80% of adults are employed, the majority part-time. Partnership with school systems results in almost every graduate from special education already doing an individual paid job in their community. Focused investment in new graduates has allowed continuing support for their employment.

- To complement a few large provider organizations a variety of locally governed, purposely small organizations provide assistance according to their distinctive identities.

- The County invests in organizing and supporting social inventions by people with developmental disabilities and their families and by staff who want to increase their capacity for effective partnership.

In 1996 the County made self-directed individual budgets available and by 2005 every adult receiving publicly funded assistance had an individual budget. The purpose of this reform is *To help the people we support to create the lives they want, connected to and supported by our communities*. Every individual budget holder has a broker to assist in planning and assure that assistance meets people's expectations.

André Brown, now in his mid-thirties, has benefited from his residence in Dane County since he was three years old. The County's commitment to permanency led to the recruitment of his foster mother, Marcie Brost, who later became his adoptive mother.

Marcie met André on a nursing unit of a state institution. Their new family benefited from intensive family support and the availability of a choice of inclusive child development settings for pre-school and after school. Even a nationally leading public school system found André's multiple impairments beyond their willingness to include him in his neighborhood school, as Marcie believed he should be. With support from a growing circle, Marcie combined vigorous advocacy with organizing an inclusive education outside the public schools. André attended public high schools and left school at age 21 with two part-time jobs.

André usually works four days a week, six hours a day. Some weeks, health issues reduce his time at work. He has paid jobs with the Dane County District Attorney and the County Courts

Read more about Movin'
Out on page 81 and at
movin-out.org.

and volunteers at Movin' Out, a housing agency. He is assisted by a rotating team of assistants.

When André was in his early teens, Marcie joined five other parents to consider how to expand the housing options available. With support from County administrators the group explored and followed multiple pathways to the different housing options that suited their sons and daughters. Their work reached beyond their own needs and resulted in the development of Movin' Out, a housing agency partially supported by Dane County that now supports a variety of means to affordable, accessible housing throughout Wisconsin.

The self-directed budget makes public funds an asset that combines with the other elements of André's and Marcie's real wealth. Circumstances made it possible for Marcie to move out of the home she and Andre shared and extensively adapted to meet his needs. Further modifications created two living areas, one for André, the other for the personal assistants who share his home.

Despite involvement of expert professionals, André has not developed symbolic communication that most others understand. He does draw people to him and inspires great loyalty. He still spends regular time with people he met as a youngster. One of his part-time assistants has worked for him for 30 years. The couple who provide most of his at home assistance have shared his home for more than 15 years and raised their daughter in his company from her birth. A network of people, identified in this diagram, hold André in relationships he counts on for social connections, the exchange of help and support, and the security of being recognized as a whole person. None of these relationships are accidental or taken for granted. Marcie tends André's key connections with great care.

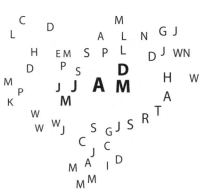

Given the County's structure and policies, Marcie and the circle have substantial room to direct public funds to make things work as well as possible for André. The diagram on the next page summarizes the current structure of his assistance, which combines public funds with the assets and capacities available from his relationships and network.

The County allocates individual budgets for supported living on the assumption that people who require substantial assistance will share their home with another person who also needs assistance. Most people who need 24 hour assistance rely on shift staff. Marcie and the circle strongly believe that it is best for André to live in

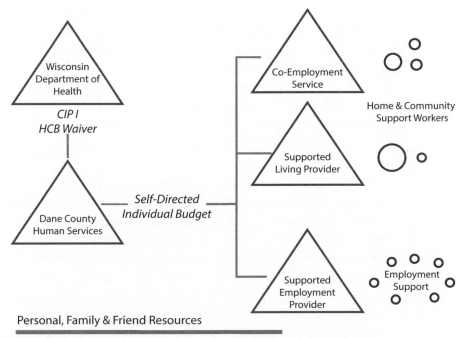

Personal, Family & Friend Resources

- Wages, Medicaid Card & SSI + Social Security (adjusted to earnings)
- Unpaid personal assistance (Average 1.5-2 days/week)
- Coordination, supervision, appointments etc. (Average 10 hours/week)
- Planning & service brokerage
- Household maintainence
- Mortgage payments

a household shared with a family, without a roommate who also requires assistance. In their judgment this offers continuity of trusted assistance that keeps what matters to André in focus and responds immediately to frequent changes in his health status. To make this possible within the allocated budget, family and friends provide substantial assistance and do a variety of coordination tasks. Much of this assistance happens in the context of activities that the people who care about André enjoy doing with him. Most unpaid assistance is scheduled in blocks of time that allow the family he lives with to pursue their other interests.

Marcie employs three at home assistants through a co-employment service organized by the County. The person who holds primary responsibility for at home assistance is employed through a negotiated agreement with a supported living provider. At work support comes through a negotiated agreement with a supported employment agency that has supported him since he left high school.

André's pattern of assistance reflects the virtues and the challenges of self-directed support: it is distinctive to him and his family. Others make different decisions about how to blend their real wealth with public funds. Real wealth varies. André's network includes people willing and able to offer significant unpaid assistance. This makes it possible for him to be the only person in his household who requires substantial personal assistance. Family circumstances make a house available. Many people can't count on these resources.

The consequences of inequality of real wealth call for deeper thinking and purposeful action. Self-direction itself highlights the problems of inequality; a return to block contracts for assistance would not solve them. Every public funding scheme in the US emphasizes the greatest possible use of people's own resources, including unpaid assistance from family and friends (administratively labeled natural support), help from churches and charities at no charge to the state, and calling on other government budgets before using publicly funded assistance to people with developmental disabilities.

André's privilege in assets and connections reflects inequalities that the whole society must find better ways to address.* Poverty of money, friends and meaning diminishes every community. Inequality hurts everyone. Advocates for people with developmental disabilities can join their voices to others who resist the bad effects of inequality. Self-direction gives André and his allies the best chance to play their part by orienting assistance toward building real wealth. Steady effort to resist social exclusion and develop capacities makes a difference to their capacity to cope with the consequences of exclusion and advocate for greater opportunity for all citizens. Reaching out to share their story with others, not as a recipe but as a guide, influences others to use self-direction of assistance as a way to act as citizens concerned with opportunity for all.

André's future is in good hands, but it is not secure. Dane County administrators have navigated the federal and state policies and structures that express the clinical services mindset with preternatural skill and exceptional results. Limits remain. The rising costs of compliance with the growing demands of rules and reporting requirements demand attention and sometimes crowd the space for social invention. The persistent lack of sufficient public funds to support people to establish their own households

---

* For a good discussion of this social issue, see Robert Putnam (2015). *Our Kids: The American Dream in Crisis. New York: Simon and Schuster.*

steadily increases the numbers of people and families waiting for this important life transition. There are opportunities to improve: more support to people and families as inventors of new ways for people to move into their own homes; better jobs at less cost in publicly funded assistance; better ways to expand people's networks and capacities and mobilize community support; more powerful approaches to developing people's capacities; more ways to build commitment, competence, and continuity in the workforce.

The County's past performance justifies confidence in steady progress on these issues but for one thing. State legislators have adopted the managed care mindset to shape funding and managing publicly funded assistance in the state. Dane County is one of a small and shrinking group of counties that continues to administer public funds locally. As the clock on local authority runs out and some form of managed care takes over the challenge to conserve and keep building on what works grows.

Self-direction break-out 3: Article 12*

The more self-evident an assumption seems the bigger the space for social invention that opens with disruption of that assumption. One common belief holds that most people with intellectual disabilities lack legal capacity –the ability to hold rights and duties and exercise those rights and duties- because they lack mental capacity –the ability to understand information, use that information to make rational decisions, and communicate decisions clearly. In this story, authorizing a substitute decision maker to act in the person's best interest obviously remedies defects in mental and legal capacity, though at the price of the person losing legal capacity.[†] In fact, in some jurisdictions simple professional assignment to the status "mentally retarded" has been sufficient to justify extinguishing a person's rights to decide. Reforms have required more refined assessment and allow people to retain their

---

* We are not lawyers. Our understanding of Article 12 has been shaped by the writing of Gerard Quinn, a legal scholar at NUI Galway who has no responsibility for any misunderstanding of Article 12 found here. Find his papers at goo.gl/zpWZzP. His writing addresses many issues we pass over in this brief discussion. Michael Bach builds from Canadian experience and offers international leadership on the implementation of Article 12, see goo.gl/uJbmLm. For US resources go to The National Resource Center on Supported Decision Making at supporteddecisionmaking.org.

† Terms for substitute decision makers vary by jurisdiction as do the mechanisms for their appointment and their duties. The may be called guardians, trustees, conservators or by some other name. What they have in common is that they appear before the law as a substitute for the person.

right to those decisions they are assessed as competent to make, but the belief that intellectual disability in itself justifies substitute decision making remains common sense to many people. This belief is so common in the US that many parents follow special educators' advice and go to court to extinguish some or all of a person's rights as a routine part of celebrating their eighteenth birthday.

Such common sense makes the words of Article 12 of *The Convention on the Rights of Person's with Disabilities* deeply disruptive. What can it mean to say *persons with disabilities have the right to recognition everywhere as persons before the law* and *persons with disabilities enjoy legal capacity on an equal basis with others in all aspects of life*? The grip of common sense leads some people to hallucinate an extra phrase into the sentence like *except for people with intellectual disabilities.*

In its *2014 General Comment on Article 12,*[*] The UN Committee on the Rights of Persons with Disabilities intensified the disruption. They make it clear that limits in mental capacity must not compromise the right to legal capacity. Difficulties in decision making that might be caused by cognitive or communication impairments determine the support a person requires to exercise their legal capacity, they do not diminish legal capacity.

The Committee demands what it calls a paradigm shift by requiring States parties to *...take action to develop laws and policies to replace regimes of substitute decision-making by supported decision-making, which respects the person's autonomy, will and preferences.*

Substitute decision making has three characteristics:

- Legal capacity is removed from a person, even for a single decision.

- A substitute decision maker can be appointed by someone other than the person concerned and this can be done against the person's will.

- Decisions are made based on what the substitute decision maker believes is in the best interests of the person concerned.

In contrast the Committee understands supported decision making very broadly. It includes a variety of approaches that people can use to assist them in exercising their legal capacity.

---

*The General Comment can be found at goo.gl/vyRGjI

- A person might trust another chosen person or a circle of people to assist them with particular decisions.

- A person might call on peer-support or self-advocacy groups.

- Support includes assistance with advance planning so a person can make their will and preferences known in anticipation of a time when they may not be able to communicate them.

- Support includes the development of communication methods for people who do not communicate conventionally.

- Support includes a duty for public services like banks to provide information to support decision making in understandable formats.

These legal words and requirements pose complex technical questions for legal scholars, judges and legislators. Lawmakers sometimes employ the device of constructive ambiguity –agreement on words that does not necessarily imply agreement on their practical meaning- in order to move negotiations along. Countries that ratify the convention often attach reservations, understandings and declarations that limit the force the Convention has in local law. It will be some time before authoritative interpretations and the means to implement them become clear, and the legal effects of Article 12 are likely to be minimal in the US.

Regardless of interpretations and solutions in law, taking the perspective of Article 12 seriously exposes much common sense to searching questions. This questioning creates a deeper understanding of self-determination which can motivate and guide social invention because people and their allies choose to treat it as a right even if it is not enforceable in court.

A first look sharpens awareness of adaptive challenges. It is never too late to explore these questions and it can never be to early for families of young children with developmental disabilities to imagine creative ways to consider them.

- Have we taken it for granted that intellectual disability produces a need for guardianship?

- Could our legitimate trust in family authority mask opportunities for the person to be more influential in their own life?

- Have we considered other legal means to support decision making and protect the person's assets (durable powers of attorney, multi-signature accounts, trusts, living wills, advance directives, representation agreements)?[*]

- Have we been purposeful and rigorous in establishing and sustaining relationships with people whom the person trusts as advisors? Are there good people with knowledge relevant to the person's interests and purposes that a person allows to influence them?

- Have we been disciplined in gathering others to plan with the person in a way that makes their gifts and purposes clear as a foundation for understand their expression of will and preference?

- If the person's cognitive or communication impairments are substantial have we searched widely for practices that let the person know that they are expected to have a voice in their lives and provide the opportunity to develop that voice?

- If our understanding of the person's will and preference is elementary –perhaps limited to our sense of their preferences about physical comfort, food or sensory stimulation– have we been purposeful in creating a variety of experiences with the person that have the potential to spark their will and offer additional possibilities to consider?

The UN Committee recognizes a small number of people who don't express their will and preference in a form that others can understand, even when others make significant effort to discover the right support for them to do so. Their instruction in these situations is clear. Any retreat to substitute decision making no matter how few people are involved would compromise human rights. So, *the "best interpretation of will and preferences" must replace the "best interests" determinations*. This leaves plenty of room to invent practices that allow "best interpretation of will and practice."

Audrey Cole, a Canadian champion of community living, leads on supported decision making with great passion and clarity of thought.[†] Her son, Ian, relies on people he trusts for best interpretation of his will and preference and, most important, for practical responses to what they detect. Thinking about Ian's will, she writes,

---

[*] Each state and province will have different rules. The Michigan Alliance for Families has assembled a set of options and guides at goo.gl/uxXZhZ. More about Representatiuon Agreements at goo.gl/k9fCF9.

[†] Follow her occasional blog at goo.gl/GbOVLs. The paragraph is taken, with her permission, from Michael Bach and Lana Kerzner *A New Paradigm for Protecting Autonomy and the Right to Legal Capacity. Part two, Section I.* goo.gl/uJbmLm

...human will - that instinctive and inherently human imperative, that sense of being, that thing that tells us we are here, that we can feel. I honestly don't think it has anything to do with intellect. Ian has it! It is what makes him stop, suddenly, and listen to the sounds of the birds or of the wind blowing through the trees. I am sure it is what makes him so sensitive to music. It is also what makes him instinctively draw back or resist things he doesn't understand (such as an unfamiliar medical procedure, for example). and it is certainly the thing that has prompted him on a couple of occasions when Fred [her husband and Ian's father] had been in intensive care to gently reach out and stroke Fred's arm - an intimacy that is not typical of Ian who usually would have to be prompted to make such personal contact. I don't know what it is but I do know we all have it! and if we take the trouble to get to know people who do not communicate in typical ways, we become very conscious of it.

The people Ian relies on know him far more deeply than this paragraph expresses. They can say much more about who he is, what draws and what repels him, what he enjoys, what soothes him. But as a thought experiment, take this paragraph as if it were all that is available as a point of departure for an interpretation of Ian's will and preference. What follows is our reading from the paragraph.

Even a few observations of Ian embodied in his world allow the construction of clear instructions to those who belong to him. Think of what just this paragraph can say about the conditions of assistance he wants his decision supporters to express and do their best to assure. Closeness to his parents matters. If his father is unwell we wants to be with him to comfort him. He wants time in nature and needs company to walk safely in the woods. His companion, whether paid assistant or friend, will be more responsive to his will and preference when they have the leisure to stop and listen to the wind and the birds without impatience. This would be hard were Ian always one of a group whose activities would be knocked off schedule by a pause to appreciate the music a moment offers. It would be hard if his assistant had a crowded list of tasks to do. Impossible if his assistant interpreted a sudden stop and a long pause as non-compliance and a signal to implement a behavior control tactic. So Ian counts on his decision supporters to be closely and authoritatively involved in choosing, orienting and directing his personal assistants so that their temperament and capacities match and complement his. He counts on them to assure that his living arrangements fit him and do not lose him in a group of clients with profound disabilities or put him at risk of being shuttled away to a vacant bed in a distant place.

Ian may give no sign of having a concept of the bank account Article 12 gives him a right to. His decision supporters express their best understanding of his will and preference when they use their knowledge of financial matters to employ whatever money assets he has in providing the conditions for a good life. This will be a life that regularly brings him the music of the birds and trees.

Audrey's mode of interpretation suspends the belief that expressions of will and preference require Ian to juggle abstractions and express himself in conventional words and symbols. The devaluing but common assumption that substantial cognitive impairment means primitive interests and expressions does not cloud her senses. The Ian we meet here is attuned to music. He comforts his father, expressing compassion. He expresses clear preference: don't expect rapid compliance with unfamiliar procedures; stop with me to listen; bring me to my father when he is gravely ill.

If self-direction demands an autonomous individual who can understand abstract ideas, gather and weigh information and advice, make a decision that others view as rational and communicate it clearly, Ian and André get left out for lack of individual capacity. This understanding shrinks the self to a single, isolated point. It allows only the most able to self-direct their pathfinder's journey and the assistance necessary to make it. A more generous understanding of self, and one more true to Ian and André's lives, understands the self in self-determination as relational. Competence results from the flow of capacities among people committed to their well being. This reveals the great vulnerability of people who lack loving relationships and are assisted in isolating and impersonal ways. Decision support begins with establishing connections to people who can start from an independent view of their will and preference and get to know them well enough to discover what matters to them.

This relational understanding of self-direction highlights a real vulnerability that advocates of individual autonomy will be quick to note. Others might manipulate or constrain the person for their own ends. A person's potential might be sacrificed to benefit their family, as when a family poor in money discourages paid employment because a person's benefits make a critical contribution to household income. A self open to the flow of other's interpretation can be stunted and shrunken by others caught in fear, certainty that they know best, and lack of imagination. This is also true when a legally appointed guardian decides

It is no use to pretend that the person alone is in charge –and for Ian and André it would be a pretense, even if the pretense were a matter of policy. The best remedy recognizes a whole person, with standing before the law and the right to decision support. This recognition asks all those involved in decisions to stay in respectful contact with the person and one another, consider different points of view, learn about possibilities and look for creative approaches to conflicting interests and differing opinions.

Open minds, open hearts and open wills among decision supporters allow appreciation of enough of a person's will and preference to make a difference. Knowledge that grows in shared time and activity, paced and shaped by the person, grounds competent decision support. The more people in good relationships, the more aspects of the person's will and preference can come into focus.

Knowing a person's will and preference matters most when decision supporters can mobilize capacity to act on what they learn. Birth families and chosen families play a central role in aligning available resources and generating the social inventions that shift expressions of a person's will and preferences into real life in community.

A new foundation for public investment

Policy recognizes self direction but two mental models express themselves in structures and rules that severely constrict self-direction. These stories answer fundamental political questions: what condition justifies expenditure of public money and what should that money pay for?

These stories are powerful because they hard to see. Their requirements for activities and reports keep attention focused on bureaucratic detail and mask the mental model. Compliance with their demands follows from the belief that whatever administrative demands attach to the flow of public funds are the only way to demonstrate accountability for taxpayer dollars.

One mental model powered deinstitutionalization and governed the flow of substantial amounts of money into local services and institution reform. Retrieved from the era of institution founding and modernized by reforming experts for leverage over politi-

cians this clinical service story created a pattern for regulation
that remains influential.

Clinical Service

*People with developmental disabilities experience the
consequences of life long physical and mental disorders,
the principle signs of which are significant deficits in
adaptive behavior and cognitive processing and increased risk of a number of co-morbid conditions.*

*These disorders are best managed by a team of experts
who regularly assess each client and develop an individualized plan of care. Based on their assessment, the
expert team sets measurable goals with input from the
person and family. The team oversees implementation,
measures the outcomes of the interventions specified in
the plan and revises the plan as necessary. The team has
final responsibility for the person's placement in clinically
necessary and appropriate services. The team manages
risks and assures health and safety, and when necessary
assures protection of the community.*

*People require supervision and activity so group resi-
dences and day occupation centers are necessary. These
settings provide the sites for implementing treatment
plans.*

*Providers meet administrative standards that govern staff
identity and training, physical facilities, programmatic
practices, and fiscal administration. Systematic inspection
and audit drive quality improvement.*

*Effective assistance meets regulatory requirements and
delivers evidence based treatments for assessed disorders
and deficits in the least restrictive settings the team judges consistent with a person's need for protection and the
conditions necessary for the treatment and management
of their disorders.*

This mental model may give clients a voice in selecting goals and a
share of responsibility for implementing plans. However, professional experts and managers remain responsible to assure health
and safety and certify the clinical necessity and appropriateness of
the assistance a person receives. They retain a duty of care for people who, by their diagnosis, have impaired capacity. People with
developmental disabilities inform the expert decision makers who
examine them; experts don't advise people who decide.

A second mental model has taken shape as administration of
assistance to people with developmental disabilities has been

grouped with management of assistance to elders and people with physical, sensory and psychiatric impairments under the heading of long term care. A leading theme in this story is containing costs through a managed market in assistance.

Long Term Care Management

People need long-term care because they are incapable of performing activities of daily living. Long term-care providers efficiently and cost-effectively perform the specific everyday tasks that people have proven that they can not do and have no other means to pay for. These tasks are specified in a plan that links objectively assessed incompetence to well defined procedures. Care management that co-ordinates long-term care with acute and chronic medical treatment minimizes long term cost.

Providers compete for membership in a network of preferred providers that will bring them business on the basis of cost, accuracy in meeting performance specifications and customer satisfaction.

People define the outcomes they want from assistance and indicate their satisfaction with what they receive. Capable people and families may choose to self-direct their care. They can shop for what suits them best from among the cost effective options they identify through negotiation with care managers.

Whenever possible long-term care is delivered in a person's family home, especially when family members and friends can provide unpaid assistance. As need becomes more intense people move into specialized settings: assisted living, group homes, nursing homes.

Those who want to promote full citizenship find these mental models disrespectfully constraining and want to disrupt them with a third story.

Assistance for Citizenship

People with developmental disabilities require life-long assistance in order to meet their responsibilities and exercise their rights as citizens. A personally tailored combination of technology, accommodation, specialist service and personal assistance enables them to develop and engage their capacities. Each person and family has the right to a decisive voice in the way opportunities for a secure home, meaningful relationships, and contribu-

tion through employment and other civic roles are dis-
covered and necessary assistance designed and delivered.
Effective assistance will be individualized, flexible and
oriented to active participation in community life. As-
sistance is co-created by mobilizing the assets of people
and their allies, other citizens (employers, association
members, neighbors, friends), and personal assistants
and experts.

This story puts self-direction of publicly funded assistance at the
center because it is a citizen's right and responsibility to co-create
the assistance necessary to a good life. It implies a different political foundation for publicly funded assistance, based on public
interest in communities that work better for everyone. A rough
sketch of a new foundation includes these ideas.

- Social exclusion is unjust and has negative effects on wellbeing, public health, security, the work of civil society and
  economic productivity.

- Solidarity, a bigger and more generous sense of WE, is a
  necessary condition of a community's capacity to mobilize
  its assets to make progress in meeting its challenges.

- People with developmental disabilities are at significant risk
  of social exclusion, unequal opportunities, isolation and
  social devaluation as less than full citizens.

- People with developmental disabilities and their families
  face continuing excess difficulties that hinder the civic and
  economic contributions they can make and unnecessarily
  limit their life chances. These excess difficulties include extra
  money costs as well as physical and social barriers to participation.

- A just public policy will offer people with developmental
  disabilities and their families better life chances. It will
  reduce excess difficulties by assisting them in removing
  social obstacles to their full participation in community life.
  It will entitle them to a transfer of funds in a form that they
  can direct to organize sufficient assistance to exercise their
  responsibilities as citizens and apply to meeting excess costs
  imposed by their impairments.

Taking the step of converting allocation of clinical or long term
care services to cash transfers in a supportive ecosystem would
provide a fair test of the possibilities of assistance based on a citizenship story.

There are resources to support this test. Jurisdictions that have already made progress in this direction, such as Dane County, are well positioned for this test if their efforts are prized and supported as test beds for new growth. If they are treated as weed patches to be uprooted and replaced with long term care management great learning will be lost. The early experience of in Control provides a prudent approach to the high level of uncertainty involved. Small, deliberately growing networks of willing social inventors who root their efforts in a deep sense of purpose will develop a variety of viable answers by learning from prototypes. *The UN Convention on the Rights of Persons with Disabilities* offers a framework of ideas to guide the selection of solutions to promote.

The shift from structures based on stories of managing deficiency to publicly funded assistance based on the values of solidarity and socially productive citizenship requires a deep shift in awareness. This shift happens as the default position of fear of scarcity and distrust of those who benefit from publicly funded assistance gives way to a recognition of fellow citizens capable of self-direction and contribution.

Politically savvy people give long odds on legislators shifting to this new awareness. However that may be, the odds improve when pathfinders with developmental disabilities and allies and their partners dare to act as if *The UN Convention* were real in its plain language. When they contribute to the work of the rapidly growing numbers of people who are inventing new paths for the economy, for the planet and for the wellbeing of all people possibilities for self-direction multiply. Regardless of short term political success, acting at the places where concerns for social justice intersect rewards all those who reach out and connect.

An ecology for self-direction

The power of self-direction grows as supports for it multiply. The richer people's sense of possibility, the stronger the webs of connection that link people, the more local solutions people have developed to recurring design questions the more resources people will have to pursue a good life.

People and families who want to increase their capacity for self-direction build real wealth by intentionally gathering a circle of support and calling on members to listen and offer what assistance they can; reaching out for opportunities to learn about what is possible and developing a critical perspective on stories that diminish the chances of contributing citizenship; investing time in organizing with other people with disabilities and other families.

Managers who are serious about self-direction will take bold steps to put their organization's resources under shared control. Even when public money comes to an organization in block contracts, funds can be allocated within the organization to individual accounts that people and their decision supporters can direct. This offers a real choice of who will assist a person and how. It challenges the whole organization to make its resources as flexible as possible: divesting real estate and shifting into more flexible arrangements; finding more ways to individualize assistance; assisting people and their decision supporters to improve their capacities to discover a future worth working towards and recruiting and developing assistants to join them; allocating as much expert time as possible to engagement with building and broadening people's capacities.

In places where people and families have to option to self-direct an individual budget, organizations can refine their offerings to become better partners. They can work out ways to set a fair price and offer a variety of specific capacities people would like to buy from them: help with recruitment, training and staff supervision; help with managing accountability requirements; facilitating plans; expert consultation; adapting and maintaining assistive technology. This has proven important to sustaining self-directed assistance when a person and their allies want to devote less time to managing their assistance and more time to other pursuits.

Administrators who are serious about self-direction will invest in people and families and partners who want to organize solutions to common design questions. Here are some of those design questions and a sample of the social inventions that have come from families and their partners organizing to develop answers to them.

DESIGN QUESTIONS

DESIGN QUESTION How might we support people and families
to create person-centered plans independent of service
providers?

> **Ontario Independent Facilitation Network** is a commu-
> nity of practice whose members assist people and families
> who want to make person-centered plans independent of
> the process for allocating funds for assistance or any ser-
> vice provider with whom they might negotiate. These plans
> start with mobilizing family and community capacities to
> support the person in living a good life. These efforts define
> the role of paid assistance. In some situations, independent
> facilitation can be a long term relationship and include
> assisting people to make planned connections to commu-
> nity roles and resources. Independent facilitators may also
> assist people without current family connections to gather
> a circle.
> www.oifn.ca

DESIGN QUESTION How might we develop leaders with high expectations for social-inclusion and self-direction and a capacity
for engagement in governing and reforming publicly funded
assistance?

> **in Control** has developed a suite of intensive learning
> opportunities for family members and people with disabili-
> ties. The courses develop a critical perspective on disability
> issues, identify state of the art practices in inclusive educa-
> tion, employment and support for life in community, pro-
> vide an understanding of how the administration of pub-
> licly funded assistance works work, how services change
> for better or for worse, and builds confidence and skill in
> participation in change efforts. The courses intentionally
> build mutually supportive learning groups whose members
> assit each other in practicing what they are learning in
> their own lives. Many graduates join a national network of
> champions for social inclusion and self direction.
> goo.gl/VHC2lW

DESIGN QUESTION How might we encourage people with developmental disabilities to create an pursue a vision of themselves as self-directing citizens who contribute to their communities?

People First of Washington State developed and delivers *Reaching My Own Greatness*, an interactive workshop led by a self-advocate and a support worker. goo.gl/QQPTsm

DESIGN QUESTION How might we support people and families to organize a circle or network of support and mobilize community assets?

Partners for Planning is a family led organization that assists families to create personal support networks, do long term financial planning and make provision for decision support, and make and implement person-centered plans. They have a growing on line resource network that provides video and print resources to illuminate possibilities and provide practical guidance. www.partnersforplanning.ca

David Wetherow, an imaginative social inventor and long-time advocate for social inclusion and self-direction, has designed **The Star Raft**, a pattern for building personal support networks that are person-centered, family friendly and anchored in natural community connections. The step by step process and the values that the process serves are described at thestarraft.com.

Local Area Coordination assists people and families to connect with community capacities before determining the role that disability services will play in their lives. Local Area Coordinators are paid community members who build a wide network of local relationships and make productive connections. goo.gl/q5Tebr

Community Circles is an effort to use person-centered thinking tools to support circle facilitation at a large scale. They seek practical answers to the question, "If circles are so great, why aren't there many, many more of them?" goo.gl/rM07Hp

Tyze is an on line tool for keeping a personal support network connected, informed and coordinated. It makes it easy to request help from network members and to keep track of documents and appointments. tyze.com

DESIGN QUESTION How might we support groups of families, or circles of circles, to come together for mutual support and purposeful action toward social inclusion and self-direction?

Deohaeko Support Network is a group of families who have been together for more than 20 years to support secure and welcoming homes, relationships that will safeguard the long term future, and valued ways to contribute to their communities. Two books by Janet Klees, the cooperative's facilitator, tell their story in a practical and inspiring way: *We Come Bearing Gifts* and *Our Presence Has Roots*. www. deohaeko.com.

Living Our Visions (LOV-Dane) is a grassroots organization of people with developmental disabilities, families and community members. It supports self-organizing groups to support one another, learn skills of relevance to them, discover and succeed in good jobs through family networks, create options for moving from their family homes with limited individual budgets, participate in civic life and enjoy themselves. It offers assistance in forming circles of support and making plans and provides the option for collective hiring of a Bridge Builder, whose task is to support people in contributing community roles. www.lovdane.org

Supported Living Network (www.sln.org.au) connects, guides and supports families and people with developmental disabilities to generate and sustain innovative approaches to community living. Adam and his family have documented each step of his moving out at adammovesout.wordpress. com. They collaborate with **inCharge** (incharge.net.au) an initiative that assists people with disabilities to act as authors of their own lives.

DESIGN QUESTION How might we assist people to organize and manage the publicly funded assistance they require in an effective way that is sustainable for the long term?

Vela provides information, mentoring and connections to people who want to manage individualized funding or form a micro-board (a group of five or more family and committed friends who join with a person to create a small non-profit organization to manage the person's assistance). www.velacanada.org

The Darrell Cook Family Managed Supports Resource Centre assists families who directly manage support workers to make plans, negotiate with the administration and meet requirements, and hire and manage. The Centre links families to other more experienced families, offers workshops and resources, and maintains a Connecting Families to Staff database. fmsresourcecentre.aacl.org

Grapevine convened young people and their families to think about the role of direct support workers and share their experiences of what works to hire them and build a relationship that supports community engagement, trying things outside your comfort zone, learning new skills, and getting everyday tasks done. They decided to re-name the role to better describe what they want from their assistants. The new name: **Future Guide**. goo.gl/vInJnn

DESIGN QUESTION How might we provide expert back up to people who live with challenging behavior and their families and people in crisis?

> **Community TIES** provides positive behavior support and crisis response service available to provide expert assistance to people and families goo.gl/3LwakO

DESIGN QUESTION How might we increase access to secure, affordable and accessible housing for people with developmental disabilities?

> **Movin' Out** provides a range of housing solutions to adults with disabilities and families with disabled children. Created by a group of families, Movin' Out offers housing counseling, assist people to get mortgage assistance and funds to rehabilitate properties, manages rental properties and partners in the development of accessible, affordable housing. movin-out.org

DESIGN QUESTION How might we open paths to inclusive, individualized post-secondary education for people with intellectual and developmental disabilities?

In 1987 Inclusion Alberta (a family based provincial advocacy association) began a family initiated partnership with the University of Alberta that offers students with developmental disabilities to participate on a non-credit basis in university courses in majors of personal interest on a non-credit basis. The effort, supported by an **Inclusive Post Secondary Network**, now involves 18 post-secondary institutions across the province. goo.gl/kuK9VY

DESIGN QUESTION How might we support people to discover and occupy roles that connect their gifts and personal interests to community life?

The Arcadia Institute, in Kalamazoo Michigan, supports people to identify their interests and gifts and match them to community people and associations. www.thearcadiainstitute.org and goo.gl/0CTf25 for video.

DESIGN QUESTION How might we mobilize local employers to provide good work for people?

The **Rotary Employment Partnership** joins Rotary Clubs, Inclusion Alberta and a regional funder of assistance in partnership to develop good jobs with career prospects for people with developmental disabilities. Rotary Clubs mobilize their members to develop jobs that match individual interests and capacities. Inclusion Alberta supports employers to assure success. goo.gl/WvO5pz

---

DESIGN QUESTION How might we give people and families opportunities to build assets outside the cash economy?

TimeBank creates a network for exchange of services and skills in which everyone's contribution is equally valued: one hour of contribution entitles a person to one hour of any other member's available skills or services. A modest investment by human service administrators supports outreach to people with disabilities and their families and assistance in getting started. www.danecountytimebank.org

Investments in answering these design questions will make little sense to administrators who understand self-direction an a matter of choosing service providers from an approved list. They will look like unnecessary expenditures to administrators who expect that the choice to hire and direct personal assistants provides away to cut costs by outsourcing management costs to people and their families. These emerge because people and their families and allies feel the importance of them, organize them and find ways to pay for what must be bought. Necessary funds may come from contributions, people's individual budgets or a variety of grants and foundation investments. Administrators committed to developing greater capacity for self-direction will find ways to invest without destroying the creative impulses that produce them.

Social inventors who create ways to multiply the power of self-direction work from these five common convictions. Offering better chances for people with disabilities to live lives that they and those who love them value living is a public responsibility. People have a right to a fair share of public funding to meet the extra costs of exercising citizenship while living with impairments, including the cost of necessary assistance. People and their decision supporters have a right to co-design and effectively direct the assistance they depend on. People, families and communities have assets that can be mobilized to support much greater measures of social inclusion than currently exist. Managers and administrators who chose to deliberately align their resources with these convictions will play a constructive part in building communities that work better for everybody.

9

Letting Go–Letting Come

The problems of life are insoluble on the surface...
Getting hold of the difficulty deep down is what is hard. Be-
cause if it is grasped near the surface it simply remains the
difficulty it was. It has to be pulled out by the roots; and that
involves our beginning to think about things in a new way...
If we clothe ourselves in a new form of expression, the old prob-
lems are discarded along with the old garment.

–Ludwig Wittgenstein

Social inventions happen when people intentionally form webs of relationship that give them courage to step into uncertainty. They listen deeply to each others' desires for a community that works better for everybody. They notice and revise stories that hide possibilities and reform structures that enclose the space for creative action. They form images of a future they want to live in. They take responsibility for their part in the distance between current reality and the vision expressed in *The UN Convention on the Rights of Persons with Disabilities*. They risk learning journeys that decrease that distance and generate new, more open-ended stories of community life.

Most people who encounter pathfinders in their homes, jobs and contributing roles form a great question:

> *How can many more people with developmental*
> *disabilities have what these people have?*

This question deserves to draw us into closer collaboration and deeper thinking because it's too easy to think that we know more than we do.

Contrasting mental models shape different responses to the question of improving life for more people. Management thinking imagines that good support is something like a manufactured product. The search is for an efficient process to greatly increase the supply of person-centered services for people with

Development and growth are not the same thing. Rubbish heaps grow but do not develop. Einstein continued to develop long after he stopped growing.

Growth is an increase in size or number. Development is an increase in competence, the ability to satisfy ones needs and desires and those of others. Development is not a matter of how much one has but how much one can do with whatever one has.

–Russell Ackoff

developmental disabilities and their families to consume. Standards and inspections assure quality.

Pathfinders suggest a different metaphor. Increasing good support is like building rich soil in which people can plant and tend the seeds of their diverse contributions to community life. It is a matter of cultivating relationships that open minds, hearts and wills to sense what wants to grow in neighborhoods and workplaces and acting to bring what's needed to life. The struggle to co-create social-inclusion and self direction developing increased resourcefulness.

Lessons from a master

The limits people show are a reflection of our incompetence, not theirs.

–Marc Gold

In the mid-1970's, we had the good fortune to make friends with a great social inventor and entrepreneur, Marc Gold.* Marc intentionally did his university research into learning in a way that overturned common sense about people with significant cognitive impairments. In his first major study he selected an assembly task that anyone would need training to do successfully –a 16 piece bicycle brake– and asked the staff in 10 sheltered workshops if they would bid to produce these brakes. All agreed that no one in their workshop could learn to do the task; they would not bid at any price. Then Marc asked them to identify the people in their shops who were least likely to learn to assemble the brake. This formed a group of 100 people who were professionally certified as totally incompetent. Marc taught a group of people with no experience in human services a method for teaching the task. The resulting collaboration between learners and teachers demonstrated that everyone involved could escape the professionally imposed story of irremediable incompetence as long as they had time enough with teachers capable of using the method to closely follow and adapt to the person's responses. This disrupted another common story that casts trainers as controllers and good learners as compliant followers.

Marc expected his results to disrupt common beliefs: assuming that people with cognitive impairments are only suited to simple, repetitive tasks; offering access to work based on professional assessments of readiness; the use of behavioral control strategies instead of offering and supporting meaningful occupation; predicting capacity to perform any task based on a person's

---

* Marc died in 1982 at age 43. For a video sample of his distinctive message (and late '70's hair and clothing styles) goo.gl/xskWzZ To learn about the way his work continues: marcgold.com. A collection of his writing, *Did I Say That?*, (1980) is currently available from used booksellers for a reasonable price.

performance on tests; and limiting people's access to real work and income based on these mistaken assumption. He expected services to change their structures and practice to offer people who had been considered incompetent for most of their lives real jobs for real pay.

When professionals and service providers resisted, he accepted their challenges. Maybe the method was too complex and costly for staff to master. He continually refined and simplified the *Try Another Way System* and the way to teach it. Maybe the people selected weren't really significantly impaired. Maybe there was something unique about the bike brake. He published additional research (27 studies). One study focused on residents of an institution unit for people assigned multiple disability statuses: severe and profound mental retardation and deafness and blindness. They successfully produced locking gas caps to a manufacturer's satisfaction. Others learned to manufacture circuit boards. When vocational program proved resistant, his associates went into partnership with employers to establish competence in the company's own training and supervision staff. He encouraged committed and talented associates to continue and develop his work.

Marc was passionate about assuring that his research made a difference to real people. He created a strong evidence base. He recruited talented and committed associates and attracted investment in training and demonstration projects. He was a charismatic speaker who demonstrated *Try Another Way* live with cooperating and paid learners nominated by skeptical professionals. Some people, including us, had mental models about cognitive impairment and employment for people with developmental disabilities exploded and reconfigured. But the core assumptions that Marc challenged still rule the lives of far too many people today, as the unemployment of four out of five people known to adult services in the US shows.

Change deep enough to bring, broaden and build what we know about support for meaningful, inclusive employment to the large numbers of people who will benefit has a price. It is not enough to demonstrate and establish a competent technology and an efficient way to teach people to use it. The change demands letting go of a story that needs to die as well as embracing and encouraging a story that wants to be born in action through our involvement. Too few people are willing to pay the price of letting go to reach a tipping point.

If you could only know me
for who I am,
Instead of for who I am
not,
There would be so much
more to see,
Because there's so much
more that I've got.

So long as you see me as
mentally retarded,
Which supposedly means
something, I guess,
There's nothing you or I
could ever do,
To make me a human
success.

–Marc Gold

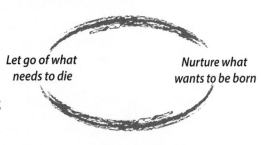

*Let go of what
needs to die*

*Nurture what
wants to be born*

The metaphor of death and birth is appropriate. If we take Marc seriously, we let go of a way of making sense of the world and our work in it. This story functions in the background to give meaning to what we do and justify our decisions. It connects us to colleagues. It's loss undermines familiar structures and practices and leaves us feeling uprooted and disoriented. What is born is a possibility, vulnerable, unfinished, uncertain –in need of us to discover and construct its meaning by re-forming our relationships and reshaping our structures and practices.

How can we expect people to take their places next to us in society if so many of the ways to supposedly help get them there force them to recognize, in one way or another, their subservient positions?

–Marc Gold

As Marc experienced the limits of his energetic change efforts he began to sense and frame the adaptive challenges that most organizations were unwilling to engage. He thought and talked more about the stultifying power of the belief that mental retardation (or any updated version of the status) is a meaningful construct for understanding and assisting a person. He came to the position that his method should only be used to teach meaningful tasks in natural settings: teaching on the job a person has rather than getting people ready. He thought and taught more about respectful relationships among equals as a necessary condition for any meaningful learning. This condition is established by hearts inspired in wonder at people's capacity rather than by technically proficient hands alone. This was Marc's natural approach, which could be hidden in people's hunger for the junk food of disembodied techniques.

Marc's is not the only voice for the capacity of people with developmental disabilities to be productive in ordinary workplaces. Many talented researchers, practitioners and policy makers have worked hard to increase employment opportunities. The glacial pace of growth in employment in the 30 years since Marc's death complicates the question of increasing the numbers of people who benefit from what pathfinders demonstrate. Those who want to make real change have to let go of the mental model that portrays change as a process that can be managed according to a blueprint and good assistance as the output of a process in which relationships are subordinate to policy commands and controls, market forces and engineered procedures. They have to become conscious of the stories of incompetence, unacceptability and vulnerability that control the lived details of so many people's lives and choose to join people, families and citizens to live new stories. They have to give up the comfortable belief that history has stopped and whatever is available now represents the best that can be. They have to puncture the illusion of a quick and clean technical fix.

Embodying ideals

Ideals are dangerous when they float, disconnected from particular circumstances. Unless grounded in a struggle for a more equal and fruitful relationship between a person and the assistance they require, *person-centered* becomes so light a phrase that it can float into any corner of current practice without stimulating any thought or action at all. The *right to choose* is only a cut-and-paste concept floating in the head when it fails to challenge mind, heart and will to do the hard work of offering real options for housing, jobs and learning and replacing guardianship and paternalistic supervision with effective support for decision making. *Inclusion* disconnected from the exhilarating risks of walking through walls to develop contributing roles and relationships is a hollow sound.

Generations of pathfinders have discovered what it takes to embody the ideals that define a community that works better for everybody. People honor and suspend their certainties and fears. They freely choose to explore what more could be possible by identifying gifts, capacities and assets in themselves, in their relationships and networks, in their community and in the economy and inventing new ways to connect those capacities together. Growing connections create the context for personal assistance and expert help. This is most powerful when the people involved develop a relationship that allows co-sensing new possibilities, becoming present together to the highest possibilities in their situation, and co-creating what they need to live those possibilities.

When publicly funded assistance plays a significant part in a person's life, freedom to discover, connect and learn is shaped by the structures and stories that service providers and public administrators enact. The extent of their courage to invest in social invention zones powerfully affects the number of people who will take self-directed journeys to social inclusion. Their capacity to create an environment for ideal seeking depends on the quality of awareness they bring to their work. Developing their leadership follows the same pattern demonstrated by pathfinders: enter into relationship with people with developmental disabilities, their families and allies, and people taking constructive action in civil life and the economy; suspend fears and certainties; open minds, hearts and wills to co-sense the highest possibilities in their situation; and take rapid, bold steps to co-create ways to realize those possibilities. This builds the soil in which many beautiful and nourishing expressions of social inclusion can flourish.

Leaders are people who frequently provide the environment for seeking ideals.

–Merryelyn Emery

The future belongs to people with the courage to join together and imagine a community that works better for everyone and then build relationships that make it possible to begin to live there.

The beloved community is not a utopia, but a place where the barriers between people gradually come down and where the citizens make a constant effort to address even the most difficult problems of ordinary people. It is above all else an idealistic community.

–Jim Lawson

Recent Additions *from* **Inclusion Press**
Resources to Support Your Work & Life

PATHFINDERS

People with Developmental
Disabilities and Their Allies
Building Communities
That Work for Everybody

John O'Brien & Beth Mount

CREATING *blue* SPACE

HANNS MEISSNER
FOREWORD BY JOHN O'BRIEN

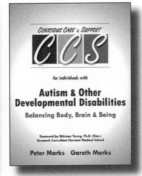

CONSCIOUS CARE & SUPPORT
CCS

for individuals with

**Autism & Other
Developmental Disabilities**

Balancing Body, Brain & Being

Foreword by Shinzen Young, Ph.D. (Hon.)
Research Consultant Harvard Medical School

Peter Marks   Gareth Marks

MAKING HOMES THAT WORK

Planning, Design and Construction of
Person-Centered Environments
for Families Living with
Autism Spectrum Disorder

www.inclusion.com

The PATH & MAPS Handbook
Person-Centered Ways to
Build Community

Make a Difference
A Guidebook for Person-Centered
Direct Support

John O'Brien and Beth Mount

ASSET BASED COMMUNITY DEVELOPMENT

**WHEN
PEOPLE
CARE
ENOUGH
TO ACT**

MIKE GREEN with HENRY MOORE & JOHN O'BRIEN

FOREWORD BY JOHN McKNIGHT

**EMERGING
RESEARCH**

STUDENTS with DISABILITIES,
FAMILIES, TEACHERS

Gary Bunch

**Facilitating
an Everyday Life**

John Lord
Barbara Leavitt,
Charlotte Dingwall

Literacy
World Wide   U-CAN

DIC
IONARY

Voice
Recognition (VR)

The
Self Teaching
Dictionary

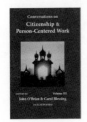

Conversations on
**Citizenship &
Person-Centered Work**

John O'Brien & Carol Blessing
Volume III

**INTENTIONAL
TEAMING**

SHIFTING ORGANIZATIONAL CULTURE

BETH GALLAGHER
& JACK PEARPOINT

NAVIGATING COLLEGE
A Handbook on Self Advocacy

Written for Autistic Students, by Autistic adults

brought to you by
ASAN

Friends & Inclusion

Five Approaches to
Building Relationships

Peggy Hutchison & John Lord
with Karen Lord

REAL LIFE AFTER SCHOOL

PLANNING FOR REAL LIFE
AFTER SCHOOL

Inclusion Press

**Download
our Catalogue:
http://inclusion.com**

FLOURISH

Who's Drawing
the Lines?

Judith Snow

Mindfulness

Gentle Heart
FEARLESS MIND

DISCOVERING
CONFIDENCE & WELL-BEING
THROUGH LIFE'S CHALLENGES

DVD

Alan Sloan

REVISED EDITION

Parents and Professionals
PARTNERING *for*
**CHILDREN
WITH DISABILITIES**

A Dance That Matters

Janice M. Fialka · Arlene K. Feldman · Karen C. Mikus
Foreword by Ann T. Turnbull

Inclusion Press

FACILITATION FOR INCLUSION
with PATH & MAPS
DVD

DVD

Personal Stories, Struggles, and Successes With Person Directed Living

my life, my choice

para